EARTH CHAKRA SHAMAN

LOUISE CARRON HARRIS

COPYRIGHT © 2020 Louise Carron Harris
All Rights Reserved

ISBN: 979-8-6945-9505-6

Cover design: Melissa Matthews

*For all our great-great-grandchildren yet to come.
May we leave the Earth better than we found it.*

Acknowledgement of the Traditional Custodians of the Lands

I acknowledge the Traditional Custodians of the land on which I have worked and written during the creation of this book and recognise their continuing connection to land, water and community. I pay respect to Elders past, present, and emerging.

CONTENTS

Acknowledgement of the Traditional Custodians of the Lands .. iv
Foreword 7
Preface 9
Prayer of Saint Francis 11
Explaining the Earth Chakras.................................... 12
CHAPTER 1: Here's Where the Journey Begins 15
    Doing the work 18
    The vision board maps the call............................ 21
    Nudges 23
Chakra Medicine Meditation 26
CHAPTER 2: Teachers, Mentors & Allies Step Into their Role .. 31
    What the heck is the hero's journey? 33
    Preparing for the quest 36
    Everyone is called 37
    Medicine teachers 39
CHAPTER 3: Red Earth Purge 43
    Leaving the nest 44
    Angels come in many forms 48
    Knowing and trusting 52
    Spiritual preparation 54
    Prayer to the lands.. 57

CHAPTER 4: Uluru & the Solar Plexus Chakra 61
    Sacred land 63
    Awakening to the truth 65
    Singing the sound of the lands 66
    Giving back what was taken 69

Solar Plexus Chakra Prayer: Abundance 72

CHAPTER 5: Unfolding of the Earth Chakra Call 73
    Guess what I just learned! 75
    Chaos and abundance 78
    Receiving from the Divine 81

CHAPTER 6: Peru's Gifts of Growth 82
    Dyslexic world 83
    Welcome to the jungle 86
    Tobacco rush 88
    Ayahuasca journeying 91
    All the visions and gifts of the past 94
    The Sacred Valley 98
    Tears from home 102
    New mesa, new beginnings 105
    Machu Picchu rising 109
    Running into the Sungate 112

CHAPTER 7: Lake Titicaca & the Sacral Chakra 117
    Ancient remembering 118
    Frustrations and divine unfolding 120
    The universe works in mysterious ways 122

Sacral Chakra Prayer: Personal Power & Divine Purpose Wisdom 127

CHAPTER 8: The Road to America 129
    Planning pressure 131
    Messages from the spirit world 132
    California dreaming 134
    News buzz 135
    The nest 137
    Road trip! 139
    Poison 141
    Flow like water 144
    Through chaos comes clarity 146

CHAPTER 9: Mount Shasta & the Base Chakra 149
    Shasta shamanic retreat 150
    Earth activation and offerings 154
    Sacred tools and divine timing 157
    Crater Lake and the Cascade Range 161
    Manifesting in the mountains 166

Base Chakra Activation: Divine Will for Greater Life 174

CHAPTER 10: Death & Rebirth in Alaska 176
    Into the wilderness 180
    This is Alaska! 182
    Death and pipelines 184
    Finally, we meet, Yukon 188
    The Inuit people 191
    Denali 194

Rebirth 197

CHAPTER 11: History of our Lands 201

    World friends 203

    A rocky road 204

    Lake Louise 206

CHAPTER 12: The Wounded Sole 210

    Defiance and derailing 215

    The gift beyond self-judgment 218

CHAPTER 13: Glastonbury & the Heart Chakra 219

    Reconnection 221

    Home is where the heart chakra is 223

    The Isle of Avalon 225

    Delivering divine will 228

Heart Chakra Meditation & Medicine: Infinite Flow of Love .. 231

CHAPTER 14: The Great Pyramids of Giza & the Throat Chakra 233

    Pyramid song 234

    Together in the desert 240

Throat Chakra Prayer: Courage to Live in Truth 244

CHAPTER 15: The Show Must Go On 245

    Everyday miracles 248

CHAPTER 16: Third Eye Chakra Magical Mystery Tour 256

    The divine duo 258

    Shaftesbury adventure 259

    Let your dreams guide you to Gaia's call 263

    Aquarian aeon activation 265

Oracle confirmation... 268
Third-Eye Activation: Innocence & Inner-Sense, Intuition & Knowing 274

CHAPTER 17: Listen to your Spirit Guides............................ 276
The King's reminder 276
The beginning of the end..280

CHAPTER 18: Leading a Sacred Journey to Egypt.................283
Discernment and responsibility 284
Pyramid problems 288
Desert dreaming 294
Universal energy of one 297

CHAPTER 19: Show Up for your Purpose 300
The next call.. 303
Harry's warrior steps up... 306
Harry and Lou 2.0 309

CHAPTER 20: Growth & Challenge in Kathmandu 313
Welcome to crazy Kathmandu 315
The Bon shaman and the Hindu swami................................318
I'm done with this crazy 320
The mud from where the lotus flower grows 325

CHAPTER 21: Kailash & the Crown Chakra 328
Chengdu... 332
Get to Tibet 336
Old Lhasa, New China 338
The road to Kailash..341
The first day of the Kailash kora 345

- Crown chakra activation 350
- Seeing angels 354
- Kailash walks me home 359
- The gift of the mountain 361

Crown Chakra Prayer: Divine Knowing 363

CHAPTER 22: Sacred Gifts from the Highest Heights 364
- The sacred cave 365
- Palm pyramids and the light 370

Epilogue 372
- Guinevere of the heart chakra 376
- As for the earth chakras… 380

Thanks 382

About Louise 384

Foreword

At various points in our lives, we find ourselves on a journey. These journeys can come in many forms. Some could take us around the world, some may manifest themselves as a difficult relationship, and some are a combination. Whatever the circumstances, embarking on a quest is possibly one of the most profound things we can do as a human being.

While not always obvious at the time, every journey will gift us a valuable lesson if not several. Somewhere along the way will be a teaching to guide us on journeys we haven't taken yet, maybe some wisdom to pass down to future generations. But if we're to find that knowledge, one thing is for sure... we have to be open to it.

When I was growing up, there was no mystery. Just things that didn't have an explanation yet. Everything was either black or white. There was nothing in between. Miracles and magic existed only in fairytales.

So, when I met Lou at the age of 17, she was the polar opposite to me in nearly every way possible, especially in terms of her views on life. The yin to my yang, you couldn't get more different.

Over the last two-and-a-bit decades, Lou and I have been on an incredible journey. Our story has meandered, twisted and turned more times that I can remember. We've had to learn to navigate our way through the challenges and find compassion to respect each other's point of view. It's this development as a team that has enabled us to live experiences that I couldn't have dreamed were possible.

Of course, Lou's calling to the earth chakras has played a huge part in our life together, not just for the two of us, but for all our family. As Lou talks about in this book, and as with all journeys, this calling has taught us so many lessons. We learned to not be defined by our conditioning and we developed a greater understanding of the power of truly accepting one another for who we are.

It has also been a great liberation to learn that our paths do not have to match exactly in order to have a shared goal. Of course, it helps that they are vaguely heading in the same direction, but trusting in unconditional love and listening to the messages we receive throughout our lives, we are always going to be guided down the right track.

The hows and whys of our journey may forever be a mystery to me. In all honesty, a large part of me hopes it stays that way. Perhaps the greatest lesson I've learnt from all of this is that I don't need to know all the answers. I just need to open my eyes and enjoy the ride.

Maybe if we are willing to look, we might even find a little bit of *magic*.

Harry

Preface

We all must take it at some point in our lives – the hero's journey – and answer the call to somewhere we have never been before, inside of ourselves and out. We all must learn to follow our own inner guidance and to conquer the seemingly impossible so as to return with the greatest gift of all – our true self.

We will meet strangers, friends and challengers along the way, many of whom agreed before entering this life to play these roles for us, so that we can learn the lessons we need in order for us to grow into who we are here to become.

You picked up this book because you know you are here for something more. You know all that is above is that which is below. As we walk together on this journey of becoming whole, be prepared to open your heart, your eyes, your soul...

Sit with Gaia, listen to her message, let her whisper to you as you turn each page, reminding you of why you are here, your own unique calling, your own unique purpose, your own unique medicine and your own divine personal power.

As you begin to say yes to love, yes to life, yes to service beyond yourself, you will absorb the blessings, healings and messages of my medicine and that of the earth chakras.

With the gentle reminder that no matter how different we are, or how we experience the world, we are one and we are love.

As our world moves into a new age, the Age of Aquarius, may you be protected, blessed and awake to the medicine all around.

My love goes with you.

Louise

Prayer of Saint Francis

Great Spirit, make me an instrument of your peace.
Where there is hatred, let me sow love
Where there is injury, pardon
Where there is doubt, faith
Where there is despair, hope
Where there is darkness, light
And where there is sadness, joy.
Grant that I may not so much seek
To be consoled as to console
To be understood, as to understand
To be loved, as to love
For it is in giving that we receive
And it's in pardoning that we are pardoned
And it's in dying that we are born to Eternal Life.

Explaining the Earth Chakras

*B*efore our journey begins, an explanatory note on the energy centres of Mother Earth. Like us, Gaia has an energetic anatomy, seven major chakras, one on each continent of the Earth. Within her sacred mountains, lakes and lands are spinning spheres of life – earth chakras, which vibrate the spiritual, physical and emotional energy of the Earth.

These earth chakras are:

- Base chakra – Mount Shasta – USA
- Sacral chakra – Lake Titicaca – Peru
- Solar plexus chakra – Uluru/Kata-Tjuta – Australia
- Heart chakra - Glastonbury Tor – United Kingdom
- Throat chakra – The Great Pyramids – Egypt
- Third eye* chakra – Shaftesbury/Glastonbury – United Kingdom
- Crown chakra – Mount Kailash – Tibet

*The third eye chakra is the only earth chakra that moves with each age. It is also called the aeon activation centre. Two thousand years ago, the aeon activation centre resided in Jerusalem at the Age of Pisces. In the 1960s, it moved to Glastonbury/Shaftesbury for the beginning of the Age of Aquarius.

It takes approximately 100 years for the ages to fully establish themselves, so it will be approximately 2060 when the Age of Aquarius is fully activated. Therefore, these times are like a bridge between the two ages.

The health of these chakras reflects the wellbeing of the whole and we all play a part in what we will bring into this new age and what we will leave behind. In the Age of Pisces, we learned about religion and compassion, but the shadow side of this led to destruction of Indigenous cultures all around the world and abuse of religious power. The Age of Aquarius is about communication and technology. Can we bring harmony with the spirit and science of this new age? It is down to us to decide what we bring with us and what we leave behind.

The Rainbow Serpent and the Plumed Serpent are the main energy lines that flow through the earth grid connecting the main chakras in an infinity sign, activating information between the chakras for regeneration of the Earth. Both have their own mysteries and magic to reveal.

There is a complex depth to the planetary grid and a vast array of intellectual understanding based on numerology, astrology, metaphysics, mysticism, history and mathematics to name a few. I am here to share with you the necessary simplicity in the grid's complexity. Before embarking on my quest, I had no knowledge of this grid or that I was *activating* it. That came much later on in the call.

It was my inner sense that took me on this journey. However, it was fully confirmed to me that the planetary grid and chakra system are true and complete, as I experienced the spirit of Gaia calling me to do her work.

For me, this journey has to be simple on a soul level because it is just too big for my mind to comprehend. (If you are interested in learning more, you can find out about this extraordinary system on an intellectual level through Robert Coon's earth chakra work.) The story I share here is told with the same lightness of spirit that called me and my wonder to join in activating Gaia's grid, preparing it for the new Age of Aquarius.

Take a deep breath, a sacred breath, a breath of innocence, wonder and deep knowing. We are all part of this earth. We all have a role to play. All we need to do is listen. Listen to the aliveness of our Great Mother.

To connect and align for your own journey to the earth chakras in this book and also your own divine unique purpose on this planet, download the sacred meditation gifted to me by Gaia before the earth chakra calling as healing and preparation for the call: louisecarronharris.com/divinemeditation

***

CHAPTER 1

Here's Where the Journey Begins

"Respond to every call that excites your spirit. Ignore those that make you fearful and sad, that degrade you back toward disease and death."

~ Rumi

There I was, watching my husband walk up and down the kitchen, head in hand, in utter shock, desperately trying to process...

"Lou, I don't know what I know anymore, but I know I don't know."

They were the most profound words I had ever heard him say. The magic was undeniable now. All I had been telling him, all I had been working towards, was real. When strange things happened to me, he would always rationalise it in some way. His only way to accept the mystic energy and synergies was to call them coincidences.

There are no coincidences, I would tell him. For such a long time, I had known *something* was going on. I could feel something big was happening to me, but I could not understand what it was going to be from the place of my mind. I just knew that I was here on this planet for a massive reason that was beyond myself.

Harry honoured the role that I took in my community as a teacher and modern-day shaman, over years of seeing people change through my work. Finally, he would have to accept that I was no longer the party girl he once married; that I could not stay like that if I was to be who I was here to be on the earth.

I had a huge appetite to grow and evolve, often beyond what he could reach or even understand. For years he had felt threatened by my spirituality and the changes I was going through: saying *yes* to life, *yes* to my inner calls, *yes* to aligning myself with my truth, *yes* to a dedicated mindfulness practice, *yes* to rigorous self-examination, *yes* to deep self-healing, and *yes* to relentless acts of service beyond myself; saying *yes* to a life of happiness, to inspiring others, to bringing conscious awareness into my role as a parent, wife, friend and teacher. Most of all, I was saying yes to my call, my purpose. I knew I was here as guardian of Gaia, protector of this planet and all of her beings.

But this latest manifestation meant I was changing fast. What if I went so far into a world he could not see or understand? How would he ever follow me there? The perfect bubble of our life together would pop! But no. I was his best friend and lover. I'd adored him from the moment I saw him for that very first time back in 1998. I was his biggest champion and he was mine. We had to find a way to both be who we were here to be on this planet. Together.

It was our destiny.

Looking at me still in shock, Harry's huge brown eyes told me he knew a miracle had just happened. Now that he could see something tangible and undeniable, it seemed to prove to him that there really was something greater than us out there: the universe, Gaia, God. Now he was fully experiencing the Divine and wonder filled the air.

Only a few days before, I had screamed and cried at Mount Illimani, the protector mountain of Lake Titicaca in Peru, who had awoken me from my sleep two nights in a row telling me I must come. I told the mountain I couldn't *just come* to Peru! I couldn't just up and leave my husband and two daughters like that, but Illimani would not take no for an answer...

"Fine, if you want me to come to Peru, you will have to send the money, and it will need to be enough to make Harry believe in all of this."

I thought that was the end of it and I told no one except my Shamanic teacher.

Thirty-six hours later, and here I sat on the floor, a £25k cheque in my hand, shaking in disbelief, wonder, excitement and knowing, while my husband paced the room. I knew now that I really did have to leave him and our little world to go to Peru. Still in shock, I began to push it away in my mind.

I can't take it. It's too big. How can I take it? It's too much. How can I leave my family? We have never been apart. I can't do this on my own.

Harry knelt. He knew me so well that he could hear the fight that had started to go on in my head. He smiled softly, stroked my face and looked at me intently. For the first time, I felt his genuine respect for me, my work, my medicine and my reason for being here on this earth.

"You deserve this, Lou. You really do. You need to go to Peru."

All I have ever wanted was to serve, to live a life of purpose, and I hadn't 'done the work' to get to this point and give up now. He understood that and now trusted that the Divine was not here to break us apart. If anything, though he was yet to see it, it was about to bring us closer than we could ever imagine.

***

Doing the work

'Do the work' is a vague and mysterious way of saying 'know thyself'. When we do the work, we have the willingness to 'go there' to heal and transform what triggers and blocks us so we can show up as better humans. And as spiritual teacher Ram Dass says, "Become the change we wish to see in the world."

I started consciously 'doing the work' when I was 21 by reading a handful of books that sparked my soul. By 27, I quit watching TV, reading the news and buying magazines. I quit fast food, ate fresh organic veg, began to meditate and started journaling. In my thirties, the road got narrower. I was called to stop smoking, drinking, and eating meat and dairy. Most amazingly to me, I learned that I actually had the willpower to master what controlled me, to abstain from addictions like social media, sugar, distraction. It was, however, a continuous journey of awareness that often got derailed. But in time, I found it easier to find my way back to my true self, the point of my personal power where anything was possible.

I also did the inner work, which was arguably harder. I sought out mentoring, healing and shamanic therapy. I didn't just have to give up substances, but also being right. I saw that I could be a dick sometimes. I saw other sides of myself that I didn't like – from being self-righteous to feeling I was undeserving or not believing in myself. I let go of fears, money issues, and co-dependency with Harry. It was all there, and I had to learn why it was all there before I could heal and change it. It didn't happen in one go. It involved incremental upgrades over years and years. In each letting go, a part of my identity had to die too! All so that I could be freer, lighter and brighter.

Reiki was my chosen tool of self-healing and it became my way of life. Every night, I healed myself, connecting with my spirit guides, journaling and honing that willingness to see parts of myself that I was yet to see, the darkness within and the light that I denied. I forgave myself for the hearts I'd broken, the things I'd said, the unconscious and conscious behaviours I'd played out. I had seen the darkness of others and I forgave them too. I healed, cleared, decluttered my head and my home, and let go of what no longer served me, whether that was businesses, friends or other attachments.

When any issues came up, I worked shamanically to clear them. I communicated as consciously as I knew how and learned to not project myself onto the world. I had learned how to manifest mindfully, not from the ego's desire, but by asking: how does the universe want to flow through me? I always got my answer.

Most of all, though, I honoured myself and my wisdom. I had learned and grown. Now I rose up and raised others around me too. The goal I had in doing the work was not to 'beat others to the top', but to ensure we all got there.

Raising and empowering others into their power was my superpower.

That was the background that had led to this moment holding a £25,000 cheque in hand, but the real magic was the letter from an old client.

> *Six months ago, the angels told me an amount to send to you. They said it would help you make important journeys.*
> *Love,*
> *Jen*

There were things I knew and things I did not. I did not know how the Divine orchestrated such magical timing, but I did know that the 10 years of dedication and commitment to learning, clearing, healing and raising others had led to this very moment, where I knew my soul was in divine service for my highest purpose.

And yet, while I *did* deserve this money, it wasn't really the money I had to accept. I had to accept that I deserved to be *called* at all. Could I even do what I was being called to do, when I didn't know what I had to do when I got there? All I could do was seize the moment and see where it led. There was a mission laid out before me, a journey I had to take. This money was not for me to buy nice clothes or go on holiday. This was a gift to go to where I needed to go and an acknowledgement of Harry for supporting me.

Being called by the mountain and having my path illuminated felt like I had met Great Spirit herself and she had finally shone her light on my true purpose. After all this time, I'd come into who I was and why I was here. And even though there was so much more I didn't yet know, my faith in myself meant I could stay present in the moment and be guided to go where I was called, where I could be in the highest service to love.

The vision board maps the call

Before I'd even connected to Peru, this journey had been divinely planned for longer than I could imagine. Of course, it was all aligned from a higher place, but that didn't mean I could make sense of what I was seeing.

When most people do vision boards, it's about manifesting what they want, but I look at it another way. You manifest what God wants to bring through you from a place of subconscious, from soul.

In one sitting, I created a picture collage, while focusing on nothing but myself and the magazine images in front of me. It didn't come from the intention of desire or want. I had to transcend the need to manifest in that way. So instead, this vision board came from a place of *what* wanted to unfold *through* me. In other words, what I was about to see on this vision board was a pathway planned for me before time. It was my destiny.

Shamanically, we call this 'looking to see what we don't yet know' and vision boards are great for doing this because you can see so much about yourself that you have not yet seen or maybe don't want to see.

There was a naked woman on a telephone 'call' in the middle of my board, another woman on a 'mission' looking fierce and walking the opposite way, a map of Australia and pictures of mountains. And words saying, 'welcome to the jungle'. When I looked at it, what I saw scared me, but there were some parts that felt liberating. As well as the images of Australia and a photo of the jungle that turned out to be

Peru, there was another image of an iceberg that my gut told me was Alaska. And lastly, a picture of a woman sitting next to a birdcage, which to me symbolised being free, though it was only just dawning on me what the cage might be.

Looking at it overall, I felt like I was on my own. Where were all the images of family and friends, sunshine and rainbows? I called my friend Mary and she helped me to understand what it may mean.

"I strongly believe you have to go to Australia. It's in the centre of your board. You can't ignore that!" she told me.

At the time, I didn't have the funds to take my family to Australia, but during that conversation the doorbell rang and the delivery man handed me a bouquet of flowers, a gift from my best friend Sandy in Australia! The flowers were all the colours of my vision board, with reds and oranges, and a message that read "for no reason other than I love you".

"Well, if that's not a sign, I don't know what is!" Mary laughed.

I text Sandy right away.

"Thank you, you have no idea how timely those flowers were. A divine message from the universe. Somehow, I'm coming to see you next year, I don't know how, but I know it will happen. I love you too!"

At the time, I didn't know that this journey to Australia was a calling, nor how or why the money would come. I thought it was simply that I needed to go see my best friend. I had no clue what was ahead.

***

Nudges

It was so warm in my duvet and so cold out of it, but I needed to get myself out of bed.

5, 4, 3, 2, up!

I rolled out of bed, pulled on my hoodie, tucked my pyjama bottoms into my socks, and headed downstairs to my little room. There, I opened my altar cloth on the floor, lit a candle, put on some music, wrapped a blanket around me, and sat cross-legged on the floor. I opened my mesa, my sacred medicine bundle.

This was my life. This was my medicine. This was how I connected to the spirit world, to my calling. It was 2016, I was 36 and I was set for the biggest year of my life. And everything I had created in my life was perfect. It couldn't get much better. I had just completed my shamanic initiation training and grown a mesa of 13 medicine stones, wrapped in an old antique cloth embroidered by my great-grandmother. Each one had been through deep initiations and ceremonies to transform them from stones into medicine stones, healing stones that shamans in Peru called 'kuyas'. These became my babies, holding the alchemy of my own sacred healing and the healing of others. A medicine woman needs a medicine bundle. This was mine and it was alive. It was a direct connection to Spirit, an extension of me.

Of course, I had no idea that these kuyas, wrapped in this old cloth, were going to play a much bigger part in a much bigger picture, beyond my Andean Shamanic teachings, beyond even my own healing or that of my community, beyond anything I could have imagined.

As I sat in my meditation position ready to begin my morning practice, breathing, connecting to my guides, I heard a message deep inside of me.

Come outside, come outside.

It was my animal guide, the serpent, one of many who speak to me. Her name is Sachamama and she resides at my base chakra. We didn't talk often. I had many guides from the spirit world that I preferred to talk to, but I knew I was sometimes avoiding the connections I most needed. She was always there to ground me when I was too 'up there' in the cosmos. I had done a lot of reiki energy healing on myself the night before and it had been flowing all night. At times, even Harry, my dear non-spiritual logical husband, would have his hands on my body and send the reiki to me in some half-awake, half-asleep state, and I would drift into other dimensions, in a constant flow of beautiful heavenly energy waves.

I felt Sachamama call again and wanted to ignore her. I had just settled and I knew it was cold, dark and probably icy out there. Then again, I knew well enough by now not to shut down these whisperings. I had to go, because I hated the sense of emptiness that filled me when I fell off my morning practice or overrode my inner guidance; all day, I would feel like I was running on two cylinders instead of six.

When we listen to that inner loving guidance – however it comes to us – we become the highest version of ourselves, the part of ourselves that knows better, that knows we can do this. For you, it may be a spirit guide, an ancestor, or something else. The exact nature of that voice doesn't matter. But when we learn to act on that 'inner nudge', magical things happen; sometimes simple things, sometimes big things, but magical things for your highest purpose nonetheless. Learning to trust the inner nudges takes us in the right direction.

I turned up my fleecy pyjama bottoms and pulled off my socks. Opening the front door, I felt the chill of the wind, and within moments, there was a freezing pain rolling up my feet as I jumped across the paving to the bit of lawn in the front garden. My bare feet broke through a thin layer of ice and I felt the squelch of not-quite-frozen mud between my toes. Since then, I have learned to like this wild sensation, but it was not something I loved at the time, a bittersweet pill to swallow for the medicine of Mother Earth, who requires us to be raw and cold, as well as warm and comforted. With reverence, I gave thanks to Gaia, Pachamama, and her reminder that everything was alive.

I reasserted my willingness to connect and Gaia herself began to whisper to me:

The lands that you are born onto hold the ancient wisdoms of your soul. You can access the information you need on your soul's journey every day. Here, with your feet on my belly, you can listen to the guidance.

I opened my eyes with love of the message still in my heart and saw a heron fly right overhead. The heron is the spirit messenger who comes to me to tell me I'm on the right path and to remind me to stay grounded. She doesn't come often, but when she comes I pay attention to the blessed guidance.

Mother Earth was right, of course. The more I had my feet on the earth, the more I could hear her guidance and the messages of whichever spirits chose to guide me. The nudges were right here. They were everywhere.

***

Chakra Medicine Meditation

As I connect to my base chakra,
I feel my gift of roots.
And they go deeper and deeper into Mother Earth.
And Mother Earth, she nourishes my blood, my bones and my belly,
and I am blessed.

As I connect to my sacral chakra,
I feel my gift of divine wisdom and service.
As I walk my path of purpose,
my roots go deeper and deeper into Mother Earth.
And Mother Earth, she nourishes my blood, my bones and my belly,
and I am blessed.

EARTH CHAKRA SHAMAN

As I connect to my solar plexus,
I feel my gift of abundance,
Where I create health, wealth, happiness, joy, laughter,
music, dancing, adventure, and discovery.
Abundance flows down into my divine wisdom and service.
And as I walk my path of purpose,
my roots go deeper and deeper into Mother Earth.
And Mother Earth, she nourishes my blood, my bones and
my belly,
and I am blessed.

As I connect to my heart,
I feel the gift of infinite love flowing through me.
I receive love from nature, the trees and plants and
animals,
and I send that love out to them.
Love flows down into my abundance,
Where I create more health, wealth, happiness, joy,
laughter, music, dancing, adventure, and discovery.
Abundance flows into my divine wisdom and service.
And as I walk my path of purpose,
my roots go deeper and deeper into Mother Earth.
And Mother Earth, she nourishes my blood, my bones and
my belly,
and I am blessed.

As I connect to my throat chakra,
I feel the gift of courage.
I begin to speak my truth, sing my truth.
The trees awaken and the world awakens.
Courage flows down into my heart and it opens up to receive more love
from the trees, the plants and the people, friends and family.
Infinite love flows out of my heart, touching all humans, animals, trees and plants and down into my abundance
Where I create more health, wealth, happiness, joy, laughter, music, dancing, adventure, and discovery.
Abundance flows into my divine wisdom and service.
And as I walk my path of purpose,
my roots go deeper and deeper into Mother Earth.
And Mother Earth, she nourishes my blood, my bones and my belly,
and I am blessed.

As I connect to my third eye chakra,
I feel my gift of intuition.
I know where to be, what to say, when to stay, when to play.
Intuition flows down into my courage where I am braver to speak my truth, be my truth, walk my truth.

EARTH CHAKRA SHAMAN

Truth flows down into my heart and it opens up to receive even more love
from the trees, the plants and the people, friends and family.
Infinite love flows out of my heart, touching all humans, animals, trees and plants and down into my abundance
Where I create more health, wealth, happiness, joy, laughter, music, dancing, adventure, and discovery.
Abundance flows into my divine wisdom and service.
And as I walk my path of purpose,
my roots go deeper and deeper into Mother Earth.
And Mother Earth, she nourishes my blood, my bones and my belly,
and I am blessed.

As I connect to my crown chakra,
I connect to divine knowledge.
And here, I pray in stillness for what I need to know
to be in true alignment with my soul's calling.
And I breathe.
Knowledge flows down into my intuition, into my courage, into my infinite love, into my abundance, into my divine wisdom and service.

LOUISE CARRON HARRIS

And as I walk my path of purpose with this medicine,
my roots go deeper and deeper into Mother Earth, gifting her this blessing.
And she nourishes all of us, our blood, our bones, our bellies,
and we are all blessed.

***

CHAPTER 2

Teachers, Mentors & Allies Step Into their Role

It was November 2015, only a week after the mountains had called me, when I first wandered through the old gardens of the college. I was still flying high on the magic of it all and the gift of the money to make it happen, and I had not come back down to earth yet.

    A chubby robin followed me down the broken path, bringing a beaming smile to my heart. Visits from the animal world raised my childlike wonder and this little guy eased my trepidation and excitement for the autobiographical storytelling course I was about to take. This was to be the first weekend of four between now and May. As I found my way to the Storytelling Hut, I passed the main college building. Then, at the bottom of the gardens, I found the entrance to the wooden hut, where I would be learning. I could feel something emerging from beyond a wrought iron gate. Taking a narrow pathway to the left, I was swimming in a pool of unlimited possibility, riding the waves of synergies, as if the universe herself had delivered me right to her door.

Here, Louise, is where your story begins.

Inside was an old-fashioned living room that had been stretched out in a Harry Potter Room of Requirement style that felt perfect for doing magic spells. Massive ancient rugs littered the floor and squashy inviting sofas were pushed against every wall. The seats were piled with cushions of all sizes, an old piano sat in the corner, and in the middle of the room was a circle of 20 or more school chairs, around a candle altar with some flowers. *Ah, an altar. These would be my kinda people.*

Then my eyes scanned the people already seated in the circle and my first glance was met with a seemingly reserved round-faced man who looked like my late grandad, a quiet woman who gave off a feeling that she was rather intimidated to be there, another aloof-looking woman, and one much older than me who I felt instantly was judging me suspiciously.

A familiar feeling of discomfort washed over me, the usual words echoing in my mind... *I am not like these people. They are not my tribe.*

By now, I was used to this feeling when stepping into a new circle and I knew that's not how it works. These people were here because they were to be part of my journey. I soothed my inner voice and found a chair. Popping my mesa at my feet like a comfort blanket, I remembered how sitting 'in circle' with people you don't think are like you was part of the transformation; they were a mirror, a chance to see the hidden parts of yourself. Anyway, hadn't I always found the most unlikely of characters could become the most awesome of friends?

It was clear from the energy of the Storytelling Hut that this was a sacred place for unravelling our 'stuff', unpacking our issues and alchemising our pain into lessons, then wrapping those lessons into gifts and delivering them to the world, as part of the great healing of the Earth. This was not just a course that would teach us how to tell our stories – and wow, did I have a great one to tell now! – but also to show us how there is healing and alchemy as well as an artform in telling our stories.

Taking my place in the circle, I opened my heart with warmth and excitement, trying to rein in my energy so as not to overwhelm the others. Even at the ripe age of 36, I was the eternal excited child. This often flowed out of me uncontrollably and I was aware now that my energy could be either terrifying or infectious to new people, no matter where I went or what I did there. People were often drawn to me, pulled into what they saw, but introverts would run a mile, hiding nervously in the corner, trying to work me out! I tended to make it my mission to be everyone's friend by the end of whatever it was I was doing. Charming people was my forte!

***

What the heck is the hero's journey?

As I settled in, the teacher entered and I was in love. Somewhere in her late fifties, Sue wore a funky hat over her short grey hair and a warm smile that spoke to me. It was as if her smile was saying, "You're home, you're safe, you can relax now. We're all going to have a lot of fun together."

God, this was just what I needed... I had been longing for this and I felt it so hard that I cried big fat tears of relief. I'm a crier and I can't hold it back! When my turn came, I shared how I had come to be sitting here in this circle.

"The universe left a trail of breadcrumbs for me to follow and I ended up here. I saw Danya Millar on stage in London a few months ago. I watched how she created magic through her storytelling, and something told me this was my path too. I followed the inner nudge to contact her, and to my surprise, she invited me for coffee. She said she felt she had a divine message for me; that all my work as a healer and teacher, with the seven years I spent presenting on local radio, would finally come together as on-stage storytelling. She told me about this course starting in a month's time to help me. And here I am."

I was bursting to say more yet conscious of taking up too much time, but Sue smiled warmly and I went on.

"When I booked this course, I had no idea what I would be learning or where it was going. I just knew I needed to be here, but then a miracle happened, and now I really do have a story to tell!"

I told them all about the mountains calling me from my sleep just one week before. I told them that I would be going to Australia in March and was due to fly back the day before the third weekend of this storytelling course. And I told them I was going to Peru in May and was due to fly back from there right before the final weekend.

"So you see," I said with wide-eyed excitement, "every time I come back from my quest, I will return here to the Storytelling Hut. Isn't that the most awesome thing ever? When I found this course, I had no idea that I would have such a huge story to tell and the story will be entwined with this experience. I don't know why I'm being called either, but I'm hoping you'll be able to guide me."

Okay, so I was a bit 'out there' for these people. Many of the group shared my enthusiasm and sat with excited expressions, loving the story. Others had confusion, and disbelief across their faces. I was used to people having mixed feelings when they met me and I was aware that my unusual energy was intimidating to some, overwhelming to others. For many though, they wanted in!

Sue was a wise teacher, a mentor, a person who knew the work deeply and understood the magic and wonder.

She said "I don't know what it is you'll be doing, or why you are called, but I can tell you you're at the start of something called the hero's journey. How wonderful that we all get to follow it with you. Normally, people who get called for such huge quests as this are single people who have the freedom to go. It's very unusual for people like you, who have family commitments, to be called in such a way. I will be intrigued to see what happens and see what stories you will be crafting from them."

I thought of my daughters, Avalon and Bella, who were now 9 and 5 years old. Our family was especially close knit. Harry and I worked from home and were used to being together all the time. And we loved it that way! The thought of leaving the house and the cats was bad enough. But leaving the girls, leaving Harry? I couldn't think of that now.

Sue went on to explain the hero's journey, based on Joseph Campbell's model, as the basis of all the great stories and fairytales, from Star Wars to Harry Potter. Every journey begins with a 'call to adventure' and the hero denying that call.

"Like when I told the mountains I wasn't going!", I said.

Then she described how there are helpers who appear to assist the hero on their call.

"Like Jen bringing the money and Mary helping me with the vision board.", I said.

"There will be tests or a crisis along the way. In the fairytales, this is something like a battle with a dragon, or it could be a moral challenge, something they call *being in the belly of the whale*."

Hearing this from Sue, my heart sank. I didn't want to think about this side of it and would make sure I didn't manifest any bad stuff. It wouldn't happen to me that way.

"There's always a victory, healing for the psychological wounds, and wisdom or medicine gained. That's called the sacred elixir," Sue said, almost reading my thoughts. "Then often, there's the final fight that brings more tests to challenge the hero, tests of his worth, challenges around returning home to integrate the new medicine," she finished explaining. "And of course, there's always the potential of a new call to adventure..."

***

Preparing for the quest

In many ways, we all have to take a journey. I had already been through so much to get to where I was, but I began to see that true calls come when we awaken to the fact that we are here for something greater than ourselves, a reason, a purpose. Before we can be called for a quest to the outer world, we must make that inner journey, I realised, like the one I had been on. Little did I know, this was part of the hero's journey too. The story so far, though, was not the story. It was just an initiation, the preparation for the call. The call was my purpose.

With a deep sense of self-compassion, I thought back on when my dedication to my spiritual calling almost broke me and Harry apart. I thought about how I'd believed I would lose my mind over that, and the time when I nearly did, crumpled up on the floor, crying alone in the darkness. These times were also when I'd had my most profound spiritual moments too. Awakening looks like destruction and a breaking apart of all you have known, death of the ego is painful, burning the attachments and conditioning, and belief looks like devastation, but it's a necessary journey one must take before the rebuilding of who you truly are, who you are really here to be.

That's the most rewarding journey. That's when there's a glimmer of purpose. In the dawning of our new selves comes a clarity of why it has all happened, a sense of understanding and acceptance of why it had to happen, a sense of knowing, seeing and feeling a path ahead. At the dawn of the new light, something will happen, something so big that we cannot deny the Divine.

This was my path. No one else's. It was incomparable to the paths others would take. I had to remember that.

***

Everyone is called

Each person's path is their own destiny, only theirs to take, no more or less important than anyone else's, no bigger or smaller than anyone else's, just their own place on this earth. It always looks impossible when we set out. The way ahead looks impenetrable. The more we listen to our mind, the more impossible everything seems, but the mind is a logical tool and not the guide, so we have to set it down. That's when a butterfly of belief lands in our heart and begins to open to the faith of "I don't know how this is going to happen – I just know it will." Doors open up in seemingly solid walls, and even though we step forward with fear at our side, this new faith holds us balanced.

At some point in our lives, we all must take a soul journey. All of us. The question is: do we say *yes*?

The hero's journey is about answering our own call to somewhere we have never been inside of ourselves and outside into the world. We follow the inner guidance to conquer the seemingly impossible. We gain power, wisdom and strength, and go deeper than we believed we could go.

At the centre, we are faced with our biggest fear, our shadows. When we come to see them, shine light on them, love and not deny them, we begin to see how they, the very parts of ourselves we have denied, can show us the greatest gift of this life: who we really are and why we are here.

When we know ourselves, we become alchemists, turning our wounds into wisdom, which we will humbly give back to the Earth as our part in the evolution of great super-consciousness. We are whole, unbroken rays of divine light. Our only limitations are ourselves.

To know ourselves is to see the whole world beyond the illusion. To know ourselves is to be free to step into our personal power. To know ourselves is to be at liberty to co-create with the universe and give our gift back to the world.

***

Medicine teachers

Before the Storytelling Hut, the last circle I'd sat in was during my shamanic training. Unbeknown to me, it was preparing me for my quest ahead. The medicine and the teachings were powerful, and I had been initiated as a shaman of the Q'ero lineage, and although I could and would never claim to be an Indigenous shaman, I was indeed showing up as a modern-day shaman, communing with Mother Earth and her medicine, creating harmony and peace and looking after the mental and spiritual health of my community, through healings, teachings, gatherings and ceremonies.

I had felt a connection to Peru since I was 13. All the threads led back to this, and the ways of this shamanism were through the mesa. My mesa was my most sacred medicine tool. Each of my kuyas had a unique gift that would be declared to me by the stone or by Spirit after a long process of initiation; then it would be ready to go into the centre of my mesa. The kuyas were medicine. They held wisdom and healing and power, like portals to other worlds, to the ancient medicines.

Shamans do not just see the medicine as something to ingest, but also as energy, a way of seeing and healing deep-rooted issues beyond the physical body and often beyond this lifetime. My kuyas were my medicine. My mesa was a piece of my soul that I carried with me. If I got sick, I would add herbs to it to help me heal. If I felt confused, I would take a kuya that spoke to me and blow all my fears into it to help lift the heavy energy and gain clarity. If I wanted to speak with mountains, animals or the spirit world, I would do so via my mesa. Having a mesa was a responsibility. And mine was a gateway, a portal to different worlds.

Though the teachers on the medicine wheel training course had taught with love, it had been tough love, and I often felt judged and challenged by them. I was due to go to Peru with these same teachers and I longed for them to love and accept me, but it was because I *needed* it that they did not. This is why we 'do the work' to see things deeper. This dynamic was triggering old childhood wounds around rejection. I had to learn to heal that need for acceptance to step into my true place of personal power, to be able to undertake greater responsibilities in my role as a shaman for the Earth. Until then, when I realised that the only person who needed to accept me was me, I had to put up with the seeming cold shoulders and constantly being triggered when I was around these people.

Teachers are sent to us to give us exactly what we need. Teachers are human with their own issues going on. Good ones will show up in vulnerability and be willing to be a mirror. Equally, as students, we must accept that if we pedestal, idealise and see them as 'gurus', giving away our power to them – or worse, seeing them as mother or father figures – they will indeed disappoint us at some stage with their humanness.

Teachers do not always show up as teachers either, but sometimes as friends, family and foe. And we also show up to teach others, not as teachers directly, but by playing roles in other people's stories. All stories need a hero, a villain, various friends and wise elders along the way to teach us to find the courage within.

As teachers, Josephine and James were here to help me become the shaman I was meant to be. Unbeknown to them, our time would be transitional, as I was not destined to follow their path, but they were here to lead me to the medicine that would not just heal me and my community, but the earth too.

Sue was here to teach me about stories, storytelling, my own stories, how to go deeper into the layers of parts of my life that I had somehow missed, and most importantly, how to excavate the gold from my stories to share with the world. This in itself is *shamanic*. For millennia, in cultures all around the world, we have gathered around fires and listened to stories that hold ancient wisdoms. I would learn to see the many threads in my own story weaving a rich tapestry, so that I could pull it all together and one day stand on stage to make the stories known to all who wanted to learn.

I needed nurturing in this process. And I needed acceptance by a steadfast woman who could hold my energy with love, not gooey love, but strong love, and also show me the teacher I was becoming.

When I first met her, Sue showed me she could be this for me. She could hold space for 30 people with love and strength, she believed in and guided even the most fearful of souls into a place of personal power, and she was wise in understanding and speaking the world. I began to see that she was the one who could make the invisible visible, bringing stories to life before our eyes with her words. Like magic.

One lesson in particular stayed with me from that first session.

"Abracadabra!", Sue said.

With her eyes wide and a glint of excitement in her smile, the whole world seemed to move as Sue did.

"It's Hebrew and translates as 'I create what I speak'. Everything we speak and every story we tell comes to life..."

Just like manifesting, I thought, *we think it, we say it and – abracadabra! – we bring it from the invisible world into the visible world in which we live.*

I knew for sure I was in the right place.

***

Teaching was my own path, too. I was a teacher and a mentor, and I was good at those roles. I had a following – hundreds and hundreds of students – that had become an incredible community. Human angels, they were, and I was their respected leader. One of the most important values I held was being well-regarded in my community and being of service in any way I might.

People seemed to fall onto my path. And to me, being in service meant helping as many people as I could. I gifted my time to people when I felt guided to do so. I would also be guided to run courses, which were always successful and transformational experiences for the people who attended. I just went with it, knowing the right people would come my way at the right time.

***

CHAPTER 3

Red Earth Purge

I woke up nervous. We were due to fly to Australia the next day for four weeks and I realised we hadn't been away from home for more than five days as a family and never flying. The only times were in our campervan, a short trip to Ibiza a few years before and a couple of ski holidays in France when the girls were babies.

I used to say, "Some people need to travel the world to discover themselves. I can discover as much just by being in my garden."

In truth, I was simply worried about leaving our home and our cats. I loved being home, especially in my kitchen, my favourite place, the heart of our home where all my people would congregate. I was also on edge about getting something 'wrong'. All I knew was I had to get to Uluru, which had been calling me from my sleep. One night, she told me I needed to bring my mesa, bring my energy medicine and collect energy medicine for my people. When I looked closer, I realised it was also on the map on my vision board in tiny writing.

The last nudge that made me book the internal flights to the Northern Territory and the hotel was when I told a friend of a friend that we were heading to Australia and she looked me straight in the eye and said, "You have to go to Uluru. It's near Alice Springs. That is where you're meant to be going. I can feel it."

It was the final confirmation that made me spend thousands of pounds on flights and hotels to get us there from Brisbane, our first Australian destination. Whatever that big red rock was in the heart of Australia, I was meant to go there.

***

Leaving the nest

The day ran away with me in manic mayhem, and during the course of packing and getting ready to leave, I realised we were flying out on a new moon solar eclipse. I looked at the dates again. *Oh my God, in two weeks' time, we'll be at Uluru on the full moon lunar eclipse!* I couldn't have made that happen if I'd bloody tried. Somehow, that knowing settled me and reminded me to let go.

Nonetheless, I was still running around busily and holding onto fear in my body. I was freaked out about leaving our house for so long, so I decided to do a new moon fire to release the fear. For me, fire ceremony is about releasing, honouring and bringing stillness, and that's what I needed in my busy mind right now.

I called in the four elements to create a sacred space, lit the fire, rattled my rattle and sang a fire song quietly. The fire roared and spoke to me.

Give me all that you are holding, it said.

And so I poured out my heart.

"I'm so scared, Grandfather Fire, the fear of leaving home and having to be responsible is consuming me. I feel Harry is looking to me to know what to do, but I'm looking to Spirit to guide me, and I wish I had an adult to tell me what to do!"

Trust, Louise. Take it one moment at a time. Enjoy the journey. Bring your heart and medicine. That is all that is asked.

That night, I curled up in bed for the last time before our huge journey and I honoured my excitement and nerves. I accepted all that I felt, lay one hand on my heart and the other in Harry's hand, and let the reiki flow between us. Immediately, I fell into a lucid dream state, visions of colours flying in front of my third eye, and then drifted into a deep restorative sleep.

***

As we boarded the plane from London to Dubai, Avalon turned to me, her huge brown eyes like saucers.

"We're going on an actual A380!" she squealed.

She was a plane geek and could tell almost any plane she saw in the sky. She could not believe all this was happening to her. We hardly ever flew on planes for environmental reasons, but I, too, felt it all hit me in a wave of wonder. I was never going to wake up from this dream, I realised. This was the reality of the unseen world calling and me blindly following the call. This was a necessary flight to take indeed.

Some Indigenous peoples in Australia say that the day is for dreaming and the night is for sleeping, but often we are too up in our heads to dream while awake. I didn't understand where my dreams were leading or why I was meant to share and collect energy medicine. I didn't know what all the downloads were about, but I believed it was sacred, that I had work to do on the lands at the other end of this flight, and that this was big stuff.

After a whirlwind stop in Dubai and a catch-up with some family friends, we were on our way to our second flight, with Harry and I bantering, trying to outwit each other and stake a claim on who was the funniest in the family. That's when I first noticed Avalon was quiet.

"How about we take you for a 9am beer? That'll cheer you up!" we joked as we passed the airport bar.

Thinking she was sad because she had forged a close bond with our friends' daughter and didn't want to leave, I sat reflecting on the nervousness I was feeling as we were about to board the longest flight we'd ever been on. And right then, Avalon threw up all over me.

"Shit, shit, shit!"

Avalon assumed a brave face and wanted to use 'mind over matter' to feel better for the plane. I guided her through some deep breaths and she put on her best performance of looking well as we boarded, despite her temperature climbing.

As we took off, Avalon slept next to me, poor thing curled up in a ball and looking rather grey. I pulled out my journal.

Everything will always be okay. I have all I need right here with me. There is nothing anymore. Nothing other than right here, right now. I don't need to plan for the future. I don't need to worry about tomorrow. I don't need to figure anything out. I don't need and I am not needed! I have Harry and the girls next to me and an innate trust in myself and the universe.

All I know is I am here to make a difference to this world. I want to die knowing I lived, loved and served. I always knew I was going to do something big, something that involved connecting people. I still hold that vision of myself at six or seven years old, lying awake and wondering how I could get every person in the world to hold hands in love. I think this is how. It's just less physical and more metaphysical! I always knew I would do something that would bring more love to the earth and it's happening. I just don't fully understand it all yet.

Uluru calls me at night. What is it with this big red rock? I hear her, I call back to her, I even surprise myself. A few nights ago, I shouted out at her, "Tell them I am coming!" And she tells me the medicine is waiting and I have to come and collect it. But how? That's all part of the adventure, I guess. I AM COMING! I will bring back the medicine to share with everyone who wants to receive it. And they will dance upon the belly of the earth, creating hotspots of energy, and all will awake to hear the calls of peace, joy and freedom.

My future is in the hands of the angels. I am washed with peace. I have literally no fear, because I know that my family and I are protected, whatever happens, whatever way it happens.

I am heading to a place in the world that called me from the heart, that gifted me the money to come once I said YES. I am BLESSED. Whatever this is, YES, YES, YES!

***

Angels come in many forms

As soon as we got to Australia, we were heading to a town near Byron Bay to stay for a week with one of my best friends. Fee-Fee was my first openly alternative friend, who I met when I was 22. I loved the seeming introvertedness about her that masked a whole host of childlike mischief. Fee-Fee, her husband and two kids had moved to Australia two years before to live off the grid.

Then, my best friend Sandy, her husband and her mum would join us from Sydney and together we would fly to Uluru! Sandy and I had been best friends since I was at uni. Connected by a force far greater than ourselves, we felt each other strongly, so when she'd left the UK to move to Australia three years earlier, soon followed by Fee-Fee, I had been left in a state of grief.

Fee-Fee was also coming on the Uluru adventure. On hearing this, our friend Ady in London had decided that he could not miss out and was going to fly out to meet us there too! This reminder of our reunion brought peace to my heart and a smile to my face.

Harry and I had never ever been on holiday alone. We had never been anywhere alone, apart from three nights in Ibiza for our honeymoon when he was 23 and I was 25. Even then, we followed up with five days at Glastonbury Festival with 30 of our friends. But this wasn't a holiday exactly. I looked around the plane excitedly. There must be others like me, from my tribe, from my 'planet'. Surely there were people on the same mission. I looked at the young man next to me, who was reading the *Welcome to Australia* booklet from the back of the seat in front of him and saw that the magazine was open at a photo of the rock. I interrupted his reading.

"You're going to Uluru too?" I said a little too bubbly and a little too loud, but surprised by his surprise at my friendliness.

"No," he answered and went back to his article.

I felt a pang of disappointment. I suddenly felt quite alone in all this and realised how I'd only really had my guides to talk to through the crazy time of mountains calling and money manifesting. Even the teachers who had guided me through my shamanic training, distanced themselves from my questions about what all this could mean.

I wandered around the plane, hoping to track down any other magical people who may have some answers, but a sea of Muggles stared back at me.

I sat back down and stroked Avalon's head, sending her reiki as she drifted in and out of sleep. I was worried for her still, but I kept getting messages reassuring me that everything would be okay.

***

"Look!" Harry said, elbowing me awake, "We're about to fly over Uluru!" I turned on my screen and there was a map of Australia... exactly like the one on my vision board!

The waves of weirdness and sudden intense energy were too much in that moment. If I'd been at home, I could have thrown open the back doors and grounded my energy by lying flat on the earth. But what was I supposed to do 35,000 feet up in the air? I had no idea what was happening to me, so I headed to the front of the plane to find some space, to meditate and calm down.

I felt Uluru beneath me as we flew over, like an intense jet of light energy. And then I saw him, clear as day. A man – my husband but not in this lifetime – coming towards me to welcome me home. For a moment, I felt uncomfortable. I was already married! Faced with another husband, I wasn't sure how I was meant to feel. I loved Harry whereas I didn't feel love for this man in the same way. I did, however, feel the bond of unity with him, a bond from another life, a deep connection but not a romantic one. In purpose, we had journeyed these lands below me in another lifetime. As he looked at me across the desert, he welcomed me not with a smile, not with warmth, but with seriousness, honour and wholeness.

Images flashed so fast before me that I couldn't keep up: lives, meaning, purpose. Unable to move, I sat with the intense download that I could not understand with my mind. I became acutely aware of someone standing by me – not a guide but a human – and I began to pull myself out of my meditation.

"Meditating, are you?" asked an Aussie man in his sixties, "I've come to stretch me legs."

He must have a message for me, I thought. And so, like it was the most normal thing in the world, I opened up.

"Wow! Did you feel that energy as we went over Uluru? Insane, wasn't it?"

He looked at me strangely.

"I'll let you get back to your meditation, darl."

I laughed, dejected on the inside that he had no answers for me, but also with the realisation that yet another person on this plane now thought I was a fruitcake. And with that, I resolved to stop assuming that everyone I met was on the same mission.

EARTH CHAKRA SHAMAN

***

"How's she doing?" asked the flight attendant, looking worriedly at my daughter.

It had been almost 17 hours since Dubai and Avalon was not looking much better. This soft-faced flight attendant was the only one of the crew not whispering and looking over at us like we were criminals.

"I'm concerned that they will want to quarantine her when we land. If that happens, they may send you all home again," she said.

Once we arrived, we would be last to leave the plane, she told us, and we would need to go see the doctors on the other side, who would be in charge of what would happen to us. Another man came to lead us off the plane and Harry carried a lifeless little Avalon on his shoulder to her wheelchair. Without warning, a steward began wheeling her away, so fast that it was hard for Bella to keep up. I picked her up and hurried after the steward, who'd come out of nowhere and who didn't say a word. We knew better than to ask any questions, but then I realised we were going into passport control. As she queue-jumped lines and lines of people, I realised she was sticking her neck out for us.

"Don't say anything. Just agree," she whispered when we got to the front of the line.

"What's wrong with the child?" the man checking passports asked.

"She got sunstroke in Dubai," the steward replied.

"Ah okay," he smiled and waved us through.

Next thing I knew, my family and I stood in baggage claim ahead of anyone else who'd been on our plane. I wanted to hug the steward, but she backed away and kept calm.

"Don't make a fuss. Just get out of here."

She winked and walked back the way we'd come.

"Just keep walking," Harry said under his breath, as he lifted our cases off the baggage carousel, of course they came through first and all together.

As gracefully as we could, we grabbed one each and left the airport, where we were greeted by a rainbow.

***

Knowing and trusting

The sun beat down on our little boat that bobbed on the rainforest-banked river. Fee-Fee's husband Shane turned off the engine and I felt an unfamiliar energy of being somewhere I had never been in this lifetime. The huge trunks of the ancient trees sunk under the water and their aliveness was strong. I didn't even have to *try* to connect with them; they were already speaking to me. I felt like a queen being welcomed by her ancient warriors.

When you connect with the stillness in every moment, you're in the divine flow of your soul, they whispered.

Everything means so much. Everything has meaning. I knew everything was just as it needed to be. I didn't have to *do* anything other than let the universe guide me and this deep sense of surrender was bliss.

Even though Avalon was still unwell, she was pulling through. She curled into my arms and I observed the sacredness of nature as waves lapped the side of the boat. I had never seen a river leading out to the sea before and was mesmerised when Shane pulled us onto the shore of a magical hidden beach.

As I sat reflecting on this paradise, I watched Avalon make what can only be described as a miraculous recovery. She ran through the crystal blue waters and danced on the beach. I couldn't believe it. I knew nature was a great healer, but these were healing lands indeed. We stayed and chatted and splashed and danced for hours that afternoon. I took it all in. I was really here in this place. And everything was perfect.

***

It felt safe being with Fee-Fee and her family. Plus, their off-the-grid eco-home was a dream! She had talked about it all her life; a dream I could see she had created. Not only was it sustainable, growing veggies and collecting rainwater, but it was uber modern, slick and massive. She was doing her best for this world and I admired her. As a couple, they had both put in the work, made the leaps and taken the risks to be more aligned with nature.

Mullumbimby was my perfect town too: full of hippies, surrounded by powerful lands, the rainforest and a sacred mountain that Fee informed me was connected to Uluru by the ley lines, the path of the Rainbow Serpent. The main town nearby was Byron Bay – a powerful energy spot and place of pilgrimage in itself. The energy was strong, often too strong for people to live there for long. I had seen that same powerful land energy and ley line connection with Glastonbury and Stonehenge. Being there was like living with a permanent full moon!

One day, we walked to Broken Head Beach and came to a vast red water lagoon surrounded by tea trees. It was an aboriginal birthing lake, filled with sacred feminine energy. We swam in the lake and honoured the women who had brought life to the world. Back on shore, I opened my mesa and felt the energy rise into my soul.

In meditation, I felt the presence of some awful horrors that had happened here. Even though the beauty of the place was breath-taking, it hit me in the heart that I had not understood the harm done to Indigenous peoples. Fee-Fee confirmed that this was indeed where mass slaughters of Aboriginal people had taken place from the late 1700s onwards in the name of colonization.

"Listen to the name of the beach – Broken Head. Says it all, don't you think?", Fee-Fee Said.

The history was not as bright as I had been taught to believe and it came with a deep realisation and shame that white people did not come here peacefully. We did not come in peace.

***

Spiritual preparation

I woke up in the middle of the night, temperature high, head pounding. And then I threw up. And then threw up some more. And then some more.

The purge.
The purge.
The purge.

I must have caught Avalon's bug. I was sure it would pass, but I got sicker and sicker until my headache was unbearable. I tossed and turned, waking Harry who was trying to sleep his jetlag away. Occasionally, he would put a hand on my head, but most of the night I was in pain and alone, not wanting to disturb my friends and their kids.

I was grateful to hear the sounds of the house stirring, hoping someone would help me. I stumbled out of bed, like a child looking for the comfort of her mum, but I took one look at Fee-Fee and found myself back in the bathroom with my head down the toilet again.

Later that morning, I tried to get up, but I couldn't do anything. I lay in the bed listening to the soothing rainforest sounds, wanting Harry by my side. He would come to my call, stroke my head for a moment, then leave. I didn't want to be alone, but he wasn't going to rescue me. I threw up and threw up, for hours and hours and hours. I threw up all day, thankful for sleep when it came and took away the pain in my head. Day turned into night, and it got even worse.

Between sleeping, I was hallucinating, seeing visions that I could not grasp. I knew this was a purge, that I had to breathe into the pain in my crown chakra, that I must go into it and ride it like a wave. I dived into the pain, looking at it, trying to understand it. It was hard work, compounded by my need to be rescued. I wanted someone to come and make it all better, but this would get in the way of the work. As soon as I resisted and held on to the idea of being saved, I would be back at square one, crying, head exploding, feeling the exhaustion and tears.

I realised what was happening. I was bringing up the *hucha*, the stagnant heavy energy. I was purging the old stuck energy from my body, ready to go to Uluru clean and clear.

I had no idea where I was in space and time, but something was telling me to look at my messages, so I reached for my phone and saw a video from my friend Simon.

Saw this thought of you...

It was old, old, old footage of a Native American shaman dancing to an old Jim Pepper song:

Witchi-tie-to, gimee rah

Whoa rah neeko, whoa rah neeko

Hey ney, hey ney, no way

Water spirit feelin' spinning' round my head

Makes me feel glad that I'm not dead.

Head heavy on the pillow, I gazed at the feathered headdress that was almost the size of the man. The headdress itself was medicine. His dance was medicine. His song was medicine. I held my mesa close and played the three-minute video over and over again, tears rolling down my face. I felt myself coming back into the world...

Water spirit feelin' spinning' round my head
Makes me feel glad that I'm not dead.

I smiled though the headache was still intense. This purge was still not over, but I was ready to move.

Next morning, I breathed deeply and made myself get up. I couldn't spend my only few days in Byron lying in a darkened room! I had to at least try to do something for myself. As I wandered through the house, it felt like I was walking on a 90-degree angle, like my head was underwater. I was weak, shaking, but determined to make it to the back door and outside. As soon as I made it, the humidity hit me, but I sat in the discomfort on the edge of a chair and stared into the garden. The colours were bright; the plants vibrant. I wished to feel well enough to enjoy this aliveness. Maybe nature was reminding me of my own aliveness somewhere inside.

Go out into the mud and get your feet on the earth, my inner guidance whispered.

I wobbled to the bare red soil and marvelled at the colour, which I hadn't noticed until now. I opened my arms and cried as the rains began to fall.

"Wash away this purge. Clear me of all that no longer serves. Mother Waters, please, wash my spirit clean."

I knelt on the mud and I knew what I needed to do.

"Fee-Fee," I called out, "I have to create a sacred space. Is it okay to do that on your lands?"

"Go ahead," she smiled, relieved to see me up and about.

I reached for my mesa and rattle and began.

***

Prayer to the lands

I sat under a tree and called in the animal archetypes, spirits from my Peruvian medicine lineage and the connection to the four directions.

"To the winds of the south, honouring serpent and Mother Waters, come be with me. Help me to shed the past the way you shed your skin. May the past and all that no longer serves be washed away in the waters, so I can walk gently on the earth, touching all with beauty and honour.

To the winds of the west, honouring mother-sister jaguar and the element of earth, come be with me. Let me see into my shadows, so I can return the hucha and all that no longer serves me back to the earth, may you transmute it back into its original form, light energy, to light the path over the rainbow bridge. I walk as a rainbow warrior, a peaceful warrior.

To the winds of the north, honouring sweet hummingbird and the element of air, come be with me. Show me where to find the nectar, the joy and love in life. Show me how to make the impossible possible as I begin to take another step upon my journey of growth and evolution on these lands and in my soul.

Calling my ancestors and grandmothers, grandfathers, and the ancient ones of these lands, all of you who have come before me, who love me unconditionally, come be with me. Whisper to me on the wind your guidance in creating a world for all who will come after me, my children and my children's children.

To the winds of the east, great eagle condor and the element of Grandfather Fire, come be with me. May I be warmed by your wisdom as I dream the world I want to see into being and watch those dreams float up to Great Spirit on your embers. As I fly high above the sacred mountains of this world on the back of great eagle, may I see from this perspective of all that is unfolding."

I touched my forehead to the earth and I felt her...

"Pachamama, Mother Earth, I come in deepest honouring of all my relations, the stone people, the plants, the trees, the finned, the winged, the four-legged, the many-legged. Pachamama, Mother Earth, I walk upon your belly every day and you nurture me. Thank you, thank you, thank you for this gift, this body, the blessing of life. I pray for the nourishment and freedom of all my relations as we dance upon your belly, experiencing this great journey of life. I rejoice."

I raised my head, threw my arms in the air with all the energy I could find, and stood up with joy.

"Grandmother Moon, Father Sun, all the star nations, please come be with me. Thank you, thank you, thank you for guiding me and reminding me that we all shine like stars in the sky and that I too am part of this great constellation and this cosmic order that takes place for all eternity.

Great Spirit, you are known by a thousand names and yet you are the unnameable one. Thank you, thank you, thank you. As I rise up, I give thanks for you giving me this life. May I sing and dance and bring freedom and love in this life.

A'ho."

Sacred prayer said, sacred space created, I opened my mesa and brought my medicine stones to the earth. I met the lands. I listened to Mother Earth speak, asking me to clean away the old so I could get to Uluru in the energetic vibration that was needed of me. My mesa was a part of me and I could heal through it. As each kuya touched the earth one by one, I could feel the healing from the earth within me. I would leave them in this place for at least a day.

Still weak but determined to move, I visited the Crystal Castle, a beautiful garden of crystals. I moved tenderly about but was in so much pain that I could not move past a giant rose quartz that was taller than me and five times as wide. I stood with my forehead against the crystal and found relief. Much as I wanted to stay this way all day, I needed to get back to the house. As we were leaving, a pyrite stone called to me from the little shop. As I held it, its healing medicine began to work on me immediately and I knew I had to buy it. Unknown to me at the time, in the coming months, this stone would play an important role in a calling way beyond anything I could have imagined.

"There's a sober rave in the mountains tonight, Lou. Reckon you could make it out?" Fee-Fee asked as we returned home.

"If there's music and dancing, I will find a way," I answered, lying face-down on the floor holding my new stone in my hand.

That night, we drove through the mountains in insane storms, fork lightning all around, and found our tiny little rave in the hills. I drank alcohol-free catnip cocktails and danced barefoot to big bass drops, laughing at the miracle healing I had experienced over the last few hours.

I was alive. I was purged. I was healed. I was dancing with new energy. And I was ready to meet Uluru.

***

CHAPTER 4

Uluru & the Solar Plexus Chakra

Maybe I was expecting a wow moment when I got there. A knowing or a feeling. Something big to happen. But nope. Nothing. No rainbows, no unicorns, no magical lightning bolts of energy. I had only learned in the past month that it was the most sacred spot in Australia and it was strange to see something so grand from the viewing platform, that huge red rock, standing before me about a mile away and feel no connection.

The cost of going to Uluru was astronomic. On booking the flight and accommodation, I saw how this big red rock – so sacred to the native peoples – was being monopolised. Undeterred, I knew I had to use the money gifted to me to go to where I was called; it never felt like it was mine to keep, but a resource for the Earth, for me to be in service.

My mind raced.

Why am I here? What's going on? What am I supposed to do next? I thought it would be more magical than this!

I listened to the mind chatter. Years of mindfulness practice meant it didn't happen so often these days. When it did, I'd learned to listen to what was really going on and navigate my way through it. I knew how to bring myself back to peace through self-mentoring.

"How am I feeling?"

Worried.

"Why am I worried?"

Because I was expecting a bigger feeling than this, a magical welcoming party, where all my ancestors would dance around the fires.

"What does it mean to me that that hasn't happened?"

That maybe I've done something wrong. That I should be doing something more.

"What will it take for me to let go of the expectation?"

To see it differently, to trust, to let go of my need to know and understand. I need to remember I've only just got off the plane. We haven't eaten yet. We have five days in this place. I need to open my eyes wider, see from an eagle perspective, see the whole moment and come out of my head.

I felt my energy shift, from fear to gratitude, and return back to my old happy-go-lucky self.

At that moment, Sandy came up to me, her huge pregnant belly and massive smile welcoming me, and put her hand on my shoulder.

"Fucking love you, bird."

I threw my arms around her.

"Fucking love you too, bird."

And we embraced, I remembered that, yes, I was here for sacred service, but also to be reunited with my best friend! Still holding one another, I looked at our tribe of nine, reunited for the first time in years, all watching the sun go down on the giant red rock in the distance. I was surrounded with love for all of them and for a moment everyone was quiet, just looking out into the stillness.

This was the beginning of the call, this love. And as the golden sun went down behind Uluru, I knew I had to trust and not chase. I would let the coming days unfold as they needed. A lesson I was to learn over and over again, layer by layer by layer...

Trust in the flow.

***

Sacred land

At sunrise, we took a tour to the rock. Uluru was bigger than I could ever have imagined. I felt like a tiny person looking up a sandstone mountain. I was grateful that we had an Aboriginal person as our guide, so as to feel the deep passion for the lands and his culture.

He shared that first nations people of Australia belong to the oldest culture known to man, dating back 60,000 years. And that all of the landscape, including Uluru and Kata-Tjuta (another sacred location not far from where we were), had been created at the beginning of time by great ancestral beings: star people from the Seven Sisters, the star cluster known as the Pleiades.

My heart skipped a beat at its mention. I had been obsessed with this star system since I was a child, feeling a deep sense of home and safety when it appeared in the night sky and grief when I could not see it in the summer months.

I loved the synergy and somehow felt like this was a piece of the puzzle I was putting together around this calling.

It would take hours to walk around the base of Uluru and most of it was closed to tourists, but our guide took us to waterholes and caves, and shared that for over 10,000 years Uluru had been a sacred ceremonial site for the Anangu people.

I could feel the hand that drew these cave drawings held the wisdom of living in accordance with natural law, passed down the ancestral timeline through all those who had walked before, for all those who would walk after. Stories held wisdom, teachings, medicine… and these stories were ancient.

It was impossible to grasp the immenseness of what it meant to stand here. It had seemed to me that life was simple on Earth back then. But it was not simple; it was far from simple. Aboriginal culture was complex, interwoven with the land. They knew how to live in balance on the earth. Then we clueless white Westerners destroyed and continued to destroy it.

This was the heart of Australia, yet I also became aware that this sacred rock was the core of a corporate village, a resort of hotels and restaurants. Even though the Anangu people requested no climbing of the rock, tourists came just for this. The depths of the wounds of these lands went so much deeper than just this though. And as I dived in, I became profoundly aware of something I was never taught in school.

My heart began to twist at the realisation.

**

Awakening to the truth

My ancestors had decimated the most ancient people of our Earth, regarded them as 'primitive'. Through eyes of white superiority, we saw them as less than us, a way to justify our invasion. We did the worst possible thing. We uprooted them, unhooked them from their life force – the land. In less than 200 years, the very fabric that held together 60,000 years of culture had been unwoven through brutal massacre. And those who remained watched their children being stolen, locked into institutions, assaulted and abused in the name of a Christian god until they rejected their Indigenous culture. And when the remaining survivors adopted the white way of living, they were still disregarded in society.

There was no place for them. While the whites thrived on their native lands, those who remained were destined to a life of poverty. This was as true today as it was hundreds of years ago. Addiction and suicide have become a path for many who carry the unhealed wounds of a traumatised culture. I wondered what had happened to my own culture to have become so cold in the quest for gold.

I listened to our guide tell the stories of the ancient ways, how boys at 13 years old would leave their mothers to be with the men. They themselves would return years later as men. And I heard the judgment of an American woman – "how awful" – and wanted both to agree with her from my own Western perspective and to shout at her for her judgment of the cultures as 'wrong', simply because it didn't adhere to her beliefs.

I realised I was projecting onto her my own shadow of being a tourist. I thought I was 'better than her', my own self-importance denying the fact that *I was a tourist, I was white, I was privileged,* and *I was ashamed.* Whatever we see in others, whatever triggers us on the outside, we have inside of us too.

Up popped my ego in that moment. I wanted the guide to see I wasn't a tourist like the American. I wanted to be like him, not her. In this denial of my shame of being white and privileged, my ego began to run the show and I could only watch myself in horror.

"Is there anywhere I could do a sacred fire for the full moon tomorrow?" I asked the guide, with the intention that he would understand I was here for spiritual purposes, as a bringer of medicine, as a healer, as a great shaman, as the chosen one.

The guide looked at me bemused, not knowing what to say. I sensed him see right through my bullshit and then he walked off!

Internally, I shrunk but I had to laugh at myself too for my ego's need to be something more than I was – a white tourist, one of the many great-great-great-granddaughters of the lands of Captain Cook.

***

Singing the sound of the lands

On the morning of the full moon eclipse, we set off at 4am for an adventure to Kata-Tjuta, another sacred rock that was 40 minutes' drive away. As we piled into two cars, I squealed like a child.

"The moon is setting on the desert horizon!"

Still half-asleep, the kids did not share my excitement.

"Today is a full moon lunar eclipse, guys, and it has rained overnight. It's a blessed day!"

We headed off on a wing and a prayer, not really knowing where we were going. As we pulled into the car park at the Valley of the Winds, dawn was breaking.

In front of us was another huge red rock, a different shape to Uluru, but just as magnetic. The darkness was fading quickly, revealing the beauty of the place. The feeling in my solar plexus was intense, the most intensity I'd felt since we'd arrived in the desert. My body was vibrating with the lands now, as though my solar plexus had a connection into the earth. This sensation was like a magnet pulling me towards it.

The light of the new day filled my heart as the rising sun made the reds and oranges glow. Hearing the kids calling me in the distance, I carried on walking, a woman on a mission, knowing Harry would be with them. I didn't have long here. The flies were unbearable already, the heat of the day would soon scorch us, and Sandy had stayed in the car with her mum, the two of them unable to climb. Whatever I had to do here, it had to be done swiftly...

I climbed into the gorge, separated myself from everyone else and pulled out my mesa, frantically rummaging for my kuyas. One by one, I placed all 13 stones in a circle on the earth.

"I am here, Mama," I whispered with tears in my eyes. "I am sorry for the hurt my people have caused. I bring my energy medicine as an offering to you. May there be healing, Mama."

Deep love flowed through me and silent prayers fell from my heart into the earth. Time stood still, as a remembering happened, a knowing that these lands had called me, as they had once been home many lifetimes before. I closed my eyes and images flashed before me. I felt my whole body vibrate with connection to new dimensions, giving and receiving, the sacredness of the land flowing through my being.

I knew then, with such gratitude, that being here was divinely guided in every way. From funding to timing, nothing and nobody could have planned this. The divine had planned this, right down to this very moment. The awareness of this miracle hit me and burst my heart open. Tears fell onto my kuyas and onto the red soil as I pressed my forehead to the earth.

"Thank you, Mama. Thank you for calling me. I love you."

Songs rose from me, through my base chakra, through my solar plexus, and out of my mouth. I had never experienced the land singing through me before, but it was unstoppable. As I let the sound out through my throat, it overrode my self-consciousness, though I could hear my ego judging me from afar. Whatever fear I felt, I honoured the flow of this gift from the lands.

"We've gotta go, Lou!" Harry yelled up from further down the gorge.

I didn't want to rush this moment, but I knew the flies were getting too much for everyone.

"Two minutes, babe," I shouted back.

Feeling like a total crazy woman in my self-consciousness, but knowing this was a gift from the lands, I grabbed my phone and recorded the song that was flowing through me. One day I would share it and it would be healing medicine for others.

***

Back at the hotel, I needed to rest and nap and integrate the downloads I'd received at Kata-Tjuta. Dreams, visions and messages flowed as I slept, and I scribbled them down in my journal when I woke.

In my dream, I got a message to return the stones that Sandy's mum had given me on the first morning we went to Uluru and give them back in ceremony. I looked now at the four pieces of red stone – "one for each of you as a memento" – that she had given with such love. Later, we had learned the Anangu people requested people not to take stones from this place in respect for its sacredness, so at dinner I suggested a giving-back ceremony for the stones. To my amazement, everyone agreed and that's when I knew this was part of the greater plan.

***

Giving back what was taken

The moon was bright as we gathered at the car park at the base of Uluru at one of the few places we were allowed to be close to the rock. There was this sense of sacred mission within all of us as I called everyone into a circle. For a moment, I was self-conscious, as my friends had never observed me in my inner shaman, but there was no time for ego now. This was sacred work.

I raised my rattle in the air and felt the veil of Uluru open. This was the connection I had been waiting to feel. As though she was opening the doors to a private members club, her energy pulsated.

I called in the four directions, Great Spirit and Mother Earth, Grandmother Moon and all the star nations, especially the Seven Sisters constellation, the Pleiades, a place I had felt certain all my life that I once belonged. Although I could not see them tonight, I knew they were looking over this moment. I called in the spirit of the lands to come be with us too and the prayers began to flow from my heart.

Around me, my friends stood with their arms in the air immersed in the prayers I was leading.

"Uluru, we come in deepest honouring of these lands and your people. We come to return what does not belong to us."

As we returned each of the stones back from where they had come, it felt like we were energetically healing not only what we had taken, but what our ancestral lines had taken too.

"May this prayer heal the lineage of our ancestors taking from these lands and these people what did not belong to us. We come in honouring and healing of the wounds of these lands and these people. May all that has been taken be returned. May balance and harmony be returned. May the medicine for the people be pure. May we all be united in love."

We knelt and touched the earth with our foreheads, and as we closed the ceremony, a deep reverence settled over us.

I looked up and saw a cloud in the shape of a perfect eagle, a sacred message. There were gasps all around, but I knew it was a sign of affirmation of our work. I felt the tiny hands of both my daughters slip into mine, knowing their own wisdom of the earth was growing like seeds inside of their hearts. We were raising rainbow warriors. I would not shield them from the truth. As I was awakening to the past,

EARTH CHAKRA SHAMAN

I was healing the future for my children, and all the children of this Earth.

***

Before we left that morning, I returned back to the base of Uluru for a final emotional goodbye and to give thanks for the deep transformation I'd been gifted by the richness of this red earth and by sharing the medicine within my mesa.

I sat in meditation in the early morning light, my medicine stones sitting on the earth, and felt the energy from them dropping into the lands and the lands feeding them their medicine. The veil was still open to me and the spirit of Uluru was welcoming. It was beautiful. Gently, in stillness, with the sting of tears in my eyes and light energy pouring from my hands into the earth, I felt a powerful activation happening in my solar plexus as if I was being gifted a blessing from the land.

Then the spirit of the Rainbow Serpent spoke to my soul.

The tide is turning, she said, *and you are part of this now.*

I was yet to discover what the Rainbow Serpent really was and how these lands played a part in the picture – both for the Earth and for my own quest. However, I was beginning to let go of needing to understand everything, instead surrendering into the unfolding. My innocence and wonder were my superpower. It brought joy and gratitude, awe and excitement into the mix. This was my medicine that fed and awakened people. This was what brought hope to many and what I was truly sharing with the Earth.

***

LOUISE CARRON HARRIS

Solar Plexus Chakra Prayer
Abundance

Rainbow Serpent, sacred feminine energy ley of our Earth,
I honour your life force,
your vitality and your wisdom that runs through Earth's grid.
I honour your spirit, your water and your light.
You are life, the flow of ancient wisdoms, the sharer of new codes.

Rainbow Serpent, Uluru, Kata-Tjuta,
I call upon you to awaken health and vitality
within and without.
In seeing all is alive,
I am abundant, reverent.
I gratefully receive aligned abundance with joy and wonder.
I share my new vitality with others.
I shine your rainbow light from within.
I will live in harmony in the right relationship with the Earth and all my relations.
I now call upon your rainbow rivers of light
to grow and evolve the consciousness
for the good of all.

CHAPTER 5

Unfolding of the Earth Chakra Call

Back at the Storytelling Hut, I was greeted with hugs, smiles and familiar faces.

"How was it, Lou? Can't wait to hear what you have to tell!"

I was jetlagged having landed back on UK soil just 24 hours earlier, so I was particularly tired and emotional, but when Sue entered the room, her bright warm smile made my body relax into contentedness. I felt teary. It was so good to see her! And I became aware of the little girl within me, still seeking a mother's guidance. Someone to say, "Well done, Louise, you succeeded", or at least listen to my stories, and understand where I had been and what I had learned.

"Louise!" she beamed in delight upon seeing me. "I bet you have some stories!"

Just the way she said my name was enough to fill me with a sense of home. She was the teacher I had been craving, someone who could see me, accept me, hold space for me with strength, safety, non-judgment and wisdom.

"Tell us a story about your quest."

I had news, a piece of the mystery puzzle, and I was desperate to share. So I settled into the circle and told them my latest revelation. I tried to tell it in a way that would embed the lesson.

"Last night, I had a vision of being in America waiting outside Indigenous lands near a mountain surrounded by ancient redwoods with Harry and the girls. I thought if I just waited patiently enough, eventually the Indigenous leader would accept me, but after three long days, we were still sitting there. In the vision, I knew Harry was showing me that he was willing to go wherever I needed to go.

Then like a lightbulb, I realised I needn't have waited this long at all. They would have called me sooner had I connected to their dreams. At that moment, I was transported to a Native American fire. I gave the elder some roses to represent love and my English roots. I was nervous, but I knew him in some way, so I asked him to show me 'the medicine'.

From his garments, he pulled out a large stone. In the same way I transfer my energy or medicine into a stone by blowing into it, he blew the energy of stories about how we used to hear the Earth, how the Earth could speak clearly to us, even through the blades of grass, and how we would hear her voice. With great sadness, he told me how the Earth was now quiet.

She is dying, Louise. What awakens her is hearing your feet dance on the Earth.

He showed me how I would create hotspots of hope on the Earth. He told me he was a new guide, who had come to me now to help me on my quest and I was to know him as 'Bird'.

We looked into the fire together and he showed me a beautiful vision that included me. I was showing people how to have fires in their gardens, how to sing and dance freely. I could see people around my fire, who then went out and had their own. People were remembering the old way, returning to an ancient part in themselves, listening to the medicine of our own lands. I saw gardens lighting up across the UK, on full moons, on new moons, people dancing with their brothers and sisters barefoot on the lands, and Gaia awakening because we are awakening back to our own ancient ways.

It felt then like we were grandfather and granddaughter, talking and talking. He gifted me and my mesa his medicine knowledge. There was so much love, hope and acceptance."

***

Guess what I just learned!

They all thought that was the end of my story, but it wasn't.

"I have more to tell you. This is just a small piece that led to something else."

I was urged on, everyone's eyes wide open, ready for more...

"Before I came here today, I had a call from a fellow shaman friend who I trained with and I told him about the Native American vision. I told him I knew this dream was a thread I had to follow. Somehow, I knew I would have to go to America when I come back from Peru and find where these redwoods are, and also a mountain."

In truth, I had shared with him a lot of the weird whisperings I'd been getting from Spirit. The name 'Alaska' had been calling to me strongly, as though a real person was standing behind me and softy pouring the word into my ears at random times of the day and night. There was an image of an ice cave and crystal blue waters on my latest vision board too, and every time I caught sight of it, 'Alaska' would echo in my mind.

"Oh my God, Lou! You're being called to the earth chakras," my friend had exclaimed.

Intrigued, I'd asked him to elaborate and a whole world had unfolded before me.

"The redwoods lead to Mount Shasta, the mountain that you must go to in America. It is the base chakra of the Earth. It is sacred to the Native American people of the area. I can feel that you are meant to go there. Of course, you're being called there, Lou. You are *indigo*! The indigo children get called to the chakras to activate the consciousness of the new Earth. That's why you're going to Lake Titicaca in Peru. It's the sacral chakra of the Earth. And you have just returned from Uluru, which is the solar plexus chakra. And you're always in Glastonbury. You're always called there. That's the Earth's heart chakra!"

He had explained at length, but I'd been transported back to that intense feeling in my solar plexus when I'd visited Uluru. I remembered how it had sung to me from my solar plexus, and on the last day, the Rainbow Serpent had sat in that same place too. I was still puzzled by the Alaska connection though.

"The Earth has a whole grid system. In fact, the Rainbow Serpent is one of the main ley lines. She runs from Uluru to Lake Titicaca. There will be a reason you need to go to Alaska. It will all unfold."

EARTH CHAKRA SHAMAN

Of course, the Earth had a grid. Of course, it had seven chakras just like us humans. It was all so overwhelming to understand on a head level, but I could feel it. I needed to know more, know where the other chakras were.

"The throat chakra is the Great Pyramids in Egypt and the third eye is the chakra that moves with each aeon. It is currently in Shaftesbury and Glastonbury in the UK, for the dawning of the Age of Aquarius. Which is now, basically. It will be here until 2080 when the Age of Aquarius is fully activated. Then it will move back to the north pole until it's time for the dawning of the Age of Capricorn, when it will move to Brazil. That'll be in about another 2000 years' time."

"And the seventh one?"

"That's at Mount Kailash, the holiest mountain in the world in Tibet."

I'd never heard of this mountain, which reinforced my instinct that my focus should stay with Shasta and Alaska. I was bemused, but I trusted all this and was now trusting my group at the Storytelling Hut with my newfound insights. Everyone listening was high on my wonder, and Sue was smiling knowingly, enjoying my revelations.

"I don't even know how I'm going to get to America or Alaska, and we spent every last drop on Australia and Peru, but I know that the universe provides when I say yes. So I say yes!" I finished breathlessly.

For the rest of the weekend, the excitement of what was to come and the space to process and talk about it with others kept me energised until it was time to go home to my bed, my cats and dancing in my kitchen. I had really missed it all!

***

Chaos and abundance

Peru was approaching and my days were full-on.

There was only a vague line between my life and my work. I was my work and my work was my life. Our home was a hub too, not just for friends and family, but for students, clients and my business as a whole. On the outside, it just looked like I was busy, always having a great time and seeing hundreds of people. Indeed, that was true, but every conversation, every action, every call had to have depth to it. Everything had to have meaning. Everything was about being in service.

Still, it was hard to find time sometimes…

I was checking my messages in the kitchen, when Harry came up behind me, kissed my neck, turned me round and looked at me in *that* way…

"I can't, babe. I have a client in half an hour!"

"We only need five minutes, babe," he joked, as he picked me up.

I was always surprised that he could still carry me up the stairs, even after all these years. He would seize those moments. I loved it when he did this. It gave me no option other than being fully present with him. I was always there for everyone else, but actually I craved just being there for the two of us.

People wanted love and I wasn't afraid to give it. Harry was a beautiful sharer of me. He was so used to everyone wanting to bottle me up and take me home that he had become so patient with it. Our house was always overflowing with people and I loved the community I'd created. To me, it was an honour to teach and share with so many men, women and kids. They were all special to me, and I would hug and kiss any of them, because I loved them and wanted them to know that they were special, unique and here for a reason. To see people rising into their power delighted me in every way.

One of my best friends Sarah would call me 'the littlest hobo', turning up in people's lives to heal them.

"They want you to stay, but you have to keep moving on," she would joke.

The consequence was that I didn't have enough time for everyone. I was always flying from place to place. I was disorganised, flighty, forgetful, spreading myself too thin. I would do my best and give all I could, but often that wasn't enough for them. Even though over-giving would sometimes be detrimental to my family, I didn't want to stop bringing people into my world and there were those who were able to accept that what I could give them was enough.

The year before, my shamanic teachers had told me to rein it in.

"Your energy is gushing out of you, Louise. You need to contain it. Why do you have no boundaries, Louise? Stop letting everything in."

But I could not see how it was a bad thing. I'd felt triggered by their calling me out for being 'nice' and being open to everything.

They could see something coming that I could not.

***

The whispering began again as I was driving a few days before I was due to go to Peru – *Alaska, Alaska, Alaska*. It was more intense this time and I was vaguely aware of people being put away in mental hospitals for hearing voices, but the voice was clear.

"Fine!" I shouted, "I hear you! If you want me to come to Alaska, you will have to send me the money again."

A car zoomed past with 888 on the registration, the number of manifestation and abundance.

"Bloody hell, that was quick, even for angels!" I laughed.

Within an hour, I was approached by my student Jen. She had been given an angelic nudge a few months ago to become my business partner, but I had pushed the idea away, afraid of working with others. However, she had received another sign from the angels, and now she was offering me the kind of money that would enable me to go to the places I was called.

Instantly, I felt awkward. Harry shuffled around in the doorway, listening but not wanting to intrude. I was battling with my ego. I wanted to be able to do this on my own, to manifest my own money, to prove to myself I was successful, but this call was bigger than that. And Jen, like me, wanted to help people and give back to the world.

Out of the corner of my eye, I could see Harry smiling and I imagined him to be thinking this whole thing was yet another ordinary day in Lou's world. I looked at him for reassurance, hoping he would tell me not to take the offer.

Instead, he said, "Jen just wants to help, babe. You'd be a great team."

"I don't know, Jen. I can't make a decision right now. Let me feel into it for a few days." I headed off to bed with a strange sense of excitement and trepidation.

***

Receiving from the Divine

The next day was spent teaching my reiki group and I shared with them my dilemma of struggling to receive the money. It was my style to teach through my own learnings and vulnerability.

"We are all eternal students of life. The more we grow, the more we have to navigate new waters and surf bigger waves. It's okay to not always know the answers, no matter how enlightened we think we are!"

I felt the presence of Jen sitting next to me in the teaching circle, like a stable partner, and it suddenly felt very right. The students shared how they could see the love as well as our potential to bring great change to the world.

"Just take the money!" everyone laughed.

Two days later, both of us back home, I called her with an answer.

"How about I say yes, I go to America over the summer and then we start work in September?"

She laughed, I laughed, she cried, I cried, we got excited and were giddy because we were always on the same wavelength, always thinking the same thoughts. Our connection was undeniable. It was meant to be. Drunk on the synergies, intoxicated with the wonder, our dreams to change the world for the greater good were about to become a reality.

It was our destiny...

***

CHAPTER 6

Peru's Gifts of Growth

As I packed my bags, my heart thumped hard and I could not stop crying. Later, I lay awake all night feeling the winds of change blowing through my being. This was not my life. This was not who I was. This was not who *we* were. We had never been apart, but now I was going to be apart from Harry and the girls for nearly three weeks. It was such a long time. How would they be without me? How would he be without me? I had no idea but also no choice. This was my destiny, my calling, and I had already said yes.

In a way, I felt like I was a superhero pulling on her suit to go on a mission to save the planet. Another part of me felt like a little girl leaving her family, because her spirit would not let her stay home any longer. And then there was the shaman in me, who silently watched me grow, patiently waiting for her moment to rise from within. I was awash with humility. I was in service, rising up, walking my path of purpose, acknowledging the call, being led only by my faith. Yes, I was still a little girl in many ways, but I was the powerful, playful woman too. Yes, I was still learning, but I was also ancient and wise, a medicine woman who had been here many lifetimes before this one.

I knew this path in my heart already before I'd even walked it.

***

Dyslexic world

I stood in the airport, figuring out where I was meant to drop off my bags, trying to take responsibility for myself. I had to take this first step on my own and Harry could feel that. I had to understand where to check in at least!

As I tried to make sense of the screens, slight panic welled up. I couldn't read it. It was all scrambled and I couldn't work out what was what. A familiar feeling of hopeless frustration that had been with me my entire school life flooded my body, as if I was back in the classroom unable to grasp anything that was going on.

I wanted Harry to just tell me what to do, where to go, to lead me there, check my bags and point me in the direction of my gate, but he held back. I could tell he was trying to step out of his role as much as I was. Tears burned in the corners of my eyes. I had to let this old dyslexic story go.

That wound, like all our wounds, was becoming my medicine, my magic, but alchemising the wound was a work in progress and these limiting beliefs around my abilities were still a ball and chain. I was a powerful medicine woman in so many ways, but I was also human and had my vulnerabilities and challenges.

"Fuck, I can't figure out where to go, Harry," I sobbed, looking up at the big screens. "I've no idea what I'm doing, babe. I can't even find my way through an airport without you!"

I wrapped my arms around his neck like a little girl who didn't want to grow up. Feeling his hands on my waist, I enjoyed the comfort and safety of this man who had been my rock for 20 years. I moved my face into his chest, trying to get as close to him as possible. I needed to stop this, to let him go and to take charge of myself.

He kissed me on the top of my head and put his hand on my face to look me in the eye.

"Come on," he said, "Let's try together. You're flying on BA, so look for the BA."

And there I saw it.

"Okay, Lima, Peru."

In a moment's relief and pride, I'd taken my first step, not a huge step for many, but it was a good start for me.

"You'll be great, babe. And Simon will be on the same flight, so he'll look out for you. This is where you're meant to be. Your mountain is waiting."

***

"Typical Lou. Always manifesting the best stuff! Your seat is like a fucking corner sofa and you've got no one next to you while I'm stuck over here with no leg room."

The jovial voice was Simon, my friend, student, second husband, brother and dad all rolled into one. I'd nicknamed him Prince Charming, because even at 60, he had a full head of golden hair, a golden heart to match, and the poshest accent I had ever heard. He was by far one of the nicest, most open and most honest people in my life. Both Harry and I adored him. In fact, Harry had said the main reason he was so okay about me going to Peru was because Simon would be there.

Simon had once been a successful and well-respected organic farmer, but at 55 years old, he'd decided to try something new.... crack cocaine! We'd met when he was in his second year of recovery, during our shamanic training. He was a walking awakening story, and a classic one at that, one where we destroy the structures of our lives unconsciously so as to rebuild it carefully with what is truly important, guided by our spiritual self, gaining wisdom, and growing into our soul's purpose.

I'd known instantly that this man was my people. And my champion.

***

It was 3am in Peru when we walked arm in arm into the hotel lobby, giggling like a pair of kids. My childlike essence was in full swing and I had tears of excitement rolling down my cheeks. I spotted my shamanic teacher Josephine and beamed at her.

"Morning!"

She looked straight through me and greeted the person behind me with open arms.

Boom! Rejection. *Am I going to have to deal with this shit here too?* I thought, trying to hide my hurt. I still hadn't shifted the deep yearning to be accepted and acknowledged by my teachers.

The other teacher James came and organised our rooms, lecturing me on looking after my passport and ensuring I didn't lose anything. I smiled to appease his apparent need to patronise me in front of the group.

"Come on, she ignored me too," Simon laughed as we headed to our rooms, apparently not triggered because his issues were different to mine.

I was well used to this default setting that I would try to please my teachers like a child. Giving away my power. I needed to shift it. If I didn't, the pattern would persist and they would keep treating me like an annoyance.

In my soulless airport hotel room, I looked at myself in the mirror. As if confirming my thoughts, I saw that the eczema had flared on my face, which only happened when I was around these teachers! I gave myself a good talking-to.

I don't have to hide my power anymore. I don't have to be ashamed of my light. I don't have to look weak and ugly to be accepted! I can shine my beauty and radiance freely. I don't need anyone to protect me now. I can do this myself.

***

Welcome to the jungle

Traveling had taken it out of me and my malaria tablets were making me feel sick. All I had seen for 24 hours was hotels, planes and airports, and I craved having my feet on the earth and being with nature. There was so much to be grateful for, but I felt alone. I sat apart from the group on the plane to the jungle, journaling and trying to process what was going on inside.

I would feel safer if my teachers at least acknowledged me and I just wanted to feel free to be myself and not fear judgment of who I was. I plugged in my headphones and listened to the Peru playlist I'd made before I'd left. Then there below me were the Andes mountains. I watched in awe as *El Cóndor Pasa* played in my ears. It was perfect timing by the song angels. Wonder filled my heart, as if I had only just that second realised that my dreams had finally become reality...

I'm in Peru.

***

As we drove down the dusty road to the Amazon, I smiled and waved at the people on the streets. I had never been anywhere like this and it was wonderful. Our old bus was filled with shamanic healers and mesa carriers, all students of my teachers from over the years, most of whom I did not yet know. On the edge of the jungle, we pulled through the huge gates of the retreat centre and stopped at our home for the next five days.

I breathed the humid air and felt my face sting. I prayed the raw weeping of my eczema would heal here.

Everyone gathered around the huge wooden table in an open-sided wooden building that overlooked the rainforest. With the sounds of exotic birds and rushing waters as a backdrop, I got to meet the other travellers. I sat down next to my retreat roommate Natalie, a warm and wonderful woman, and became an instant sister as we all started getting to know each other.

"What do you do, Lou?" one guy asked.

I told the group about my community back home, the healing, the teaching, the mountain call, the earth chakras I'd just learned about and how I was flying blind.

"I'm so excited to see where this is taking me," I finished.

As I spoke, I tried to ignore the spiky energy of my teacher James, who was doing his best to tune out of the conversation I was having with my new friends, but as I looked across the table, I caught him rolling his eyes. My stomach sank. What had I done to receive such hostility from him? I sensed envy but couldn't understand it. He was my teacher. Why would he be envious of me? When I'd first told him and my other shamanic teacher about the mountain call, neither of them had celebrated with me. I'd wanted them to help me understand it, to celebrate with me and not regard me as an irritation, but I knew I could not expect others to do what I would do, to act how I would act.

I breathed through the tears that were brewing and carried on chatting away, trying to hide the insecure child within me that was feeling pretty vulnerable. This was my lesson. I had to let this go! I had to not care about what he thought, what anyone thought. I had to learn to stand in my own personal power.

This mission of mine was bigger than this drama.

***

Tobacco rush

I had come here for a five-day ceremony drinking the powerful plant medicine Ayahuasca; a 5,000-year-old shamanic hallucinogen from the Amazon that brings you into a state of wakeful dreaming, allowing you to cross the bridge into the spirit world and go deep into the parts of yourself that need to be seen and healed. I was at this retreat to enter the landscape of my soul, to let Mother Ayahuasca speak words of wisdom to me, heal me and guide me on my journey.

EARTH CHAKRA SHAMAN

Ayahuasca makes you very sick and preparations had started a month before. I had abstained from sugar and sex to purify the body, but there was much more to come. Local shaman Javier made us a tobacco tea to help purge everything from our bellies before the main Ayahuasca ceremony later that evening. I took my place in the tambo with the rest of the group, sitting on the wooden floor with my bucket and water bottle.

Javier was a friendly-looking Peruvian man, who had been working with Ayahuasca for 30 years. He spoke next to no English but his energy made me feel safe. When it was my turn, he handed me the tobacco medicine and I drank. In no time, my stomach churned and I had a familiar sense of needing to be sick but not quite being able. It reminded me of my entire life when I used to drink alcohol, because I got sick every time I drank. I'd been sober for six months when the mountains called; it had been something my spirit guides were indicating I needed to do for a while and I could see now that I'd had to be free of alcohol and everything it meant before I could be called. Everything we do is a detoxification, a shedding, a decluttering before reaching a new level.

As with many others in the tambo that evening, the sick came like a flow and I purged my self-consciousness along with my fear, my sadness and my dinner! Leaning back onto the wall for support, sweat dripped down my cheeks, stinging the sores on my face. I drank some water and puked some more.

"Drink! Drink!" Javier encouraged us.

For a moment, a rush of light came in and I saw flashes of highs, times I'd thrown up in the garden at house parties when I was younger, times when the waves of ecstasy had become too much, times when the energy coursed through my body taking me higher and higher, opening my heart. I recalled the euphoria that flowed through me on the dance floor or at festivals, the undeniable rush of love. *Were those times so bad? How is this any different?* I thought. But it was. That was escape. The back door to spirituality. This was sacred.

I was slipping into a similar state of euphoria, though. The tobacco brew was strong, beyond what I had expected, but it was meeting me with a gentle warmth. I'd had a relationship with tobacco for most of my life, from as young as 11, and only freed myself from the cage a few years earlier. I had abused this sacred plant, colonised and monetised by the West, and in time, it had abused me. In my younger days, I'd even had some spiritual experiences with tobacco, but I knew our relationship had to end if I wanted to free my soul. Yet here in ceremony, it was different, sacred, and I was grateful to meet it in this way.

Rain came and the smell of the jungle was wonderful in my heightened state. I heard heavy drops against the tambo roof, as if it was singing just for me, rejoicing, speaking directly to my heart a simple message for me alone.

You are here. You are here.

Awash with love and contentment, free of fear, safe in the arms of Mother Waters, I arrived. Fully in my body, I connected to the elements, the lands, and finally felt at one with the group, the people with whom I would journey these next few weeks.

Afterwards, I sat on a rock in solitude listening to the trees, feeling the warmth of the sun, still in a state of bliss. It dawned on me then that I wanted to stop hiding my power from my teachers, stop fearing that they would be envious of me, because tobacco had shown me there were parasites in my energy field.

A question came then...

What is hiding inside that creates this disempowerment in me?

***

Ayahuasca journeying

I pondered for hours what to ask Mother Ayahuasca before I drank her, but in the end all I knew was that I wanted the courage to be myself.

When the ceremony began, I received my medicine from Javier, sat back down, and was heaving into my bucket in no time at all. I closed my eyes.

Immediately, I found myself in a dark room, following a light into another world. The colours were beautiful, like those I would see in reiki but more alive. Deeper I went into the space, where millions of little green and orange serpents ate away at the parasites in my energy field. I stayed still, knowing I had to clear what I could here before going into the next dimension. In this space, I could see that I was not strong in my body and that this was holding me back.

I came back into the tambo, into normal life. I'd gone in fast and strong, and wanted to go back down there beyond the waiting room, to know what was blocking me from a strong body. I was restless and ready to go again, but I feared the judgment of my teachers for getting up and asking for more. Since this was the exact issue I needed to clear, I made myself get up. I walked over to Javier, knelt in front of him and looked him in the eyes. He nodded, then as he blew my prayer into the medicine, words came from deep within my soul.

Take me to the belly of the Mother.

I drank, knowing this was a big intention...

***

Mother Ayahuasca rose from the Earth and, like a hand scooping up my tiny body, pulled me down. I crossed over into the spirit world.

I was no longer in this world, but inside the tambo was all the medicine of the jungle, the trees, the plants. I felt these spirits enter my body, and I became them, exploring my body for the first time in pure amazement. I touched my hand, amazed at the sensation of the skin, amazed at what it felt like to be in a body. I felt my hair, amazed at how it looked and how beautiful I am. I giggled and giggled in the pure wonder and delight of feeling this body for the first time.

The shaman sang his medicine songs taking me deeper and deeper and deeper. The nature spirits wound themselves around my veins, pulling me, disembodying me, until the only thing that remained were my wings. Every part of my body was exhausted from the convulsions that felt like they were ripping something out of my stomach, but I was beyond the conscious mind. Scared, amazed and courageous, I had no idea where I was or who I was. Now there was no space and no time. I was in the centre of a kaleidoscope, being moved through the dimensions, dying, being reborn, dying, being reborn.

Between dimensions, I saw my teachers and how they had chosen to play this role to be my challenger, to make me feel uncomfortable so I could learn to be a strong leader and not give away my power. Seeing them beyond their egos and their roles, they were me and I was them. I had so much love and gratitude for them.

"Thank you, thank you, thank you," I said as I passed by.

I was reborn as a dragon, coming out of a cave, the spirit guide asking me, *What do you want to bring to the world?*

"Love, of course," I replied.

The medicine songs Javier sang took me again, each time going through the whole process, diving deeper into what hid inside me.

I was lost in more lives, many lives, one after the other. And I was so tired of all these lives! Yet here I could see that each life was getting lighter and lighter. I saw that nothing was so serious after all. We don't need to take things so seriously.

The lives kept going and going and I kept laughing and laughing. Each life, I kept being given the ability to choose what I wanted to bring to the Earth. I began to get tired and wanted the cycle to stop. Was it ever going to end? Then I realised my soul was tired of living life after life, hoping this was the last time. But in this journey, Mother Ayahuasca was cleaning the hucha, the heavy energy, for each life I was reliving, so that my soul could be free.

I retched again, stuck in a life that my body was trying to purge of hucha. I felt the shaman near me, helping me clear it.

Back in my body, I could hear myself crying, "I'm so tired. I'm so tired. When will this end?"

Physically exhausted from the journey, yet fully aware it was my soul who was crying, tired of all these lives, I held onto my bucket as my anchor to this world. I held on, as I began to go in again. I held on, as the deeper I went, the more I was sick. I held on, as I went past the room again, past the green and orange serpents eating the parasites, for life after life after life.

***

All the visions and gifts of the past

I lazed in the swing chair in the morning sun on the veranda of the communal area, hugging my mesa like a child with her dolly. I gazed across the jungle vista into the distance and down at the tambo below me. Immersed in the sounds of nature all around, I enjoyed the warmth on my body as I sat in a blissful, peaceful haze, physically unable to do much else.

We were still eating lightly, knowing there was to be another ceremony that evening, and still weak from the last purge. I relished the freedom of feeling too weak to do anything, even pick up a pen and write. Having guilt-free rest time, fully off-duty in every way, I was unsure if I had ever felt this before. I smiled to myself and pondered the visions of the night before.

I'd had a few visions with dragons and past lives. In fact, the very first time I'd known undeniably I was having a vision of a past life and was being called was just after doing my reiki masters. It had been a strange but wonderful time of awakening. In that vision, I'd been a dragon being freed. I'd flown so high, but still had chains around my foot. I flew to Glastonbury Tor, and there, the chains had fallen from my foot, and I'd flown higher and higher… I'd had another vision, where I was human and been taken to the Tor. I lay next to my dragon as I was cut in half and my blood drained, then filled instead with golden light. Next, I was transported to an old cathedral, filled with angels and kings, where I was crowned Guinevere and told I would receive a ruby when I was ready for my purpose.

Six months later, on my 34th birthday, a ruby had indeed shown up in a miraculous way. And it was the beginning of many gifts along my journey that would become powerful medicine tools.

Just before I'd come to Peru, my sister-in-law had sent me a yellow sapphire ring, which I'd researched and found to be related to the sacral chakra. The card that came with it said her mother had left it to her when she died, but she'd been guided to send it to me. She'd had no idea about a dream I'd had three months before telling me I would receive a sapphire ring to assist me on my journey.

I'd been gifted many special items from the universe and I felt so protected. I had come so far, and all the time, it had been preparation for this. Yet as the afternoon came, I noticed apprehension for that evening's ceremony. I feared how much deeper I could go. I wasn't sure I could take another session as deep as the night before, knowing now the power of Mother Ayahuasca.

I stood up and wandered around until I found her, then sat with the vines of the plant, in prayer.

"Thank you for last night, Mother. Thank you for the visions. They were intense. I am coming back to you tonight, but I wanted to speak with you first... I'm unsure what to ask of you in the ceremony."

Within moments, she replied, *What would you ask if you had no fear?*

I reflected on the question, but when it arrived, the answer came from beyond my mind.

"To be fully in my body and fully in my power so that I may serve."

Still scared, I sat with her, letting her soothe away my fears. I touched my rings, reminding myself that everything was in the divine plan.

Surrender and trust.

***

I reached for my bucket, knowing this sensation now. The evening ceremony was here and I stepped gently into the journey this time. First, I saw rivers and waterfalls, a polar bear, a stag, a boat on the water, a sunrise. I didn't think anything much was happening, not like the night before, but then I felt a shift as I entered the plant world.

In my vision, I found myself in Alaska and I knew I had to connect to the waters. There was something I needed to do in service. Then, I was a plant in the jungle. The nature spirts became me again, embodying me and laughing as they touched my skin, my hair, my legs as though they had never experienced humanness before.

The tambo was alive. I opened my eyes, and yes, we were indeed all plants, experiencing each other! Javier was an angel shaman with cream wings that reached down to the floor. He was hunched over and weaving his way through the jungle, speaking with the plants, blessing us with kindness. He was looking after us and we were all one. The spirits were laughing. I was laughing. This was incredible!

I closed my eyes again and the spirits took me into the kaleidoscope and detached me from my body. I was unnerved. I didn't want to be separated from it now that I was finally feeling fully connected. But the spirits were powerful and commanding. I had to trust and have courage to deal with what they were about to do. They pinned me down and split me apart. Then Javier arrived to extract something from my head.

I opened my eyes again, and I was laughing and dancing freely. The jungle was incredible and I watched Javier as a memory. Was this something I was meant to be doing too or had I done this in the past?

Eyes closed, and I fell deep into Mother Earth, and there I met her spirit. It was like meeting God. She was God. I was in awe. I had never met such love and it amazed me to be in the presence of such light. This was love beyond judgment, love that was pure.

She touched my hair and my face and spoke softly.

This is my gift to you. Love the gift I have given you.

I looked at my fat belly and cried for all the times I had not loved the beautiful gift of my body. Hating on it was like hating on a newborn child, when really, I was perfect. This beautiful gift was perfect.

"Oh my beautiful body! I'm so sorry! I love you. Thank you, thank you, thank you."

Louise! What have you done to your womb? she said then in her grand voice.

I stared at her bemused, not knowing what she meant.

You have been doing my work. You need not take the traumas of others into your own body to heal them.

She showed me past lives then. She showed me how I had led happy communities, and that other tribes had been jealous of how happy my people were, but I'd had no idea it was making me sick. My people would be happy in themselves because I would take on their darkness and sadness so they could be free. I would store it in my belly, instead of giving it back to the earth.

This is my job. You don't need to do it.

She was wonderfully non-judgmental in her loving of me, as she healed my womb, teaching me like a mother would teach a child.

My body tried to throw up the hucha of all these past lives, but it was hard to let go. I screamed, maybe in my mind, maybe in the tambo, maybe in the spirit world, maybe in all of them as it came up into my bucket, lifetimes of other people's heaviness leaving my body and soul.

I began to cry with compassion for all that I had done to my body, the pain, the scars, the ill-talk. I cried with sadness. And I cried with gratitude for this beautiful gift. I had never felt such love for my body and such a connection to Mother Earth.

As the pain eased, she left me with a parting message.

Learn to speak with the waters, Louise. Work with me and become the healer you are here to be.

***

The Sacred Valley

I woke to the mountains. It was so early that the sun was just rising. I sobbed as I woke because I knew this was home. As the rains had celebrated my arrival back in the jungle, so the mountains whispered to me now.

You are here, you are here, you are here...

"I *am* here!" I whispered back.

In the Sacred Valley of Peru were the most ancient sacred sites of the Earth, sitting among rolling green hills, giant mountains, Inca ruins, and breath-taking scenery.

Husband and wife Don Francisco and Donna Juana were the Q'ero shamans I'd pictured: tiny round bodies, huge smiles, dark skin and creased faces, wearing bright colourful regalia. They could have been 50 or 500 years old and I was amazed how fast they moved up the rocky mountainside, while I puffed and panted away. At the top, we sat in ceremony, as we would every day for the next week receiving rites, blessings, activations and visiting the sacred sites.

Every time I paused to take in the green lands, the mountains and the curved terraces of the ruins, I was blown away. I couldn't stop crying in gratitude for simply being here. Even when James and Josephine were short and sharp with me, I could not stop the flow of love. They had organised this whole thing. They knew this place and they were showing up for me, until I got my shit together and stopped needing them to like me!

The stunning Andes passed by as we drove from sacred site to sacred site, ceremony to ceremony, and a small group of us sat at the back of the coach like the rebel kids on a school trip, doing healings on each other, talking for hours or sitting in silence. In between times, I played with my mesa, relishing the time I had to think, be and learn. I loved this group who were fast becoming family.

During our time in the Sacred Valley, the waters spoke to me.

Water is alive. It must be freed. Only the earth and the water are ours to offer. Not our children. Not other animals or energy. Be aware of gifts.

The winds spoke to me too.

Careful strategy must take place. There are some who you can trust and others who you cannot, because they don't understand you. The call is much greater than you can imagine. Keep saying yes and the universe will provide.

***

Get out of the drama triangle

Nat and I had become so close in such a short period of time that we had practically merged. It was easy and honest when we chatted together.

"I wish they would just talk to me! I hate being disliked and it's really triggering me. It's bothering me so much that I lie awake thinking about it over and over in my head."

"Are you going on about James and Josephine again?" she joked.

I blushed.

"I do go on about it, don't I?"

"You kind of won't let it go, yeah."

"Argh! I know! It just feels so strange to have thoughts whirling. It's years since I eradicated that kind of overthinking and I'm pissed off with them more because they're in my head!"

"You're pissed off with them for being in your head even though you put them there!"

She had a way of speaking the truth playfully.

"I've done the fucking work, though. It shouldn't be like this. I'm the most present person I know and they are ruining my zen, man!"

I buried my head in my pillow, pretending to scream.

"Lou, what do you want from them?"

"Just to be fucking nice. Why can't they just be nice to me? Why can't they just say, 'Morning, Lou, how are you?' or even just say hello?"

Nat looked at me straight-faced. She wasn't joking any more. If anything, she looked annoyed.

"Lou, why do you keep playing the victim in their drama triangle?"

It was a stab in the gut. A perpetrator will always attract a victim, a rescuer will always attract a victim, and a victim will always attract a perpetrator and a rescuer. We keep playing into these roles, until we decide to stop.

"Shit! I am, aren't I?"

"Yes! And now you can get out of it, because you're even boring me now!"

"Alright there, perpetrator!" I laughed.

***

I lay awake, asking my guides for the lesson and how to claim back my power, and I realised that I treated James and Josephine like teachers, in the same way a child does. A teacher has power in that situation. If a teacher didn't like you, you were in a vulnerable place. *But I'm a grown adult. I pay them to teach me and take me places. Come on, Lou!*

From the next morning on, I started a new practice. If they were rude to me, I thanked them in my mind for teaching me to be stronger and not be a victim. I stood a little taller and pulled them up on their treatment of me, not in dramatic ways, but in small empowering ways.

"James, why do you feel it's okay to keep speaking to me like a child?" I asked, finally, "You don't speak to anyone else like that."

Startled at my speaking out, he stumbled for words and denied it.

"You do, though, James. You really do and I'd like you to stop."

***

Tears from home

I got some sketchy reception, but it was just enough to facetime home.

"Hey guys! Oh my God, look at you!"

Bella had a new haircut and looked beautiful, and Harry looked so handsome, but Avalon seemed sad. The girls both wanted to speak with me and started talking all at once.

"Hey! Hey! One at a time, girls!" I said, conscious of giving them individual attention.

"Bella, you go first. Avalon, you second."

About three seconds into Bella telling me about school, I could see Avalon was upset and obviously desperate to tell me something.

"Avalon, come tell me what you wanted to tell me."

But she wouldn't look at me.

"I don't feel like it now," she said with tears in her eyes.

She was pained and I was pained for her.

"Baby, I want to speak to you and I know you want to speak to me. How about you take the phone and go into my healing room with a blanket?"

She went and curled up on my chair in the healing room. God, I missed her. I missed home. Then she began to sob and sob and sob. I watched her through the distorted connection and my heart broke. I could not wrap my arms around my little girl or wipe the tears from her face. I could only sit and watch helplessly as she sobbed her heart out, because she missed me, and because she'd lost a tooth and wanted me to tuck it under her pillow.

"Mummy, I want you to come home now."

I could not bear the pain and started crying with her.

Through my tears, I managed a reply, "Baby, I can't come home yet. I have to stay here."

***

I joined the breakfast queue with a face still streaked with tears.

"What happened? Why are you crying?" came a voice.

It was Josephine. I blurted out to her the conversation I'd just had with my family and saw the warm smile that I'd seen her give others in the group. For the first time, it was directed at me.

"I can see it's hard for all of you, Louise, but you're in the right place. And they will gain so much from your experience here."

I felt her love and empathy for me. She left me there. It was the one time I had no expectation of her. And the one time she acknowledged me.

***

James triggered me all day though. Like siblings who were just annoyed at each other's presence, we were pissing each other off and I had had enough.

So that night, the sacred fire was a soothing balm for my agitation. Stars flickered above and the shadow of the giant mountains held us. I knew this land under my feet as my home for many lifetimes and I felt safe here, but this aggravation between me and my teachers was owning me.

Something took over. I held in my hand a stick, my offering for the fire, and I blew into it all my fury.

"Grandfather Fire, I've had enough of this drama. I give it to you. I have no time for it. I've been called here for a reason and that reason must be beyond this drama. I give it to you. Rid me of it now."

The mountains whispered by return, *You must learn to not judge the judgment of others.*

In that moment, I knew something had shifted and that night I slept more soundly than I'd slept since I'd left home, knowing the power was within me. No one has the power to take our power. That's an illusion we create. If we think someone does, they will show up in the world acting like they do. It was a lesson that was going to meet me time and time again on this quest until it became my truth.

Over the next few days, my teachers engaged with me and included me more. They were like different people. And everyone noticed. Although I wouldn't go as far as saying I felt liked, at least I felt safe and accepted, while being aware that I must not put my happiness in their hands.

I was here for bigger reasons.

***

New mesa, new beginnings

My morning practice was to rise before the sun, sit in the front gardens of the hotel, and connect to the wisdom of the mountains before the day began. The day before we left for Aguas Calientes, the town below Machu Picchu, I found myself unable to get up from my morning mountain time. These mountains had been so special to me for the past four days and I was sad to say goodbye.

Don Francisco and Donna Juana arrived and came to sit next to me. I had grown a lovely silent relationship with them and always felt like they had one eye on me, despite our group being large. They watched as I played with my mesa, and the new cloth and stone that I had picked up in Písac the day before, which activated memories of a great former lifetime. I had been holding this stone when it was confirmed to me that the Inca Q'ero also believed that many of us here on Earth were from the Seven Sisters star system. For me, this stone represented home.

"Ahh, new mesa, new beginnings..." he said in his small amount of English.

He picked up my Písac stone and a stone from another sacred site that I had been gifted in a profound moment of teaching where I learned that the stones were alive. A giant boulder had spoken to me about a stone that I was to receive, and this smaller stone was it. I had collected it with the deepest of gratitude for the stone people that spoke to me, knowing I would never forget this new bond.

I watched Don Francisco lean over and place the stones on my new mesa cloth. I observed how he folded it up and gave it back to me. He beckoned me to kneel in front of him and blessed my new mesa with his. Then he winked! I felt instantly conspicuous. Having a second mesa was not the 'protocol'. I wanted to hide it! But I respected myself and Don Francisco, knowing what he was doing for me was right and reflected the feelings I had inside.

There was something new ahead of me.

***

The train to Aguas Calientes from Ollantaytambo is possibly the most beautiful journey in the world, cutting through the mountains alongside the river. I didn't stop smiling for the whole two hours, looking up through the glass ceiling in awe of the colours in the sky, the mountains, life everywhere. As we got closer to the town, even though I couldn't see it, I could feel the energy emitting from Machu Picchu. It was incredible to feel its power, but it was also clear to me that the waters held as much as the mountains.

Our hotel was modern and our room had floor-to-ceiling, wall-to-wall windows overlooking the river and the mountain face.

Nat and I stayed up for hours, sitting cross-legged on our beds, talking and playing with our mesas and kuyas; as though they were alive. They were alive, after all, and they spoke to us. Our relationship with each of our medicine stones being a reflection of our relationship with ourselves.

There were two layers to my first mesa: the inner layer held 13 medicine stones and the second layer held trinkets, such as a small eagle figurine, a Pachamama and Pachatata statue, two stones from Australia and a glass salamander made by my friend's mum. I had always had a connection with salamanders and newts, and my friend had given this to me during our shamanic training the year before, as a memento for the time a little newt had found its way into the conference centre and into my open mesa. Weird things always happened to me!

It was 11.30pm when we realised the time and started to pack up. As early risers, it was the latest we'd been up all week. I closed my mesa briefly, but Nat continued to play with hers, so I opened mine again, shuffling the trinkets around in the second layer.

"What the fuck?" I screamed, as a live salamander – or was it dead? – stared back at me. I flung the mesa cloth over it, not wanting to see it, and jumped off the bed shaking.

"There's a salamander in my mesa! Holy shit! How did he get in there?"

Once my heart had stopped racing, I crept over and gently unfolded the cloth. Yes, there it definitely was. I swiftly closed it again. Nat giggled. She wasn't even surprised.

"Well, isn't that curious?" she said, as she wrapped up her mesa and snuggled down to sleep.

Tenderly, I moved his tiny almost-lifeless body to the centre on my mesa and left him some water in a dish. *Why was he here? What was his message?* I was worried for him. I didn't want him to sacrifice his life to be a messenger for me.

I settled him in for the night and went to bed myself, but I couldn't sleep. The salamander was talking to me, sending me information that I couldn't grasp, as it went in and out of my head.

The water is dying. It wants to live through us...

At 3am, salamander told me I had to do ceremony! I placed a bottle of water in the centre of my mesa and began a ceremony to bring life back to the waters. I was to drink all the water and feed the now purified water to the salamander too. He came back to life as I fed us both.

He asked me if I wanted to go further into my purpose to serve more deeply. *Yes, of course*, I answered silently. *This is why I came to this Earth – to serve.*

By 5am, I was back in bed reiki-cuddling myself, the energy flowing and more messages from salamander coming through. At 6am, I was up again, feeling wired. Nat rose too.

"Have you slept at all?" she smiled.

"Hardly. He's been talking to me all night, saying the waters are dying. There's so much hucha."

"Come on. Let's sing," she suggested, hopping out of bed, and pulling on her poncho. We grabbed our rattles, and led by nature, we sang songs that I had never heard before, singing our hearts out to the salamander, to the waters, to honour our missions and give thanks for being here in service.

***

I wanted to take the salamander to the rainforest to let him go, and since we were going up there for ceremony that day, I went downstairs to speak to my teachers about it. I wanted them to tell me what it all meant, but I was faced with stern faces.

"Take it and release it right away," Josephine snapped.

I didn't want to release him in the town, but I'd been given my orders. As I set off, I passed one of the Q'ero shamans, and showed him photos of the salamander.

"Ahhhh, Pachamama blessing," he said.

I wished I spoke some Spanish, so I could ask him what it all meant.

"Louise!" Josephine called out from the hotel lobby, sounding like my mother when I hadn't tidied my room, "Have you set that salamander free yet?"

"Not yet," I admitted.

"Go and do it now!" she ordered.

Like a dutiful daughter, I did what she told me, but I felt so bad and moaned to Simon the whole way.

"Oh God, he'll never survive in the city."

I found a patch of green, and though it didn't feel enough, I obeyed Josephine's orders and let him go.

"Please be okay," I whispered.

And then It came to me, maybe my little messenger was more powerful than I had led myself to believe. After all, he was magical enough to have teleported or shapeshifted into my mesa. I had to hold faith that he would be just fine.

***

Machu Picchu rising

There were a thousand coaches taking people up to Machu Picchu from the town that morning and I had to remember that this was a tourist trap. So far, our journey had been anything but touristy. Our teachers and Q'ero shamans had created a truly sacred journey, but now I could see crowds of people ahead of us who would be climbing the mountain without any such sacred awareness. This was not just a place to take photos, tick a box, and return home to say you've been there. Just like Uluru, Machu Picchu was more than what you can see with the human eye. When we approach sacred sites with an openness of heart and mind, with reverence and offerings, there is a veil that lifts and an invitation to explore the sacred energy that it emits.

Away from the crowds, we sat for sunrise and I was overcome with joy as the light illuminated the mountain range. I could have watched for hours. Looking over the green mountaintops for miles, I could see how vast this ancient city had once been. And there was much further to climb for our secret ceremonies if we were to get away from the hoards of people.

The messages of the night before were still with me. Frustrated that all we could buy was bottled water owned by Coca-Cola, I unscrewed the cap on mine and did reiki on the water, awakening her, bringing her back to life and giving thanks. I felt the heat in my hands and blew energy and love into the bottle, then took a sip. As I did, I felt a presence behind me and turned to see Don Francisco beaming down.

"May I share with you?" he gestured.

I passed the bottle and he gave me his cheeky smile and drank, then passed the bottle to Donna Juana. I had been seen. I was used to doing things like this in hiding for fear of persecution. That old story still ran through my soul, but Don Francisco and Donna Juana had seen me, and they had honoured my medicine. Indeed, they had done nothing but honour my medicine. No judgment. Just lightness.

I looked back over the mountain range, tears now flowing down my face. Behind me stood all my teachers and shamans gazing out at that beautiful view with love in their hearts and I could feel their souls. It was as if God was showing me how far I had come.

"I am beyond grateful to you all," I said in my heart.

Bring joy and play to the messages, the mountain answered.

It didn't make sense, but I showed the mountain my joy by offering up more thanks.

***

After wandering the old walls of Machu Picchu, imagining what it was like to live here and feeling the reverence of what this place once had been, a shining beacon of light for pilgrims in the Andes, we regrouped at the Pachamama Stone to share snacks.

"Special mesa," Don Francisco said, indicating my mesa.

I laughed but the word 'special' reminded me of the shame I'd felt when Josephine had once pulled me up in front of my group asking me why I thought I was so special.

Maybe she was right, though. I did think I was special. Magical things happened to me daily and it was hard not to feel special. Equally, I thought everyone was special and had always felt my work was to awaken the *special* in others, to help them see their own unique medicine and to be blown away by the synergies that come when we step into our calling. To me, my mesa was special. And old. And sacred. And I was blessed in every way.

Don Francisco passed me a stone from the ground. Shocked, I realised it was the exact same kind as the lineage stone I'd received from Josephine during our shamanic training six months before.

Before the mountain had called me to Peru, I'd had a dream in which I'd asked her where my lineage stone was from, but she hadn't known. In the same dream, she threw another stone at me. When I'd caught it, I'd seen it was a rock full of symbols and knew I had to decode something. The following day, these exact symbols had shown up on an Incan ruin in a museum. The pieces were coming together.

In thanks, I placed Don Francisco's stone in the new mesa that he had blessed a few days before, knowing this was my lineage stone to this mountain, to the Q'ero and to Don Francisco. I loved the idea that I had matching kuyas in each mesa, both representing the lineage to these lands and to my Western teachers. Although the relationship I had with Josephine was fractious, she was my biggest teacher and I loved and honoured her, just as I knew she loved and honoured me.

It wasn't until much later that I realised I'd left one of my medicine stones on the ground where I was sitting. It must have fallen out of my mesa and it broke my heart when I realised, but I knew this was the way of things. Giving and receiving. Even our precious medicine stones. Unknown to me, this unconscious offering was the start of a new way of using my mesas, and I often wondered if Don Francisco secretly knew the divine plan and if that was why he initiated me into my second Mesa.

***

Running into the Sungate

It was getting hot, but a few people were heading up to the Sungate and I was keen to join. I was not prepared. I needed a wee and I only had a few sips of water left with nowhere to top it up. I'd been told it was a real hike and would take a couple of hours, which was making me hesitate, yet something deep inside was telling me to go.

I had to trust.

I always have what I need, I told myself, *I'll be fine*.

Once we awaken to the next level of our consciousness, there comes a moment when we realise we always have exactly what we need, and somehow we manage to survive with what we have. This faith was real within me now. And so, I set off to the Sungate, about to climb miles uphill in the midday sun, with nothing but a dribble of water and a prayer to the mountain to carry me.

I hiked and hiked and found myself alone, away from the group. I was hot and exhausted, going higher and higher, but as I climbed, the view rewarded me with ever more beautiful views. The Sungate was near. The Sungate, where once pilgrims would enter Machu Picchu, having walked across the Andes...

Something told me to plug in my earphones. It felt weird using technology at such a sacred moment, but l did as I was guided, and a song came on that I had never heard before, even though I must have put it on my playlist. I heard the up-tempo drum beat and a beautiful voice singing.

"Sing me baby home, sing me baby home, run baby, run baby, run baby, run."

And I began to run. I ran and ran like I had never run before. Up, up, up the 500-year-old cobbled pathway, not stopping for breath.

The song ended and there in front of me was the Sungate, the highest point of Machu Picchu, the old gateway. I finally felt like I knew this place, like I knew the essence of leading my people through this gate after a great pilgrimage.

I looked down on all the mountains. I cried and laughed and danced around. I was so high! I had come so far! There were a few people dotted around up here, all in the same state of bliss, sitting on rocks in silence, staring into the magnificence of these lands. Smiling, I found a spot on a high-up rock to take it all in. People of all ages and from all places saw me and smiled back. Wherever we had come from, we all came to this place for a reason, for the expansion of our soul. They felt what I too was feeling: the essence of all life in every drop of breath.

I hadn't heard the next song before either, but it was as if a higher version of myself had prepared the playlist for this very moment. The lyrics described how people on Earth had fallen from the stars, landed where hearts gather, been guided to take leaps in our lives even when the ground had shaken, and come back home to our hearts.

I stood up and spread my arms, letting the wind hold me, feeling like I could fly. I called the energies into my hands and then pulled them into my heart, collecting the energy from the mountain into my body. My body tingled and radiated.

"Thank you, angels. Thank you, Gaia. Thank you, mountains, for orchestrating all of this. I love you."

The wind, the earth, the sun, the moon, the stars, the ancestors, they were all with me here. This was why I felt so free here in Peru. I was free to be the way I am, to talk to everything, to hear its reply. I was in sacred lands where knowing the aliveness of all things was just the way.

I had spent my entire life hiding this connection, apologising for crying when I saw the beauty of existence, quieting my wonder because it confused people and made me appear mad when I was just happy. I knew we all had this earth connection though, and I knew why so many couldn't feel it. In the Native American vision, I'd been told that the land used to speak to us, but she was quiet now because she was dying. The land had spoken to me purely because I was willing to listen. *If everyone began to listen to her again*, I thought, *they would feel what it is to be truly alive. And then they would not harm her.*

I was whole, free and opening. I felt my energy was bigger and I could emit it for miles and miles. I looked down at the name of the track playing. *Hummingbird*, it was called. You couldn't make this up, but the song angels had! I felt light in heart and body, just like a bird, as though I could fly, as though wings had grown on my back. Before I knew it, I was running, running, running, skipping, jumping down the old Inca path, flying faster and faster downhill, back down the mountain. It was dangerous. I could have fallen to my death. But I couldn't not run.

And the mountain held me...

I found myself back where I had begun at the Pachamama Stone. As I rested my head on her to give thanks, she spoke to me.

A rock's energy is like bliss. It is source energy. You too will return to being a mountain.

For a moment, I was scared at that message. I didn't want to stand still, but she soothed me, reminding me that the mountains were pure energy, holding the energy of the Earth.

The rocks and mountains hold you grounded. They are happy to be of service and used as medicine stones.

Before I left, she had one last message for me.

Write the book, Louise.

It was the first time I'd heard it but I agreed without hesitation. I would write a book to empower people to walk their own path, to be fearless, to keep the faith as they followed their hearts.

***

CHAPTER 7

Lake Titicaca & the Sacral Chakra

I felt settled inside of myself. All the way to the lake, I noticed how different I was from the little girl looking for her teachers' love and acceptance way back in the jungle. I had grown and was no longer afraid of hiding my magic, my powers, my medicine or my mesa for fear of rejection. These old stories were aches from many lifetimes before, but I had done so much healing on this journey and now I was ready to meet her.

I lay top-to-tail with the others in the boat, as the Uru man took us out to the centre of the lake. The highest lake in the world and I was on her. The sky was bright blue, the water rocking us peacefully, and I drifted into a sleepy state. I felt the lake's energy like a mist coming into my own energy field and I felt deep love for my teacher next to me for bringing us here, for bringing me to the medicine of Peru, and for challenging me.

I recalled the message of Ayahuasca. Josephine had carried all 20 of us here, each with our own issues to heal.

James too had shown up to be a challenger to push me into my power, so that I would become unwavering. At times, they had been perpetrators, but here on the lake, we were all one and there was no drama. There was only peace.

I felt my journey with Peru coming to an end. Yet it was also just beginning.

***

Ancient remembering

Everywhere we went around Titicaca was beyond sacred. We visited caves that I felt would absorb my very being if we'd stayed long enough. We went to the Stargate of Amaru Muru where I could have been transported into other worlds forever had I allowed myself to go.

This part of Peru was cosmic. It was so different from the mountains. Sometimes I would sink so far beyond the lake that I could connect to deeper waters, deeper earth, while also having my head in the stars. The whole place was an energetic portal and the downloads were constant.

On the way out to the island homestay, James turned to look at me and, overriding his usual state of annoyance, pointed up.

"There's Illimani, Lou. There's your mountain."

The mountain that had called me here.

I smiled, grateful for this moment of warmth, resisting my inner child's need to connect further with him. He had opened a gateway to talk, but we were past that now, and neither of us needed to pretend anymore. And so, I sat in silence.

EARTH CHAKRA SHAMAN

We landed on the island and met our new guide, shaman Jorge Luis, who had amazing wisdom and English to translate it. He told us how Titicaca was the birthplace of the Inca and about the ley lines in these parts. Finally, I felt like someone was giving me the answers I had been seeking.

"There's a ley line called the Truth Line that goes from Lake Titicaca to Mount Shasta. If you follow it, you will see that many churches are built on the line because this energy is very powerful."

At the mention of Shasta, my heart jumped. He knew Shasta, the base chakra of the Earth, where I would be going in a few weeks' time! I wanted to tell him, to jump up and down, but contained myself and my need to be acknowledged by teachers.

I could see how the earth chakras were connected by ley lines, energy running between each chakra, just like in the body. Part of the process of me healing people was placing the stones on their chakras to create more vibrancy, clear blocks, and ensure flow between the chakras. I realised that this was why I had been called here to the sacral chakra of the Earth; to bring vibrancy, to send healing energy and to collect healing energy to share with others in my healing. It was reciprocal. Everything was reciprocal – to bring balance.

***

From the island, I stared out at the far Bolivian shores of Titicaca where Illimani looked over us, the protector of the lake.

"So, I made it," I said. "You called, you sent me the money, and here I am. Thank you."

I opened my mesa and intended that all my medicine fly across the lake and kiss the Illimani mountain top.

Welcome home, Louise, said the water mountain, as gentle as the Mother herself greeting her child at the door. *You must learn to connect deeper to the waters, Louise. You must make your offering to the lake.*

Feeling Illimani nearby, as I lay awake on that tiny yet powerful island in the middle of the lake, I processed all that had happened here in Peru. I knew the outer world was a reflection of my inner world, and I wanted to truly see the last of what my teachers were showing me.

I wanted them to accept me. Where was I not accepting myself? I felt them judge me. Where was I judging myself? I believed they were more powerful than me. Where was I not owning my own power? They triggered my rejection issues, but I also triggered other people's rejection issues, sometimes in my own students. They were sharp, but I too could be sharp and sometimes taught my clients with tough love.

A seed had been planted in Peru and the lesson would grow inside of me. To do this work, I had to stand in my personal power, believe in my own medicine and trust in my own path. I had to be courageous to show up in all my light and not give it away to anyone. I had to back myself and stay aligned with my own path of purpose and service.

***

Frustrations and divine unfolding

Our last few days were spent visiting sacred sites not too far from Lake Titicaca on the mainland. Despite our magical time here, something felt incomplete. I felt frustrated and restricted and had a desperate need to get to the lake, even though we'd been told we wouldn't be going back, because there wasn't enough time.

I needed to get there.

I had not said my goodbyes or made an offering. I had not swum in her waters or been on my own with her. There was a kuya in my mesa that I had dreamed the night before of giving back to the lake and I was determined to get there.

The schedule for the day was back-to-back right up until 9pm and we were leaving at 5am the next morning to catch a flight back to Cusco. Throughout our farewell dinner, I was itching to get away. Then from our last fire ceremony out the back of the hotel, I could see the lake in the distance. I was so close and yet so far. It wasn't near enough to get to on foot, but maybe I could get a taxi. It was 11pm by now and I was exhausted. And as we finished the fire ceremony, the news came that we would need to leave at 2am, because there was going to be a local protest the next day, and the roadblocks would go in at 5am.

"You need to be back on the coach in three hours," James instructed.

Ugh!

I'd been hoping at least to have a chance to meditate and connect with the lake that way, but it was clear we needed to get our heads down for an hour. Cuddled up with my mesa, wallowing in unfinished business, it was time to let go and trust that one day I would come back to this place to finish what I'd started.

For now, there was nothing I could do...

***

The universe works in mysterious ways

Cold, tired and fed up, we climbed onto the coach and drove along the lake in the dark, which was as frustrating as it was beautiful. I was tempted to ask to stop, but there was a sense of urgency in the air and tensions were rising. Something wasn't right.

I rested my head on Simon's shoulder and let out my tears. I had expressed my exasperation to him the evening before and he had assured me graciously that I'd be back one day.

Then braking sharply, the coach came to a rapid halt. In front of us was a fire. On the road! At first I thought a car had exploded. It looked like a war zone after all and I could hear men shouting. Then I saw the hay bales and car tyres producing the thick black smoke. The coach reversed along the narrow lane, which honestly seemed more dangerous than the flaming roadblock, but behind us the road was now blocked with hay bales and car tyres on fire too.

For a brief moment, I was fearful, but it parted, and a strange sense of joy welled up in me. My eyes flitted to the lake. Was this how the universe was going to ensure I made it? I watched the scene unfold while everyone else around me was freaking out and a sense of deep wisdom settled over me. This was all aligned.

"Did you just manifest this so you could get to the lake?" Simon laughed.

"There's only one way out of here and that is by boat!" I jested in my worst Spanish accent, trying to conceal a cackle.

I couldn't hide my delight in the situation and I threw myself into his chest so it would seem to everyone else that I was terrified at the act of war we may or may not be encountering. Inside, though, I knew how it was all going to unfold, as if the lake had planned it and showed me already.

"Seriously though," I whispered to Simon, "I feel pretty awesome right now. The only thing that I would really like is a cup of coffee."

At that moment, the coach driver got back on board with flasks.

"How do you do that?" Simon joked, amazed at the randomness of it.

We had got stuck next to the only hotel on that stretch of road and it happened to have a jetty, so we lugged our suitcases off the coach to wait for a boat. Most of the group were miserable and shattered, but I was stupidly drunk on synergistic bliss and carrying a sense of smugness that I knew I would need to drop. I had to return to humility before making my offering to the lake.

Within a few hours, a little boat came to collect us and we boarded as dawn turned the night sky from jet black to inky blue. In voices usually reserved for speaking to naughty children, the teachers told me where to sit and what to do. I sat down in the undercover passenger seats but something overcame me.

"No! I need my mesa. It's in my suitcase at the back of the boat."

James made some sarcastic remark about me being a nuisance, but I ignored him and left my seat to go find my luggage, before he got a chance to tell me to sit back down. With a sense of urgency as the boat pulled away, I headed outside to the stern of the boat to grapple with the mountain of suitcases. I was relieved to find mine was right there on the top. Both nervous and excited, I grabbed my mesas and realised I did not want to go back inside. Nor was I meant to. I knew what I needed to do...

I climbed over the suitcases and found a tiny wooden ledge to balance on while I opened my mesa. I selected the orange medicine stone, orange being the colour of the sacral chakra, and leaned over the edge. I could almost touch the dark waters. And in that sacred moment before I made my offering, I felt the buzzing energy of this medicine and remembered I held in my hands the gift of perseverance. *How reflective of this journey*, I thought. I had to let it go, though. This was my offering. Gently, the boat turned and there, like the greatest gift of all, was the rising sun, lighting up the entire lake in a golden orange glow. I gasped. The Inca believe that the first morning sun is the holiest, which is why we must rise for it every day. I felt it.

Against the stillness of the vast lake and with my mountain far in the distance, the orange light illuminated my hand, my face, my body. I reached down to touch the water and let the kuya go, dropping it in and watching the tiny ripples it made on the lake's surface.

Humbled by God's greater plan, I said my final prayer to Peru.

"Thank you, Mother Waters, Lake Titicaca, Mount Illimani for calling me. Here is my gift to you. The gift of this medicine stone was perseverance. I gift it to you with my new level of consciousness, lessons of standing in my personal power. Here is my activation. This is my growth that I gift to the grid. May all humans wake up to the consciousness of their own personal power."

Hypnotised by the magic of the light dancing on the waters, I heard the message to replace this kuya with 'the orange stone'. There was indeed another orange stone in the outer layer of my mesa – a stone from Australia.

The gift of your new medicine stone will be the gift of the Indigenous medicines of the earth, the lake whispered into my heart.

I reached for it now and blew the gift of the lake into it. I kissed it and popped it into the centre of my mesa with the other kuyas. I felt the change of my mesa within me. I was more grounded and more certain in myself. I was no longer using the medicine in the way I had been taught. My mesa was becoming a portal for the earth chakra medicines, which must have been why Don Francisco had encouraged me to begin a second mesa.

One for me. One for the planet.

***

The sacral chakra of the Earth awakens the divine call within us, reminding us that the journey is lonely when we're about to access the great energies within ourselves. The birthing of our path and divine purpose cannot be guided by anyone else. Our only guide is our inner sun, our innocence, our inner sense. Only we know our path.

I packed up and turned to see James standing there smiling at me, the lake and the sun. He had seen me, I knew it. He had seen me giving away my medicine. 'Breaking the rules' as it were. I returned his smile and realised I was completely free of him and the drama. I had learned all I needed to learn from him and no longer had to hide my power. I had freed us both from the long and tiresome dynamic. He had seen me fully in my medicine woman, no longer the fearful little girl needing approval from her teachers.

Our time together in this lifetime was over. I turned back to face the waters, grateful for the whole experience.

***

I Facetimed Harry, as soon as the boat pulled to shore, and laughed at what I saw.

"Oh my God! Where are you guys?"

He moved the camera view to show me the old ruins behind him.

"We're in Glastonbury," he said.

"You have to be kidding me, right? What on earth made you go there? I used to have to drag you kicking and screaming!"

"We all got the urge to come," Harry smiled.

Seeing them at Glastonbury and seeing my image with this golden glowing lake behind me took my breath away.

"Oh my God, Harry! You're on the heart chakra of the Earth and I'm on the sacral chakra. The Rainbow Serpent flows between us. She flows from Titicaca to Uluru to Glastonbury"

The universe had worked in mysterious ways indeed. And there was yet more mystery to discover.

***

Sacral Chakra Prayer
Personal Power & Divine Purpose Wisdom

Divine Mother, Pachamama, I give back to you what no longer serves
So you can return it back to light energy.
I release and heal.
In this healing, I grow.
In this growth is a code.
In this code is my offering
to the great Grid of Gaia.
And you rejoice in the awakening of my consciousness.
I grow, I give, I receive, I awaken.
Mother Waters, bringer of life,
Lake Titicaca and all the sacred sites of these ancient lands
of Peru
that shine the light on the pathways to our heavens,
I come in the deepest of honouring
of the divine feminine and the divine masculine.

LOUISE CARRON HARRIS

Rainbow Serpent and Plumed Serpent,
I honour your dance of sacred union
through the sacral chakra of the Earth.
May I awaken to the truth of the power and creativity I hold within me.
May the divine feminine and divine masculine birth my purpose with passion and play
and awaken my medicine and soul purpose on planet Earth.
May I share my gifts from Gaia with the world with unconditional love.

***

CHAPTER 8

The Road to America

To help us see deeper into where we were meant to be going in both the calling and in our lives, Harry and I decided to create vision boards.

For hours, we sat in our own spaces in silence, going through boxes of magazines, flipping through the pages, letting our heart guide, cutting out images that called to our souls. When we had finished, we shared with each other.

First, we looked at Harry's. I laughed right away, as so many of the images were the same as my own, including the Great Pyramids of Giza.

"Wow! We've both got the same image in the centre of our board."

It was a picture of a bright multi-coloured hand.

"It reminded me of the way the reiki flows," he explained.

"It reminded me of reiki too," I responded.

I was surprised that it would be as important to him as it was to me. Harry was reiki-attuned, but not because he wanted to be a healer, just because I had attuned him when

I was practicing to become a teacher a few years before. Now he used it on me all the time. It was part of our morning flow, sleepy cuddles and the reiki flowing between us. But he didn't really talk about it. I hadn't realised how much he valued it and I was touched.

I noticed that I had chosen the right hand and he had taken the left… much like how our minds worked.

We both had water, lots of blues and mountains on our boards, but details of where we were meant to go were very loose indeed. But my inner fears of failing such a big quest were soothed knowing that I wasn't alone and that Harry was willing to be a little more mystic with me than normal to honour the call.

***

"Wherever we're meant to be going, it's got something to do with the Yukon," he said when a truck pulled up in front of us with YUKON written on the back.

We had been tracking the nudges of where to go for weeks, and it turned out that Alaska was a big fucking place! However, Harry and I had both been seeing the word 'Yukon' everywhere, and in the end, it was Harry who confirmed what I'd been wondering. Now I stared at the map, recalling a dream I'd had.

"There's something I am meant to do around healing the waters in Canada. In Lake Louise, I have to take the medicine there to heal trauma in the waters, which will help the whole of Alberta," I told Harry trying to understand what the dream meant.

"And there's something about the waters of the Yukon, some sort of healing or activation."

Later that same day, a friend who lived on Vancouver Island in Canada got in touch, then one of our friends who had moved to Calgary messaged me randomly, or not so randomly. It turned out that she lived near Lake Louise. The universe was giving me tiny little pointers, like pins in a great map. It still wasn't fully clear, but it was enough information to get us going.

***

Planning pressure

All the flights were booked. So many flights! To LA, then Seattle, then Alaska, then Canada. And then we had a road trip to the south of France for the wedding of one of my best friends where I was to marry her and her husband in front of 100 people. And *then* I was due to go to a festival for another girlfriend's hen weekend. It was all too much. I just wanted to close all the doors of Lou's world, hide in my kitchen and make playlists on Spotify!

The responsibility to get it right, to trust that I was enough, that I could do enough, and lead us to where the Earth wanted us to be, was eating at my usual light-hearted serendipity spirit.

"I just feel like I'm having a 'non-spiritual, non-trusting' moment. I'm worried we're going on a humongous trip to the other side of the world, on a sacred quest to the middle of nowhere with our children and with no adults to tell us what to do or anyone to look after us!" I confided in Harry.

"Only you know what needs to happen, babe. I can't tell you or even advise you. No one can. I can only follow you on this, but you seem to have got everything right so far, so just keep doing what you're doing," Harry said.

"What if I take us to the wrong places?" I moaned with my head in my hands.

"Cross that bridge when you come to it. You always make the best decisions in the moment. What would you advise yourself right now?" Harry said.

"I'd say breathe, stay present, ask God to heal my fear so I can turn it into gold!" I answered.

And like that I breathed away the thinking and came into my body.

"God, Gaia, universe, I give you this fear. I cannot carry it. Here, take it, so I can go to sleep."

***

Messages from the spirit world

I needed some final guidance before we headed off on the quest, so I turned to my trusty ally, Angela, a medium who had prophesied so much of my calling up until now. I trusted her guidance.

"You need to beware, as there will be challenges when you go away," the medium warned, looking up at me from the six tarot cards she had in front of her.

"You must be still when you reach the waters of your destination, meditate and look around you. They are asking you to be present. You are being blessed in sacred turquoise waters too. There is beautiful light coming from below."

She went quiet for a moment and I wasn't sure if I was meant to talk or not, but her eyes remained closed, so I sat tight. Then she took a deep breath.

"Louise," she said in a gentle grandmotherly voice, "this money, you must be careful."

She opened her eyes, looking at me seriously before she went on.

"It will go just as quickly as it came."

She moved on.

"You must be gentle with Harry. There will be times when he is not comfortable in your world. It's when you're on a mountain. You must learn to give him space and accept that your world sometimes takes much longer for him to process."

She went back into her trance.

"There is a falling-out in August, with a woman, a friend of yours. The angels are cutting the cords strongly. They are telling me you don't have a choice in this. They are forcing this situation. The relationship no longer serves and it has gone bad. They are intervening. It's unusual for them to do this, but they are doing it for your own good."

I was triggered and I felt it deep in my core. I hadn't had any major fallings-out with anyone since I was in my early twenties and three friends 'broke up with me'. I'd been devastated for years.

"But how or why would such a thing happen?" I asked.

"It's not for you to control, Louise. They cut the cords. You are not to go back."

Viv? I gasped at the thought.

She was the only friend I would be seeing in August while we were on our travels. While Viv lived in America now, she had been my friend for 15 years and had been my bridesmaid. There's no way we'd fall out. I had offered to pay for her to fly to Mount Shasta, to come on a five-day shamanic family retreat that I had booked for us. She had seen it pop up on her social media feed too and said she would love to go. I was excited for her coming and Viv being there would help Harry be more relaxed on the retreat. I could not see how we would ever fall out. Angela must have got this reading all wrong.

"There is a Peruvian guide speaking to you in a lost language. You must listen to him. There is another guide with you. He is African, possibly Egyptian, I can't tell. He is quiet but strong by your side," she said, coming to the end of the session and opening her eyes again.

"You must speak with him. He will guide you a lot on this journey."

***

California dreaming

Staying with my family in California was the ordinary before the extraordinary, and all part of getting ready for the journey ahead. Uncle Jay picked us up from LAX, wrapping his arms around me for a welcome hug.

"Hey, baby girl. You're here! What's this the boys tell me about you not drinking anymore?"

I rolled my eyes and punched him playfully in the arm.

"I'm pure now, Uncle Jay."

"Naw, you're just outta practice, girl!"

Apparently, it wasn't the hen weekend two months away that I needed to worry about pulling me off the sobriety wagon, but my wild American family. Next thing I knew, it was 4am and my aunt was outside telling off me and my cousins for keeping the entire neighbourhood awake with our singing, shouting and mucking around in the hot tub after sinking the four bottles of margarita that my uncle had loaded us up with. I was nearly 37 and about to embark on a journey that was going to teach me to grow up. Ahead of me in the coming weeks, beyond the safety of my family's nest, was my mission. I was scared and relished acting like an 18-year-old for one night, like savouring the last piece of chocolate before giving it up forever.

But first, I spent 12 hours puking.

"I tell ya, you're just out of practice, baby girl."

"Uncle Jay, this is *why* I can't drink! It poisons me and detaches me. I can't hear the Earth. I can't feel my energy. My head hurts!" I cried over the toilet bowl.

He had absolutely no idea what I meant.

***

News buzz

My aunt and uncle's home was the beating heart of their family. Their kids, grandkids, neighbours and friends were always coming and going and I loved being a part of it. I found it easy to just be Lou for a while and not have to worry about being a shaman or in service to the Earth. I woke up every morning to my uncle cooking up pancakes and treats and playfully entertaining all the children at the breakfast bar. It was heart-warming and comforting to watch the intergenerational interactions. Family, to me, was everything.

While I loved being here, mornings were very different to starting the day back home. Like most homes around the world, the TV was always on in the background, playing the latest news. We never had the TV on at home. We didn't even have the radio on. We only played our own music and rarely had any external media interference.

The constant buzz of the news bulletins soon began to wobble my sensitive energy field. No matter how much I paid no mind to it, I found the unavoidable presence of the flashing images would capture the eyes of my children and Harry. Fury washed over me as I saw them entranced and unaware as they munched their breakfast. I would shout with rage in my mind, *Harry! Wake up! Stop staring into that fucking box! Come back!* His energy spoke louder than words. Aggravated by my prickliness, he came back on the defensive, building an energetic wall and looking on, motionless, transfixed, captivated by the drama. Then, boom! It had *me* too! Like a hook in my soul, I was drawn in.

Riots in Turkey... All the airports closed... This is really bad... People are rioting in the streets.. Tourists at high risk... The government is going to fall... Could be kidnappings... No way out... Catastrophic effect on the whole world...

Realising I'd been ignoring all this, fear penetrated my belly and I paced the house with my phone, hands shaking. *Oh my God*, I thought, *I am so damn ignorant. I need to understand this stuff!* My friend Claire was in Turkey on her first holiday on her own with her kids and I had an urge to speak to her. Was she okay? Was she scared? I desperately messaged her, knowing it was the middle of the night over there. I also texted her ex-husband to see if he knew anything and to check she was safe.

After some time, he responded but seemed bemused at my worry.

"What's the drama? They're fine."

Eventually, I heard from Claire too.

"It's fine! Life is great. We love Turkey. There's been a bit of trouble in one of the towns but we're having a great time."

I had been spoon-fed a taste of sensationalised, media-circus drama... and I *had swallowed!* I loved the timing of this lesson. When I came to my senses, I was sent more information from the universe to help me get my head around what had happened. My teacher Sue happened to be in Turkey too, teaching some classes over there, and posted on Facebook that she'd seen some American news reports of the town where she was staying, but nothing was actually happening there. She expressed her fury that the media footage used was from a bombing in Paris a few years before.

I was cross with myself for having even been sucked in. The adrenaline of the drama had controlled me, like it does with everyone. The media is toxic. We must be truly aware what we consume and what it does to our mental health and our vision of the world. It was a wake-up call to be aware of the thieves of my presence of mind.

***

The nest

On the last night, music played from the pier bar, soundtracking the Californian dream as the sun set on the sea behind us, the warm glow reflecting the glow in my heart for my family. I watched the way my uncle held court over cocktails at the beach bar, my aunt rolling her eyes and laughing at the stories we'd heard a hundred times before. My cousins, their kids, more friends pulled up chairs and joined in the banter. The girls' eyes sparkled, their hands holding their bellies, as they chuckled harder than they knew they could. They were so happy! We were so happy!

It was the end-scene of a feelgood movie where everyone lives happily ever after....

As the inevitable journey loomed closer, I desperately clung onto the child inside, the part of me that just wanted to be looked after, told what to do and where to go. I didn't want to grow up. I didn't want to go.

***

"You okay, babe?" I asked Harry the next morning as we closed the suitcase.

"I suppose I'm nervous about driving the RV and getting it out of LA central," he admitted.

"Me too," I replied, rubbing his back and kissing him on the cheek. "This is way bigger than anything we've done before, isn't it, though? Maybe we should honour the nerves. We've never done any real travel. We're never alone at home, let alone on a 1500-mile road trip to Seattle with a sacred quest! When we went to Australia, we were surrounded by friends. When I went to Peru, my teachers led the whole way. Now we are about to be fully responsible adults, without a plan, two kids to look after, and no parents!"

"Yeah, it's crazy really," he said quietly.

"Are you nervous because we don't know what the fuck we're doing?"

"I guess, but I'm leaving that in your hands. I just need to make sure you're all safe," he said, not looking at me.

I felt sick.

"I suppose faith is about letting go of expectations, trusting the flow, allowing it to go however it is going to go. If we honour the feeling of uncertainty that lies ahead then it lessens its grip on us," I suggested.

If we just stayed present, observed the signs and slowed down, surely we could walk the path one step at a time.

***

Road trip!

I held my breath as we pulled onto an eight-lane freeway, then held it for the next four hours. On some weird level, it felt like I was making us small enough to squeeze between the thousands of lorries and cars flying either side of our RV, as we left the city on our way to nowhere.

The only plan was to drive as far north as possible and find somewhere to sleep for the night.

We are exactly where we need to be. We are safe. We are guided by the universe. All will be well.

I recited little mantras to reassure Harry, but really, they were for me as the van wobbled and veered through the traffic. I was the leader on this mission. And it scared the shit out of me.

"We're proper road tripping now, kids!" I announced, as the music flowed and we sang, stopping only to chew my nails and never taking my eyes off the road.

"This is your journey, babe. You just tell me where to go and I'll go," Harry said with an essence of service that I'd not felt from him before.

With WIFI too expensive to use over here (I had already racked up a £200 bill in Peru) and a semi-working dongle that was already proving near useless, we had to go old-school and use a map. I hated maps! We also had one day less to get to Mount Shasta than I had planned because I'd agreed to pick up Viv from the airport, which meant taking the shitty freeway and not the scenic route through Yosemite National Park. My cousin had thought I was mad when he'd found out.

"You came all the way to California to take the I5? You're crazy. That's the worst freeway in America. You're taking the worst road trip ever!" he laughed.

It had been the only way I could make it work, so I did my best to override the sadness of missing out on seeing the redwoods. The first seed of failure had been planted, though. The redwoods had been in my vision and I wasn't going to get to be with these magnificent trees.

Playfully, I outlined the plan for Harry.

"Okay, here's what we're going to do. One, drive 300 miles north, sleep somewhere near San Luis. Two, drive another 350 miles north, pick up Viv from the airport 100 miles from Mount Shasta. Three, drive 100 miles back to Mount Shasta. Four, go to the retreat. Spend five days dancing around a shamanic fire activating the base chakra of the Earth and downloading all the energy medicine for my mesa. Six, drive 700 miles to Seattle. Seven, fly to Alaska. Eight, fly to Canada and drive 700 miles. Nine, fly back to London, sleep for six hours and drive 700 miles through France. Simple!"

I smiled as we left the city behind and squeezed Harry's hand, knowing it took all his concentration to glance at me and return my smile. He felt the magic too. But on top of everything else, he carried the load of keeping us all safe.

***

I relaxed as much as I could into the drive, gazing out the window with the feeling of blessings warming my soul. The view of the San Gabriel mountains breathed life back into my soul. I was like a fish put back into water; no longer gasping for breath in a concrete city. Here, I could see and feel Mother Earth again, even if it was from a gas-guzzling RV on a freeway. I had missed her so much.

We sang along to our road trip playlists, the kids content in their own little worlds, loving the novelty of a table to do their colouring on. *Life couldn't be better right now*, I mused to myself as I watched them.

Once again, I'd trusted. I knew we would be fine. We'd find a place to stay. We'd be protected and safe. I had only one concern: the constant pressure I put on myself to honour this calling and complete the mission I had been sent to do.

***

Poison

Chocolate bars, burgers and refillable Coke... How do people live on this shit?!

We'd pulled over and were experiencing our first American service station stop, which turned out to be my idea of hell. Not even the kids wanted to eat any of the food. My raging disgust at the food industry was as hot as the desert air that hit my face as I stepped out of the van. Even at 5pm, it was sweltering and dry. I hadn't realised it would be like this.

We got back into the van, having had hardly anything for dinner, and the kids made themselves beds and were soon sleeping. We hadn't got as far as I had hoped, having sat in three hours of bumper-to-bumper traffic. The landscape began to change, and the mountains got further away. I fluctuated fast. One minute, I was saying, "Look at those lovely mountains in the distance". The next minute, I was thinking, *This is all wrong! I've made a huge mistake.*

I reached for my oracle cards for guidance and pulled out my pendulum.

"Am I on the right track?" I asked.

Everything pointed to no!

I was not in the right energy to use divination tools and I knew they could be confidence-destroying if read the wrong way. I wanted to trust in myself. I was on the journey for a reason. I was called for a reason. Yet within hours of setting off on my quest, I had begun to feed the doubt.

As the outer world changed, so did my inner world. Distanced from the mountains, all I saw was factory farming, barren lands, then 'conventionally' cultivated fruit and nut trees. The plants didn't feel alive to me, though. Man was fucking with nature all around, and not one tree seemed free of that control. I felt a constant niggling that something wasn't right. The land was not vibrant or living, and my mind could not compute. It was like seeing a dark side of the world, coming out of my rainbow bubble.

Just then, we passed a sign for the redwood trees in Yosemite National Park and I shouted out from my despair, "Let's go that way!"

Harry jumped to it and tried to move lanes, but it was too late to get this huge RV off this godforsaken freeway and to be with real nature. I was kind of shocked he'd been so willing to do what I asked. I'd spent 18 years with this boy whose first response to anything I suggested was no. Then we'd follow our usual pattern of me having to convince and coax him into my ideas. This made me see he truly *was* at my service on this journey.

"I just wanted to see the real trees," I cried, "The alive trees! Not these dead ones! What if I was meant to go to those redwoods and I've fucked it all up already?"

I got the feeling Harry really understood, but I was watering that seed of failure and it began to grow inside me. *Have I failed my mission before I've even started?* I wondered as I watched the sun set on the barren California lands. *Come on, Lou. You can choose to see this differently*, I thought, and I turned up the music to honour the beauty of the sinking sun. But the sadness of seeing trees being forced to grow in the desert stayed with me. None of this made sense!

I later learned of the California water wars, where there is not enough water to farm in the desert, so they drain the reservoirs and drill down into the groundwater. I was yet to understand this fully, but glimpses kept coming my way of the long-term ecological devastation this would create.

Signs next to farms: "No water, no jobs."

Then, in the dusky sky, I could see what appeared to be a dust storm and it unnerved me.

"Slow down, babe," I gasped as I grabbed Harry's thigh and detected a terrible smell outside.

We proceeded slowly through the fog, trying to figure out the awful stench. And then like a punch to the heart, I knew the smell was methane as I saw them... Thousands of cows! Packed together in interconnected pens. For miles and miles along the freeway.

Horror.

Hell.

I had never seen so many cows. I felt sick with pain for their suffering and with rage for them being hidden away here where no one could witness the farming of these souls, the death camp for these living beings, all for money to feed human addiction.

"Welcome to Harris Ranch, California's Largest Beef Producers," read the sign with a big American smile. It taunted me.

Eat, drink and be merry. Only you can't drink from the tap because of the chemicals we've used to pollute the local water. None of it is safe to drink. But don't worry... You can always get a Coke! I thought sarcastically.

It seemed to go on forever and so did my silent tears. I already knew the staggering numbers of cows that were raped every year, the animals fattened up on corn, crying for their stolen babies, trapped in their own shit and squalor to be slaughtered and sold for millions. Yet even though it was now in front of my eyes, I couldn't comprehend what I was seeing and could never unsee. I hated humans in that moment, for raping the earth, for raping the animals, as if it was our right.

Fuck you, Harris Ranch. Fuck you and the whole fucking industry.

***

Flow like water

It was nearly midnight when we entered the gates of the San Luis campsite, greeted by a swooping white owl that brought joy to my exhaustion. Was it a sign that we were on the right road after all or just a messenger to soothe my aching soul? Either way, I was desperate to ground on the earth, so as we parked up, I flung open the van door into the pitch black and let my bare feet breathe in the dry sand and leaves.

Next day, we walked to the edge of the San Luis, the reservoir for San Francisco and LA, but it was pretty empty. The drought meant they would have to pull down water from Shasta lake, 500 miles away to top it up. I felt sick awakening to this unnatural control of water. In 2016, half of all the water used in the United States went towards raising animals for food. I felt my rage. It seemed that us humans couldn't stop ourselves. When we have used all readily available water sources, we drain the aquifers and deplete the Earth of her water. Wells dry up, reducing the water in streams and lakes. Wildlife suffers and water quality is greatly deteriorated. In time, land subsides. Nature no longer stands a chance.

"We need to pray for the waters," I said to the girls as we stood there.

I shook my rattle and sang a song that came from somewhere beyond myself. I cried for the lands. I cried for the waters. I cried for what I did not understand. And I cried because I felt ashamed to be human.

Then I remembered...

I am water!

We all are.

Humans are made up of over 70% water and the spirit of water is alive in us. But just like the plants and the animals, she comes to us from a place of human containment. She is not free to flow where she knows she must go. We control her like we control everything. How far removed we have become from the essence of what we are: earth, air and water. Living in cities and towns, alone, eating poisoned food, drinking polluted water, we have forgotten the sacredness of the waters. We buy it in bottles! We turn a tap and let it run! She was not ready to emerge from the earth or come off the mountains to be trapped into man-made lakes or drilled from the aquifers. And everything has consequences.

She was showing me this, I realised. I was meant to see this! Water was going to be a bigger part of my journey. The messages were becoming clear... Even the names! San Luis. Harris Ranch. Luis and Harris... I couldn't ignore it. This was my path. I was here to witness the darkness, not bask in the light. I needed to see the issues before I could bring the medicine to the base chakra of the Earth, the base chakra which represents our basic needs of shelter, food and water.

The mission was to become aware, to whisper to the water spirit and to awaken her within...

***

Through chaos comes clarity

Avalon had been quiet for the last 24 hours, and now wouldn't move from my lap. She was tired and her little body was burning up. When she started crying about the pain in her ears, I knew we had to get her some help. Half an hour later, we pulled up to a medical centre where the concerned doctor diagnosed an infection in both ears. $300 later, we were sent across the car park to the Walmart to get some antibiotics.

"Where did you get this prescription?" the pharmacist asked sharply.

"The medical centre," I replied, increasingly fearful.

"Where are you from?" she shot back.

"England," I answered, feeling like I was under interrogation.

"Come back in an hour. We need to check this prescription," she said, frowning and walking off.

There were no trees for shade in the car park and the heat reminded me we were really in the desert, so I headed inside with Avalon on my shoulder. I wandered around Walmart trying to get some paracetamol to help her while waiting for the antibiotics I didn't believe in and I began to cry. Walmart stood for everything I did not: unethical corporate domination; pedalling poison for the masses.

Avalon's sobs fell down the back of my neck. She was in so much pain. I realised traveling always took it out of her, just like it did me. I longed to be back in the safety of my home. I was low and missed my joyful self; the Lou who would get up every morning, dance, sing and enjoy life. And I still felt pressured to get everything right... for the quest, for the Earth, for humanity!

I managed to get enough WIFI to reach out to my students in our online group and everyone responded with kind words. Over 30 of them offered to send reiki. Then realising we wouldn't make it in time to pick up Viv that evening, I typed out a quick message to her.

Avalon is sick. We're not going to have the time to get you. Can you get a taxi or a lift down to Shasta?

She replied straight away.

Lou, this is all just too chaotic for you, so I think it's for the best if I don't come. Have a good time. Hope Avalon gets better soon. Love you.

I was devastated, desperate to see a friend, to see her. And there was that story in my head again. *This is all going wrong.* I thought back to what Angela the medium had said about a cord being cut with a friend in August. It wasn't possible. Not with us. Our friendship wasn't like that. Viv and I were so laid back with each other. There was never any drama. And I knew this wasn't to be true. Viv was playing a necessary role in my quest, ensuring I was exactly where I needed to be.

I hurried back to the counter for the pharmacist's verdict.

"This is too strong for your daughter and too expensive. This is $280 when there is another one the same for $12. I don't know why he gave you this, but it's not right and it's too much money. I can give you the cheaper one if you like, but it'll take a couple of hours to get it changed."

Her warmth made more tears tumble from my eyes. And for two more hours we waited. As we left Walmart at long last, I waved the bottle of antibiotics at a kind shop assistant who'd seen us anxiously coming and going.

"I think we can finally get out of here," I said.

And like an angel, she held her arms out and hugged me. I surrendered to her motherly embrace and sobbed with gratitude for her love, for this love, and for the final acceptance that I had no control over what happened. I just had to let go.

"Dry your tears now," she said, "All will be well."

And I knew it would be.

***

CHAPTER 9

Mount Shasta & the Base Chakra

The road to Mount Shasta was long and the sense of bewilderment I'd felt over the past 48 hours began to fade. I caught sight of a real tree, then another, and another, and even though there were still buildings in view, I could breathe. *Trees!*

"I reckon we'll make it to the Shasta lake campsite in time for a full moon shamanic fire," I said joyfully.

"Can we have marshmallows, Mummy?" Avalon called from the back of the van beneath all her blankets, so much brighter now.

"You can have whatever you want for being such a warrior these past few days."

It was like we had just travelled a 300-mile road of death, where I couldn't connect to anything. It had messed me up, but now as we cranked the music and danced in our seats, the high vibrations were back and I felt the connection with the trees, the air, the land, with my family, with myself.

On our first day in Shasta, I rose with the sun with a rush of gratitude and excitement... *Nature! I can get into nature!*

Without waking anyone, because I knew they needed the sleep and I needed the alone time, I grabbed my headphones and mesas from my bed and snuck out of the RV to the shore of the lake. The blue of water, the green of the trees lining the hills, the colours of the birds and butterflies, they took my breath away.

"Good morning, Mother Waters," I shouted across the deserted lake, as I jumped in. I was all alone in this vast space.

"Good morning, eagles! Thank you, thank you, thank you!" I called out, as I watched them fly overhead.

My heart was bursting with love and reverence for the aliveness that was being brought back to life inside me. I breathed it all in.

Back on the water's edge, I sat in silence, my mesas open and meditated, processing all that had happened and giving it all to the lake.

***

Shasta shamanic retreat

A hundred people gathered in circle around the sacred fire on Mount Shasta, Harry sitting next to me, a girl in each of our laps, watching the group we would be a part of for the next five days. I observed Harry's energy. He had come to some of my community shamanic fires in our garden, but this was indeed going to be a lot further out of his comfort zone. Yet he seemed relaxed, so far, and happy to be in someone else's hands for a while.

The shaman stood and everyone rose to their feet, shaking their rattles towards the sky. It was an invitation to join the dance, the sacred dance of the Huichol tribe, the dance of the deer.

"Ho!" and the dance began.

Clockwise we followed each other, like ants, round and round and round the sacred fire. Dust flew into the air as we dug our feet deep into the earth, heel, toe, heel, toe, heel, toe, stamping, shaking our rattles. Deeper into the dance I went. I did not know these people, but I knew this way. I did not know this tribe, but I knew this connection to Spirit. I knew the deer! Sweet, strong, wise, discerning deer who had been coming for six weeks into my garden at home, but also my dreams. The spirit of the deer rose up through my feet and entered my soul. The rattling sound in my ears, I was taken.

God, I feel home, I thought to myself as I danced between the two worlds, dropping deeper into a meditative state, dancing into the mystic, dancing on Gaia with my children.

And then there was Harry. I could not believe what I was seeing. He was dancing the deer dance. My insides grinned. I sent him a message in my mind. *Someone found their inner shaman!* I caught his eye and winked. He smiled back, a cheeky look on his face that I had not seen for a long time. Something had overridden his usual self-consciousness and sometimes crippling introvertedness, and he was two feet in, stamping, dancing, shaking a rattle in the air.

Avalon clocked that she had the power to change the direction of the dance. "Ho!" she sounded and delighted in 100 people shifting from clockwise to anti-clockwise around the circle. Now we were dancing backwards. Spirit was strong enough to keep even us newbies on our feet.

Never in a million years would I have thought this possible if you'd asked me a year before. The four of us, here, doing the deer dance? No chance!

Turns out you can always expect the unexpected. Always.

***

A family weekend of ceremony on the base chakra of the Earth was like a dream to me. It could not have been more perfect. Divine times, indeed! The camp was full of kids, so the girls were off playing in streams, running through tall grasses, hiding in each other's tents and messing around from dawn to dusk in Mother Nature's playground.

The shaman, a charismatic 70-year-old American, had been initiated into the Huichol tribe when he was just 18 years old. He had taken a shine to us and nicknamed me Miss England. There was one sure way to become popular in America, I realised, and that was to be English!

"Hey, you guys are Brits?" another American guy asked as he grabbed a chair next to me. He wasn't much older than I was, and I clocked his rings, Inca bracelets and various Peruvian jewels. Comforted seeing something from my own initiated lineage, I replied.

"That's right. We're from a place just outside of London in Buckinghamshire."

"No way! My girlfriend used to live in Beaconsfield."

"That's where we live! Harry was born in the area, but I grew up in a place further north called Wolverhampton."

"No way!" he said, going bright red in excitement, "I was born in Wolverhampton too."

"You're not American?" I asked.

"I've lived here for 10 years so I picked up the accent," he explained.

Nothing surprised me anymore, not after all the synchronicities I'd experienced now, and I knew he was part of my journey. In the five minutes before the next talk from the shaman, my new friend Mike and I dived deep. We were born in the same hospital, both moved to London and worked in sound recording studios, both loved music, both connected to Peruvian shamanism. The more we talked, the more we laughed. I was inwardly curious at what had brought us together and how this soul brother was going to play into my journey, or maybe how I would play into his...

Turning back to the group, I was amazed to see Harry in deep concentration making prayer arrows. His willingness to dive in humbled me.

"I really enjoyed that rattling meditation," he said, relaxed and sounding as surprised at himself as I was.

***

At night, Mount Shasta kept me awake, talking to me through my dreams, as I went in and out of worlds.

You create your own reality, Louise. There are a multitude of dimensions. There is no right or wrong, just the way you see your own world.

Each night, visions would come and go. The deer spirit visited me, guiding me across ancient lands, and in those dreams, I knew where I was going. Every morning, I would get up and sit next to the ever-burning sacred fire, telling it my dreams and listening to the wisdom of the flames that came back. The more I told the fire, the more the messages revealed themselves.

Earth activation and offerings

By day three of the retreat, Harry had gone a little quiet. Part of me wanted to probe and to make him happy, but then I recalled the message from my medium to give him some space. So, when he chose not to join in the morning teachings, instead of pestering him and making him tell me what was wrong, I simply kissed him on the forehead and honoured his wishes.

He appeared back in circle later that day in time for the ceremony where we were to make offerings to Shasta. We walked through tall grass in the heat of the afternoon sun, towards the ceremonial area, men, women and children, all making their way together to honour this sacred mountain. Everyone had their own intention. For many, it was to ask for prayers and wishes for themselves, their friends and family. For me, it was to share my medicine to activate the base chakra of the Earth, to give all that I could give.

We stood in a line, looking out to the snow-capped peak. To be in ceremony in this way with so many people was joyful, blessed, and exactly why I was here. I could feel the mountain's energy opening up effortlessly, welcoming us. Before the mountain spoke, I saw a perfect energetic rainbow around its peak and was in awe of the energy field of the mountain. The shaman smudged and blessed us with sage before we made our offerings. I held my rattle in the air and called to the spirit of the mountain in my mind.

"Mount Shasta, I've come a long way to be here today and bring you the offering of my medicine stone. This kuya has been through the fire. It was once one but split into two. It holds the gift of individuality, unity and power, and of twin souls walking alongside each other, honouring that we are all one."

I lay it on the ground with a prayer arrow I had made and a piece of chocolate, then placed my forehead to the ground and allowed my tears to flow. I felt the mountain instructing me to only leave one half of the kuya and take the other half for another offering elsewhere on my journey.

I went into a deeper trance and communion with Shasta, the messages flying through me so fast I couldn't catch them, yet somehow they landed in my soul. I pulled myself out of the trance and took a breath, trying to keep a foot in both worlds so I could recall the messages. I closed my eyes again, this time intending to stay present while slipping behind the veil.

"Mount Shasta, please tell me... Why me? Why have I been called to the earth chakras?"

Because you have a pure heart, Louise. And that will be the medicine of your new kuya.

I knew this was a reference to the pyrite stone from Australia that I'd got on the day I'd been sick. It had been sitting in my outer cloth all this time, waiting for its moment to be transformed into a medicine stone and now was that time. I blew the mountain's gift of 'pure heart' and popped it in the centre of my mesa with the other kuyas. My heart filled and I thanked the mountain.

"Shasta, I honoured your call and I came. I stand here with my family at my side. I ask you to bless me with your wisdom."

And what will you do with the wisdom I bless you with, Louise? asked the mountain.

I was more surprised at my own request, which had come from nowhere, than the mountain's question. I had never asked anything of the earth chakras before and was unsure why I had done so now.

"Mount Shasta, I want to bring love and light to the Earth, to help people so they can learn to connect with her again and find peace within themselves," I said in my mind.

That gift is always with you, Louise. The more pure the heart, the more wisdom is received.

My heart was vibrating so much that it took my breath away and I heaved with uncontrollable sobs. Conscious of the girls nearby, I breathed through it.

God, I'm always crying! I thought.

"Shasta, please tell me why I have to go to the Yukon?" I tried again.

You already know the reason. You hold the energy in your mesa and in yourself to bring balance to the waters. Take the energy of the great power spots to the waters. Help them heal and inspire more people to do the same. Lead your people to these places, Louise, so they too can restore balance to the Earth. You can do this for the rest of your life if you wish, Louise. In doing so, you will discover a new earth node and take people there too.

I envisioned myself taking people around the world in my own unique shamanic way.

There is no need for lineage, Louise. You have the medicine within you. Love is your power. The more you love, the more your mountain wisdom awakens. You will become divine in your ability to love if you can look at what you do not love, and learn to truly love and honour that too.

***

Sacred tools and divine timing

It was time to leave, and given our English charms, everyone was fascinated with our journey ahead.

"Where are you guys heading next?" the shaman asked.

In truth, we had no idea. The name Saint Helens had come to mind in a dream on the flight over. I had learned a few days before that this was in fact a volcano close by, but we'd have to take the I5 to get there and that damned road was no longer an option for me. I knew the soulless freeway was not my path, so I had to trust.

"I feel there's an energy line we need to follow, but we're just going to drive north and ensure we're in Seattle in four days' time to get our flight to Alaska so who knows!" I said.

"Mount Rainier is very sacred. It's the protector mountain of Seattle. You will do well to go there," the shaman suggested, "And please make an offering for me!"

"I will," I promised, hugging him as we left and feeling grateful that we had some sort of direction.

Having said that, I had dropped so deep into nature that I was beyond laid back about the journey ahead. I was so fully connected that I knew the lands would guide us and I trusted we would go where we needed to go.

I looked all over camp for Mike but couldn't find him. It seemed he had left without saying goodbye. I was yet to work out why we had met, but I mean... how often do you meet someone with such synergies? There would be a reason, I knew it.

"Let's go to Shasta town for lunch. We can jump on the WIFI and figure out where we're headed next. I'll send Mike a telepathic message to meet us there!" I said to Harry, half-joking, but not. I knew it would work. I just hadn't learned how to say the batshit crazy stuff with conviction yet. Even with Harry!

I closed my eyes. *Come meet us in the town, Mike!* I thought, with a certainty we'd see him again.

***

We tucked into some lunch in a little cafe off the main street and got chatting to another couple on the table next to us.

"Oh man, you need to go to Mount Mazama. It's totally on the lines of what you're doing here," the guy said, once we'd got over the 'cute accents' conversation and told him about our quest. "And head to the city park in Big Springs. It'll be on your way. Bottle up as much of that mountain water as you can! It's sacred and will really top you up for your journey. That water is ancient and comes right off the glacier. You'll have time to get to Mazama by nightfall if you leave in the next hour or so…"

We thanked the couple and finished our lunch, then out of nowhere Mike appeared. We all jumped up to hug him.

"Oh my God, you guys, you'll never guess. I was in the car park looking at the beautiful view before I left, and something nudged me to turn around. And there you were! So weird."

I smiled knowingly.

"Wanna come crystal shopping?" I asked him.

Mike had told me about all these crystal shops in Shasta, as he was a regular in the area, and by all accounts had quite a collection back home.

The crystal shops here were more intimidating than the tiny hippy shops in the UK. I felt inadequate looking through the windows into a vast museum of shaman drums, wands and crystals the size of my small humans. Stepping through the door, it felt very 'serious shamans only'.

Immediately, a stunning translucent crystal drew me in. 'Lemurian' it said on the label. I had never heard of a crystal with that name, but I couldn't pull myself away. Somehow, I knew it wasn't mine to buy, but that maybe there was a Lemurian crystal somewhere that was meant for me.

"Hey Lou," Harry called me over, "You need to get one of these."

He pointed to a beautifully carved wooden wand that had a crystal on top. He was being serious, which sort of freaked me out.

"I'll buy you one," he offered.

This freaked me out even more, but rather than taking the piss out of his sudden support for shamanic paraphernalia that I wasn't sure I was even comfortable with, I shut my mouth and felt into the thoughts that were coming up. I noticed I didn't feel 'enlightened enough' to have a wand. And yet, there was something else saying there was a wand here for me, so I played along.

"I love the colour of the turquoise wrap, but that's not the wand for me. I suppose if I was to get a wand, maybe it would be like that Lemurian stone over there," I told him.

Mike popped up.

"I know exactly why you're here! Follow me," he said, leading us to the back of the shop, and a hidden area I hadn't noticed until now. He crouched down to a shelf almost on the floor and reached for a wand.

"Oh my God! This is my wand! And it's Lemurian crystal on the top!" I shrieked.

Mike placed it in my hands and tears stung my eyes. It was amazing – turquoise and absolutely beautiful. Mike was bursting to tell me why he knew it was mine.

"There were only two made like this: a male and a female. I have the other one."

Stunned, I replied, "Oh Mike, you really are my brother from another mother, or maybe brother from another lifetime!"

As we said goodbye, I felt like it was some kind of karmic exchange, like we had been fleeting passers-by, messengers of truth and wisdom for a short while.

And I also knew I would see him again someday.

***

While Harry filled the bottles with melted glacier water and the girls took off their shoes and splashed around, meditating on a rock by the waters with my medicine tools was my perfect goodbye to Shasta. The sacred waters were so clear, and I asked them to bless me, my wand and my mesas. I laughed out loud as an old man turned up and began to play the Peruvian song 'El Cóndor Pasa' on a harp – a universal reminder that I was on the 'truth line' between Shasta and Lake Titicaca as well as the sacredness of the waters. All is connected. The universe, the elements, the chakras, the ley lines were all guiding me.

The 'truth line' was also called the Plumed Serpent or Quetzalcoatl, this divine masculine ley line met with the Rainbow Serpent, the divine feminine ley line. Together, they formed an infinity sign over the Earth. Years earlier, Harry and I both had an infinity symbol tattooed on our wrists and were learning to embody the divine masculine and feminine within us, and bring balance and harmony to the Earth in our truth.

***

Crater Lake and the Cascade Range

Onward we went and arrived at camp in the dark, heading straight to bed as I was keen to get to Mount Mazama for first light. When I woke and pulled myself out of Harry's embrace, I felt my wand digging into my side. I'd fallen asleep with it on my chest!

"Morning, babe," I said kissing Harry's soft lips. He tried to wrap his arms around me and pull me closer.

"Only thing standing between us and an act of passion is my wand, two mesas and two children sleeping two feet away," I laughed, pinching his cheek and kissing him again on the forehead.

I climbed down the ladder, giggling that this was our reality now.

"Wake up, kids. It's a new day! More mountains, more lakes, more adventures! Wakey wakey!" I sang as loud as possible without waking the neighbours.

"Morning, baby," I said to Avalon, kissing her cheek. She opened her eyes and smiled at me, "Mummy, I had the best dream last night. We were on a rollercoaster down a mountain."

"That sounds like the most awesome dream, baby. Now, where is that sister of yours?"

Bella had somehow wriggled all the way down to the foot of the bed and I found her sleeping in a ball there. She was the most curious kid!

"Morning, Babybel, ready for more adventures?"

Bella's big brown eyes peeped through her mass of knotty blond curls.

"Can we have chocolate milk, Mummy?"

"No! You can have an avocado! That's your bloody fault, Harry. One taste of chocolate milk and marshmallows and our children have been taken to the dark side."

Jokes aside, I was food-anxious for the kids. They hadn't eaten anything healthy, green or organic since we'd left the UK, and eating out was taking a toll on my own body so much that I was constantly craving broccoli!

***

It was crisp outside but the sun came up as we reached Mount Mazama and warmed us. I was curious to know this volcano and its 8,000-year-old lake, the deepest in the USA, which like so many places I was learning was a Native American sacred lake now 'owned' by the national park. We pulled over at a viewing spot to see a vast basin of clear blue water and a gorgeous green island 800 feet below us.

"Harry, I need to get down there. I need to have my body blessed in that lake. This must be the place Angela the medium spoke about, a lake so sacred that I must honour it with the other half of my medicine stone. This is what Shasta wanted: for me to deliver the second part here."

Down in the overflowing carpark, it was already so busy that I could feel Harry's concern of parking this huge RV among all these tourists.

"There's a space with our name on it. I know it. The lake is calling. It wants us to go down there. Just trust, okay? Your fear of not being able to park is blocking your flow. And we have to be free of fear on this journey," I said more to myself than to him.

Harry wasn't listening anyway, but I knew it had gone in as soon as we pulled into the next carpark and there was a space for us right at the back.

The walk down the rugged tree-lined path was two kilometres long and the trail was steep, and for a moment, I wondered how the kids would get back up. We had a little water and a few snacks, though. I had to have faith.

At the edge of the lake, I stood knowing I had to get into these freezing waters in my bikini and the thought terrified me! I remembered the medium's message that she could see me in sacred turquoise waters. I had imagined they would be warm, and I would be basking in arms like a scene from a cheesy 1980s movie.

Easing myself down the shiny rocks, my toes touched the water and it was indeed as freezing as it looked. I had no desire to go in, so I created a ceremony for the waters on the edge of the lake. I raised my wand and allowed the sounds and words and songs of reverence to flow through me, coming from deep beyond what I could think or feel. From Gaia herself maybe? It was love. I knew that much. It was ancient and it was an honour. The crystal of my wand was an activator for these waters, I realised then, as it vibrated strongly. All of a sudden, I threw my kuya into the waters and jumped in after it.

"Fuck!" I screamed unglamorously and unceremoniously, unprepared for the shock of icy cold mountain water that paralysed my body.

This was an abrupt cleanse! As the reciprocation of my offerings, I wanted to enjoy the blessing like a goddess, but I was gasping for air, unable to control the fucks that fell from my mouth. This was joy. Pure joy, pure love, pure reverence for the whole. I was human, real, imperfect, and I knew the waters gave no fucks for my fucks and loved me unconditionally.

As we made our way back up the steep hill, a gentle angelic woman looked me in the eye and then at the mesa in my hand.

"Oh, it's you guys! I saw your mesas in the window of your RV earlier."

She accepted me as one of her own without question and introduced us to the group she was leading.

"We're looking out for UFOs," she said.

"Oh wow! Have you seen any?" I asked, like it was no big thing.

"Of course! Shasta is a hub for them. We've seen so many."

"Is this where I catch my ride back home then?" I joked.

"Where are you from?" asked another guy in the group, knowing what I meant and being serious.

"Pleiades, Seven Sisters," I answered, without apologising for my weirdness.

All the way back to the car park, they shared stories of mythical Atlantis and Lemurian civilisations. I told them about my wand.

"Well, you are a starseed, Louise. It's no coincidence the wand chose you."

They shared that the Lemurian were a peaceful and innocent civilisation that deeply loved the Earth and that we would have been a part of that time too. They told us how the Lemuria was connected to Mount Shasta and that their energy was to rise again, that my work here was leading to a new Earth, a utopian one.

EARTH CHAKRA SHAMAN

I was grateful for the unapologetic mystical conversations, the food for thought and another reminder that I was on the right track.

***

We had two choices of road to take to get to Seattle and we settled on the scenic route. For the next few days, we would drive through the Cascade Range of mountains and volcanoes all the way to Mount Rainier. The drive was unreal. The road drove us, and the flow moved us. We had a direction, a destination, faith, confidence and freedom. And whatever happened between sunrise and sunset was up to the universe over the next few days.

Oregon was ethereal in so many ways. Loads of the music we had listened to over the past few years had come out of this dreamy state. To feel the lands where that music was born was beautiful and suited every view we set eyes on as we weaved through the peaks.

The sun was setting as we reached Mount Hood, and the chatter between us faded on that last stretch of road. The surrounding nature demanded our attention as it changed from forests to vast wild rolling grasslands, held together by huge mountains. An old euphoria dance track played as the golden sunlight touched the open plains. Without even knowing it, we had arrived on sacred lands and a Native American reservation.

I looked behind me to see the girls staring out the windows, their chins resting on their tiny hands, as their tired eyes gazed into the orange vista. The lands had demanded they pay attention too. Unable to say a word, the air was thick with stillness and the four of us fell into deep reverence.

The energy of the lands held stories of sadness of the Indigenous people and the understanding of what had truly happened was slowly unfolding for me. Tears of grief and shame came then, followed by more tears of hope. *Can we bring peace, innocence and utopia back to the Earth?*

***

Manifesting in the mountains

"Rise and shine! Let's get on the road. If you get up now, I promise we'll manifest somewhere that sells pancakes for breakfast!"

In wing-and-a-prayer style, we'd turned up to the next campsite with no booking in the dead of night again. Having no sat nav and no plan unnerved Harry a little, so to honour his need for stress-free driving, I had the whole day ahead all figured out. This time, we were going to get to our destination in the daylight.

The town where we'd landed was clearly a ski resort in the winter, and as we made our way in for breakfast, Avalon started screaming and pointing at the chairlift.

"Mountain roller coaster! Like in my dream!"

"Avalon, you are by far the greatest manifester I have ever known. How did you do that?" I laughed

The morning on the mountain was just what we needed. Not just seeing these lands from the van, but feeling them under our feet, breathing the air, being present with the aliveness.

"Couldn't you have manifested something less steep?" I yelled to Avalon as we flew downhill in her mountain roller coaster, half-laughing, half-screaming all the way to the bottom.

We clambered into the van elated and buzzing with excitement from the alpine slide.

"It's a four-hour drive to Mount Rainier, girls, so get settled in. Now, Avalon manifested a mountain roller coaster. What you do want to manifest, Bella?"

"Chocolate milkshake!" Bella shouted. I gave Harry a look.

"Well, I want to go to a waterfall, because it's been at least 24 hours since I put my body into shock and swore like a crazed banshee!"

The deeper we went into the mountains the narrower the road became, until we were unable to see beyond the trees on either side. It was mystical and all so new. I loved the feeling of wonder, not knowing how the road was going to twist and turn. I opened my window and let the cool mountain air stroke my face with its purity and presence.

"You're enjoying this aren't you?" I laughed as I observed Harry's confidence and speed soaring.

Being out of his comfort zone, his love for me, his respect for this call, so much had changed since a year ago, when I had broken down exhausted by having to hide and dumb down my spirituality. We had danced for years like this. Him loving me so much. Me feeling unsupported and unaccepted in my spirituality. That had changed gradually. But here in the mountains, he changed day by day.

As the trees passed us by, I tried to hide my tears, not overwhelmed by love this time, but remembering the pain we had gone through to get to this point. I recalled the moment six months before when I'd cracked during a major argument about me going down a path he didn't get or want me to go down. I knew something big was about to happen to me, but I didn't know what.

"If you ask me to choose between my calling and you, Harry, I need to choose my calling. This is what I have been put on this planet for, and I love you, but my purpose is bigger than you."

The memory stabbed my heart like an arrow as I realised now how that must have felt for him. I took a deep breath. *It's okay. We're here. We made it.*

The winding road descended, and we crossed a bridge over a mighty river.

"Oh wow, look at the waters! I'd love to stop for a dip," I said aloud.

Harry swung the van into the car park just in time.

"Come on! Let's have five minutes," he said.

Shocked at his spontaneity, I noticed how much I loved it. I had been leading all the way, but today I was honouring his request to get to the campsite before sunset and just look at his response. He was relaxed now and leaning into the flow.

Down at the river, the waters were again so incredibly cold, but I made myself stand in them, in just my knickers!

"Ahh Mother Waters, I feel like it's been a lifetime since you touched my body, but it has been only a few days. The more we connect, the more I need to connect to you. So much has happened since Crater Lake. We are following the divine flow and it feels so good. We feel the signs along the way, knowing we are on the right path. Mother Waters, do you have any messages for me?"

Crouch down and pick up a rock, she whispered.

So, I did. Out of the icy waters, I pulled a stone that was not grey and smooth like the others, but black with little holes, almost volcanic looking.

A new kuya for you, Louise. Work this medicine stone. It holds something you are yet to understand, but it will be the gift from the mountains and the waters.

I thanked the waters, feeling a sense of peace within.

***

Harry had known I needed to come here. He was following the nudges too. And if his driving was anything to go by, he was fully in his freedom and faith. I loved it.

"I feel a mountain near us beyond these trees," I said.

"We *are* in the mountains, you knob!" Harry laughed.

"I know! I mean I feel something big," I said, my stomach churning and my head spinning. I sat on the edge of my seat, eager to see, but couldn't see past the trees as they were so close around the road.

"There is something here we are meant to see," I said with certainty. "When we get a chance, let's stop, if there's a lay-by or something."

Around the next bend, a lay-by came into view and we stopped and jumped out. There in front of us was the most incredible outlook where the trees parted and we could see wilderness for miles and a huge mountain peak in the distance. I jumped out and stood in awe as an eagle flew overhead.

"What mountain *is* that?" I asked dreamily, as we soaked in the view.

I ran back to the van to grab my mesas while Harry checked the information board to see where we were. He walked back with a look of pride in his eyes.

"Guess what! That mountain is Mount Saint Helens!"

As he pulled me close, his hand behind my head to kiss me passionately, I knew he was feeling the wonder, seeing me, honouring the call... and the mysteries of this ever-unfolding journey. That kiss meant so much more than a kiss. It was a seal, an affirmation, an honouring of us and the earth.

***

I leaned into my mesa. There was a small white medicine stone that was calling to be offered to Mount Saint Helens. It held the medicine of 'the god within'. It was one of my very first medicine stones and my attachment to it was deep, but I was called to offer it.

I felt into my pocket and there was the stone I'd picked up in the river. I laughed. It all made so much sense to me now. This was volcanic rock from Saint Helens. This was her gift to me in exchange for my medicine.

I stepped to the edge of the lookout, raising my wand in the air, and singing prayers and words from my heart. Overflowing with love from my entire being, I threw the medicine stone far into the ravine and shouted to the mountain range, "Mount Saint Helens, I am here!"

I heard Harry laugh with endearment. He knew my rituals by now and honoured them as he honoured me. With every ritual, with every blessing, with every exchange of energy, we flowed more, we soared higher, and we became more blessed. He had seen that.

"Mount Saint Helens, you called me. Without mind, you brought me to you. You gifted me a stone from your river and here I am to share with you my medicine, my love. May this resonate throughout the lands and drop into the earth for every being to feel the medicine."

The ceremony completed, angels flew over in the form of eagles, as if thanking us and giving permission to leave.

Why am I always surprised? I thought to myself as I sat in silent awe. *Because I'm in a constant state of wonder*, came the answer. Long may that medicine last.

***

"Waterfall!" Harry shouted as he saw a sign and pulled into a turning on the other side of the road so suddenly that I was forced to grab the armrest.

"Come on!" he said, jumping out.

"Who are you?" I laughed, jumping out too.

"You said you wanted to manifest a waterfall. Let's go find it!"

Bemused and still getting used to this man who usually said no and resisted what I wanted to do as his default setting, I loved watching him diving into the adventure and responding to every call. This was Harry's moment. As we walked into the ravine, I was aware that it was past tea-time and he had overridden his fear of arriving in the dark just to provide me with a simple want of seeing a waterfall.

Having not seen or thought about waterfalls for the entire trip, I wondered why the universe had put that desire in my head. Was it part of the call? Did this waterfall need my medicine? Was this for Harry to overcome more of his programming? Or did I just want to see a waterfall?

Harry held my hand as we wandered down and found ourselves in a water oasis, with giant stepping stones and the rushing sound of the falls. I didn't feel the need to jump in this time. It was chilly and the day was coming to an end. Instead, I watched Harry roaming around, jumping from boulder to boulder, investigating like a curious child, enjoying his time with the kids. That's when I knew that this was for him. This was his transition, his awakening, his transformation of fear into faith.

***

It was the end of the most blissful part of our journey and some part of us knew that. These past four days had been beyond sacred, and indeed reciprocal, as it felt like a job well done. Having risen early, we had made it to the top of Mount Rainier by 10am and now gazed out through clear blue skies that contrasted the rich green trees and patches of snow. It was time to do my final ceremony, at the peak of our last mountain.

"Hey Mount Rainier! I'm Louise and I know you know me. I come in the deepest honouring as I end my journey through the sacred Cascade Range, pulled by divine flow to this very moment. I am not the woman I was when I began this journey. I have gathered and shared medicine along the way, making offerings and receiving gifts. I have made it here to you. We have let the lands guide us, discovering each destination though fresh eyes, not through thought, but through wisdom. I am at your service, Mount Rainier. How can I serve you now?"

I listened and the mountain spoke.

EARTH CHAKRA SHAMAN

Remember the ancient ones, the ones who came before you. Put right the wrongs that happened. Through love and through the construction of a new Earth, you will rise and those who you touch will rise too, for your heart is open and connected beyond the veil of any known thing. Rise up and take your place in this great turning of the world.

I reached into my mesa and gifted a medicine stone from the Andes. I lay it down with some chocolate and the offering that the shaman at Shasta had asked me to make.

And as I kissed the earth, I whispered, "I thank you. I will do. I love you."

***

Base Chakra Activation Divine Will for Greater Life

Mount Shasta, base chakra of the Earth and Plumed Serpent,
I come with the deepest honour and reverence.
I call upon you from the purest place of my heart
to activate my divine will to be of service to greater life and planetary rebirth.
I let go of all that is not in alignment with the will of greater life.
I see and heal all that is out of balance and harmony.
It is my will to unravel energetic entanglements,
to see all that is dark and bring it into the light
to stand in my personal power and dream the new Earth into being.
Where all is in balance, all is in harmony.
Honouring those who have walked before me,
I listen with love and compassion.

EARTH CHAKRA SHAMAN

To the elders, the wisdom keepers and the whispers of the divine will of Gaia.
I promise to tend to my mother as she tends to me
to work with her energy as she works through mine
to pilgrimage to the earth chakras and nodes
and gift my growth to the grid performing sacred acupuncture with my light.
My gift of light codes flows through the entire grid,
spinning new consciousness through the serpent leys.
The chakras awaken and expand.
All life on Earth has the will to create greater life through divine will and love.

***

CHAPTER 10

Death & Rebirth in Alaska

Apprehensively, I looked out of the window of the plane, recalling how I'd had it out with Alaska only six weeks before sitting at my kitchen table.

"Okay Alaska, where the fuck do you want me to go to? You need to be clearer with me. I can't figure this one out!"

We had seen signs everywhere for Yukon, but it turned out that the Yukon was 500,000 kilometres squared of unpopulated nothingness. And after days of staring at a laptop, trying to make things mean something, I had admitted defeat. I had no idea where we were meant to be going.

"It's a massive fucking state and a massive fucking river!" I cried.

I felt burdened with the responsibility of making the right decision, feeling the weight on my shoulders. I'd had dreams of meeting Indigenous people up the north of Alaska and had formed an ideal that an elder would take me under their wing. Some part of me still yearned for someone wiser than myself, a grandfather, to scoop me up and tell me that I was doing well, that he was proud of me.

One night, I'd dreamed of mountains with crystal clear rivers, and flying in a plane to get there, and I woke up just *knowing*...

"We have to go to the Yukon River! That's where Alaska wants me to go."

In naming it out loud, my entire body had vibrated, all my hairs stood on end and spontaneous tears flowed. The *knowing* was always a full-body experience for me. And a relief!

Within days, the song *Denali* had popped up on my Spotify, and through my research, I found this Alaskan mountain to be the largest in the USA and a vortex of some kind that was connected to the earth chakra grid. That was enough of a sign for me. Following the synergies like breadcrumbs through a forest, I had got the spirit message that I had to 'land' on Denali on my birthday to 'let die' a part of myself. And that would mean taking a plane to the summit.

I'd tried to plan it, book it, get something concrete locked in prior to arriving in Alaska, but it wasn't flowing.

"Just show up, Lou. Trust it will all happen as it must," I reminded myself out loud.

***

It was surprisingly hot when we landed, according to the smiley woman at the car hire desk in the airport.

"Don't let this weather fool you. It's going to rain for the rest of the week."

She looked at us adoringly like all Americans seemed to do.

"Ah, you guys have the best accents. Are you from England?"

Our voices had been like wearing a royal badge and I noticed that we sometimes even played into it and became even more English.

"From just outside of London. We've been on a road trip between LA and Seattle. Now we've got six days here before we head to Canada."

"That's one helluva trip, guys!" she beamed.

"I'm on a spiritual quest. These guys have to follow me into the unknown," I joked, gauging her reaction to see if she could be a messenger before I continued.

"Oh, how interesting," she said, unsure how to respond to what I had said.

I didn't pursue it. I had learned that there was a fine balance between sharing enough so that the right conversations could open up and just baffling people, which could get pretty uncomfortable!

She pulled out the forms.

"So, let me confirm, you're going to take the car from here at Fairbanks and you're going to drop it off down at Anchorage in six days' time?"

"That's right. We've got a lot to pack into six days, that's for sure," I said. "Could you show us on the map how to get to the Yukon River. I couldn't work it out on Google Maps."

"Oh my!" she laughed, "You can't just drive to the Yukon. Gawd, no!"

She laughed some more and my heart sank, like someone had turned up the dial on my fear of failure.

"There isn't any tarmac as far as the Yukon. You would need a specialist truck with a satellite radio, hard-wearing tyres, and at least two spares tyres. You need to take all your fuel with you. You don't just go off into the wild in your hire car," she explained, teasing us now.

"How much is a truck to hire?" I asked with a blank face.

"Oh no, sorry mam, you misunderstand me."

She was looking a little worried now. Clearly I was naive or mad. Or both!

"We don't hire trucks. And if we did, you wouldn't be insured to drive out on your own."

"But I need to get to the Yukon River! It's part of my spiritual quest. I need to get there tomorrow or the day after at the latest before we head out to Denali, where I need to be on my birthday."

I glanced at Harry for help, but he just looked back at me.

"Erm, how the fuck do we get to the Yukon?" I asked him, laughing nervously, trying to stop the tears from welling up.

Digging deep, I used the only way I knew to get this situation under control – charm! I turned back to the car hire woman and smiled.

"Somehow, we clueless English people, who just turn up in Alaska and think they can just drive to the Yukon, will find a way to get there, right?"

She smiled. She was going to help.

"I'm sure you can get someone to drive you there," she suggested, then disappeared out the back for a while to get a number.

"Call Frank," she said when she came back, handing me a scrap of paper.

Before we had even reached the hire car, I was on a £5-per-minute call to Frank.

"Sure, I can take you," Frank said. "No, mam, we can't take children. The roads are hell for the best of us. We'll leave day after tomorrow. Set off at 4am and be back about 10pm. See you then!"

And like that I was going to the Yukon River with a stranger named Frank. Without Harry or the girls.

***

Into the wilderness

There was nothing to do for 36 hours other than twiddle our thumbs in a log cabin in the middle of nowhere under a vast grey drizzly sky with only mozzies for company. It was hours to the next town, but it seemed like a good idea at the time of booking! I was underwhelmed, tired and disconnected. We decided to go out and have a little walk around the cabin just to get out.

"Alaska is a bit like a shit Americanised Scotland," I said, instantly ashamed of my judgment. "I suppose we just need to get to know the lands, meet them. Maybe we can do a little fire ceremony outside in the fire pit tonight?"

As we walked down a green forest path, unsure if we were trespassing or not, I babbled on about fears, about getting it all wrong and about feeling like I was underappreciating the Alaska vibe, when I noticed Harry was preoccupied.

"Are we meant to be here? Is this okay?" I asked him.

"I think so."

"I feel a bit weird about it, like someone is watching us," I admitted.

"Yeah, I do too," he said.

Then he stopped, looking at the tree in front of us.

"Erm, we need to go back," he said calmly touching the trunk, his hands running down some scratches.

"These are fresh bear claw marks."

My heart raced.

"Fuck! Maybe it's not someone, but *something* watching us!"

I tried to ground and manage my energy as I called to the girls, knowing we could give off fear vibes.

"Girls, get here now and stay close. We're going back to the cabin."

We started walking. Fast! With Harry and I trying to act 'normal' and chat away about daily things.

"Oh, how lovely is that tree? How lovely is the sky?" I mused aloud, overcompensating, trying to convince whatever was about to eat us that I was calm, cool and definitely not scared at all, therefore it should leave us alone. On seeing the cabin, I pretty much forced the kids to sprint to the front door.

Fucking stupid English people, I thought as we shut it firmly behind us. We hadn't given it a second thought. We'd never had to before. The scariest wildlife I'd ever seen in the UK was a fox!

As it transpired, unless you were prepared to carry a gun or bear spray, or you were on holiday with a cruise ship company, who make Alaska look delightful from their distant windows, there wasn't much to do here. Because Alaska had wildlife! Lots of bears, big bears, brown bears, grizzly bears. Oh, and mountain lions!

And since I'd rather have been eaten by a bear than sell my soul for a cruise ship package deal, we twiddled our thumbs in that log cabin, passing the time with an indoor fire, mindfulness colouring books, and old VHS videos, until it was time for me to meet Frank and go to the Yukon River.

***

This is Alaska!

Frank was around 65 with a smile that reminded me of my grandad. In the truck were the smiling faces of two other tourists who had managed to escape the cruise ship.

"We wanted to see more of Alaska than an all-inclusive hotel!" they joked. I liked them instantly.

Then there was the driver Tom, who wasn't far off Frank's age, but could still have taken on a bear!

"God, if only we'd had Tom with us on our walk," I joked with Harry as I kissed him and the kids goodbye, aware they had another day of nothing ahead. "He would probably have tackled the bear for us with his bare hands."

The road out towards the Yukon didn't seem too bad at all, but as if he could read my mind, Frank spoke up, "Don't get too comfortable, folks. This road goes for another 30 miles and then it gets rough, so enjoy the peace while you can."

Frank was a 'good Christian man' who shared his love for Mother Earth openly. I adored this about him.

"Here in Alaska we have nine months of winter and then all three seasons in three months. Everything grows really quick for a short period of time. Where it takes your vegetables nine months to grow, ours will grow and fruit in three."

I was amazed this was even possible, but it was true, and it proved to me how nature works with us when we work with her. I noticed how tiny the trees were. They went on for miles and miles but were all no more than eight feet high or so. I thought they looked about five years old, but Frank told me they were more like 300. Now I understood why I found the landscape so unusual.

"When you live in Alaska, your life depends on you honouring Mother Nature. If you don't, you will not survive. You can't ignore nature. We must protect her, so she protects us. Do you know what permafrost is, Louise?" Frank asked.

I shook my head, feeling ignorant.

"This ground is frozen and some of it has been frozen for hundreds of thousands of years. In some places it's 12 inches thick. In others, up to 2,000 feet deep. And when it gets disturbed and broken, it begins to melt. So here, when they built this road, it damaged the permafrost, it started to melt and we can never replace that. It needs to remain untouched. This is the wonder of Alaska, our ecosystem and our soil. Very bad things will happen for the whole planet if the permafrost melts. Our planet is heating up and we can feel it."

I shuddered.

***

Death and pipelines

"And we're just coming up to the biggest threat to our permafrost now. Keep your eyes open," Frank said.

Soon, he was pointing out a huge white line; a pipeline snaking through the valleys and over the hills. I sat trying to process what I was seeing. Was it gas? What was it doing out here? Why was it so important to the Earth? It looked so alien in the vast landscape.

As the penny dropped, a heaviness came over me, an awareness that my mind could not understand. The darkness of this pipeline was visceral now. How could I not have known that what was out there was the epitome of what was destroying Mother Earth, harming the lands and the waters, feeding the planet's fossil fuel addiction and lining the pockets of government-protected corporations?

Out of nowhere, I saw a raven by the side of the road. This archetype had been trying to get my attention since I'd landed in Alaska. I knew he was journeying with me now and I paid attention.

"What is your message for me, Raven?"

Nothing. I couldn't hear any message. All I noticed was my body responding. All I felt was sick. I was not going to like what I was about to learn.

Frank began talking.

"This you see here is the Great Trans-Alaskan pipeline. It zigzags its way through the wild Alaskan wilderness, 800 miles from the very north to the south."

I could not process what I was seeing.

"This is Alaska's scar, right through the middle, and up to two million barrels of oil are transported from below the sea every day."

Defying all odds, defying science, engineering, laws and the rights of the Indigenous communities and Mother Earth herself, the pipeline had become an unstoppable darkness that held no other vision than going where no man or machine had been before in its mission to extract and transport oil across Alaska.

Between 1975 and 1977 for over $10,000 a day each, pipeline workers sold their soul and disconnected their spirit to go underground. They worked in temperatures below -27°C, winds of over 100 mph and lived in isolated 'men's camps' with no daylight for months on end. Drugs, prostitutes and trafficking of Indigenous women was heavy within the culture. The vast amount of money flowing through the main cities meant the pipeline became a law unto itself through unruly behaviour of its workers and desolation of the wilderness. Wildfires rampaged as the pipeline dripped oil across the lands, tearing apart not just the Earth, but communities too.

I could not believe what I was hearing. I had never realised the true cost of oil extraction so that I could drive my petrol car, fly around the world, and buy the products I used every day. I had known that pipelines existed. I had seen animals covered in oil from spillages on the news, but that hadn't affected my world enough for me to truly get it on the level that I was getting it now.

Now it was my world. Now I had seen it with my own eyes. It was my responsibility to be the change.

***

"We're going to pull over so you can go and touch it."

Frank seemed almost impressed to show us. I felt sick. Gathering my wand, my mesas and my coat, I stepped off the truck and headed out on my own to stand underneath this immense snake. Above my head was the pipe, on brackets seven feet in the air. My stomach cramped and my anger flowed. I fell to my knees sobbing and opened my mesas preparing to make a prayer to the Earth under the pipeline.

"Oh Mother, how we have raped you. I am so sorry. I am so sorry for my part in this fucking oil industry. I am so sorry for the damage my people have brought."

Raven came and sat with me, speaking the words of Gaia.

Do not hate my blood, Louise. Please bless it as it flows above your head. Love all of me even when I am not flowing where I should. Bless me as I pass. Bring peace to the wound from which it comes.

I raised my arms in the air and the light passed from my hands. I began the words of prayer that passed through me from the place beyond my mind. All I knew was I was healing. I was bringing my blessings to this wound.

Little did I know that, at the same time and for the first time in history, tribes were gathering and awareness of pipeline corporate corruption was coming into the media. It began in North Dakota with the Sioux tribe protesting another pipeline through their sacred lands, polluting their waters; now people from all over the USA were coming together to stand in solidarity as water protectors and protectors of the Earth against the Army Corps who were brutally attacking peaceful protestors.

I waved my blessings, protecting the waters here in Alaska, bringing light to the darkness and really seeing how man had mined, drilled and taken more from the Earth than we needed. The consequences were coming to light. We were coming close to learning the vast and painful repercussions of our actions. The Earth was heating up, the planet was overflowing with plastic, and humanity had turned against nature, forgetting that we humans too *are* nature. Like the white man in Australia, like the Spanish in Peru, we invaded and destroyed lands, rivers, mountains and people for gold and profit.

"Thank you, raven, for your love. I pray for the reconnection of us all, for the remembrance of who we are and why we came here, and that we harm not ourselves, each other or Gaia."

***

I stared vacantly out of the van window as the rains came. This trip to the Yukon was indeed long. I was tired and feeling the stark reality of how I travelled around the planet on the blood of my mother. Okay, she had asked me not to hate her – or *it* – and to honour the oil and how it was used. She had called me and opened her wounds for me to come to these places, but never again would I fly for any other reason than to be in service to her.

"Louise, we'll be crossing the bridge of your Yukon River soon," Frank said.

I looked out as we crossed the bridge and was stricken by how brown the waters were. The sky was brown too. Even the rain was brown and getting heavier. And I couldn't hear what I needed to do. I worried. *Come on, Louise. Trust that she will tell you what to do when you meet her.* I forced myself to accept that this was a mere glance of the river. Just because you walk into a room and see someone doesn't mean a connection is made; that only came when you met face-to-face. *She's waiting for me,* I thought, *she's waiting to meet me.*

The truck pulled up at a café, originally a camp for the pipeline workers and now the only place to stop on the pipeline road. The moment I stepped inside, I was transported to 1975. Nothing had been modernised in 40 years! The plastic tables and chairs reminded me of the original McDonalds interiors. The music playing on a record player and the falling-apart toilets reminded me of primary school. And it wasn't deliberately retro, done this way to be cool or hipster. It was just Alaska.

I left Frank, Tom and the cruise couple to their coffee. It was time for me to meet my river.

***

Finally, we meet, Yukon

It was a long, wet walk down to the river. I had had expectations of bright blue skies, crystal clear waters, eating a picnic by the river with Harry and the girls, maybe even having a little dip. Erm... not exactly. This was not crystal clear or even beautiful. But she was the *biggest* river I had ever seen, vast, fast and terrifying. Had I really travelled all this way to be here in the wet, all alone, irritated by my ears that were raw from mosquito bites and with nowhere to even sit? And when I looked around, there was that goddamn pipeline looking back at me.

I took a deep breath and exhaled. I knew that expectations were resistance to being in the now. This was exactly as it needed to be.

I took a seat on the cold rocks and wedged myself between the manmade wall of the café grounds behind and the gushing brown river in front of me. *What do I need to do? What do I need to do? What do I need to do?* I wondered as I pulled my mesas and offerings out of my bag. The rain hammered down harder, pouring down my face and under my top. Then something took over me. I took over me!

I raised my wand in the air, rainwater trickling down the inside sleeve of my raincoat and I laughed and laughed. It was perfect in every way. I let go and joy flowed as I called out loud...

"Mother Waters, great Yukon River, I am here. I heard your call and I answered. I have come all this way to be at your service. Mother, guide me in what you need from me and I will do it."

I began to sing, louder and louder, words of songs that I did not know. For a brief moment, I became self-conscious about what I was doing. What if anyone else saw me? But the waters brought me back into the song, into my trance, into the energy, water all around. Prayers that I did not consciously create fell out of my mouth just like they had before. I travelled on the love flowing from my heart into the rain, into the river, into the waters of my own body.

When I came back to myself, I looked for a safe place to open my mesas and sat down. Instantly my mesa cloths got soaked, but I opened my first mesa anyway, knowing that the Yukon wanted the very first of my medicine stones. I recalled the medium telling me I needed to stop and listen to the birds when I got to the water of my destination, but there were none, and I wasn't sure how long I could sit here at the side of the river waiting. Then again, raven was watching the whole time. Was this what she'd meant?

"Mama, I have an offering for you. I have made you a prayer stick with the blessings of my dream for the future world, a world of love and reverence. I offer flowers with prayers for the illumination of humanity and for the illumination of my own purpose on this path. I make an offering of this beautiful pinecone that I brought from Shasta and also one of my medicine stones. The kuya holds the medicine of 'understanding'. I am bringing this medicine to you to share with all of humanity to bring understanding to all."

I made my offerings to the powerful river and sat in stillness, soaking in the medicine of that moment, accepting all that it was. I felt her lap at my feet, and she spoke to me, telling me to take the stone from Saint Helens as my new medicine stone. I washed it in the waters and felt the blessing of the new gift.

Realise your dreams, she whispered.

I waited. Was that the gift or was that her message? Then I felt the energy change within me, and I knew with that familiar certainty, this was the gift.

"Thank you, thank you, thank you..."

I blessed my mesa with Yukon waters and packed up. That was it. It was time to go home. It had taken me pretty much three weeks and all of the money I had to get here, for all of 20 minutes on the side of the great Yukon's muddy waters. Exhausted, I laughed. Jesus hadn't walked out of the waters and told me I'd done a wonderful job. I hadn't transformed into some ethereal water goddess. I was still me, looking like a drowned rat, on the edge of a brown river.

But I'd done what I came here to do, to share the medicine, to collect the medicine. I had to be the one to validate myself.

The person I was becoming was getting clearer and clearer. I was growing up and having faith in myself and my connection with Gaia and God.

***

The Inuit people

I watched the kids' faces light up as the little aircraft dipped below the clouds and we saw the territory stretching out ahead of us, miles and miles and miles of vast untouched lands.

"Guys, we're about to fly through the Gates of the Arctic," the pilot said.

I could feel it and the name was very deserving. The Gates of the Arctic were two mountains meeting each other. I became overwhelmingly aware that we were flying where very few humans on the Earth had been. The reality of this privilege struck my heart, as I looked down and wondered about the parts of these lands that had never been touched by the foot of man.

The plane flew over the reservation and I began to understand what 'reservation' truly meant. These were people who had once been nomadic, who had had lands and a way of life taken from them. These people had been pushed into these reservations and forced to live a poverty-bound Western lifestyle.

I got off the plane, feeling ashamed to be a tourist, to be coming here to see this unhooking of people from their rightful place on the planet. A tall Inuit guy with a beaming smile greeted us off the plane. He was warm and seemed genuinely glad to meet us. His name was David.

Bella and Avalon ran off with the other children, the way kids do, and one of the local women asked if she could take them all to a park. There was a distinct lack of money, but there was an abundance of kindness. As we walked through the reservation, we saw houses that were poorly built, but felt like homes. We saw an ancient and vast culture squeezed into a modern way of life. We were here for just an hour, and while inviting tourists here was the only way they could make money, I was deeply aware of infringing on their privacy and their community.

Another wave of shame washed over me as we were invited into the only modern brick building in the reservation and I smelled a rat right away. This was a museum clearly 'just for tourists'. I could feel that the history depicted was not the truth, but what the American government wanted tourists to see.

"Something doesn't quite feel right," I said to Harry under my breath.

I found a local woman and followed my hunch.

"May I ask you some questions? It says that in the 1950s the tribe wanted to settle and not be nomadic or hunt anymore. Was that true for all the members? Did everyone really want to stop living the nomadic life?"

"We had no choice," she answered, cool and sharp in her reply. "Of course, we agreed to settle – so they wouldn't keep taking our children. They stopped the caribou and we could no longer hunt or do anything, so we had to agree."

She was angry, and I honoured her anger as I became deeply aware that my innocence and ignorance was no excuse.

"I'm so sorry," I said.

She shared with me her own story, but I felt she spared me the full details.

"I was sent away. I had to go to school far away from here. When I came back, there was no place for me. I came back when my own children begged to return here so they could learn their roots."

I could feel tears coming and struggled to stop them. I felt her pain and the pain of her people, but I didn't have a right to cry. I touched her hand over the counter and said again how sorry I was. But sorry was never going to be enough. I had to take action, and that began with staying open to learning the truth of the way the world has been set up.

When it was time to leave, I walked back towards the plane with David and asked, "So, where are your shamans?"

He stopped and looked me in the eye.

"I asked my grandma this when I was young, and she told me, 'We are Christians now. We do not speak of such things.'" His last words would land time and time again in my memory as I tried to comprehend the depths of that statement.

Before we took off, I prayed to the waters and a raven landed next to me, then flew off again, leaving a jet-black feather. A beautiful shamanic message of transformation and healing from spirit.

The golden glow of the midnight sun was a sight I would never forget as we took off over the Yukon. With mixed emotions, of blessings and sadness. I was doing what I could to heal the Earth's wounds and the wounding my ancestors had caused across the world. I wasn't about to stop here. I hadn't even made it halfway through Alaska, let alone the earth chakra call.

***

Denali

Every adventure calls for a minor emotional meltdown in order to reset! When we got to Mount Denali, I was clueless, disconnected and void of any universal nudges in any direction. We had missed two buses to the tourist office of Denali National Park, and when we got there, we were given the bear talk, reminding us that nowhere was safe! To top it off, the new moon energy was intense, and I was scared.

"Why the fuck are we traipsing around Alaska, clueless, like dumb tourists? How the hell could we go walking? We were not at all safe. We were so stupid!"

I burst into tears and the girls looked dismayed. Harry pulled me into his chest as the girls gathered around me.

"I think the pressure of getting it right and constantly waiting for guidance from the universe is taking its toll on you, Lou. Can you stop asking your tarot cards for guidance and just relax into wherever we are?" Harry asked.

I unleashed all my pent-up worry.

"But I can't, babe! What if I make a mistake? This is the only day we have to walk around Denali National Park. And it's now 2pm. We haven't been anywhere yet and we can't go out because of the bears! I miss home. I miss knowing what I'm doing. I miss waking up, having sex, dancing around to loud music before school. I miss eating fresh organic food every day. I miss broccoli! I miss feeling the blessed moments of nothing and watching the birds from the kitchen. I miss friends and flowing with life. I miss the wonder and the magic. I feel so responsible for doing these activations and blessings and making every second count!"

"Love you, Mummy," the girls said, clinging to me.

"I love you too, girls. Sorry Mummy is having a meltdown, but sometimes we just need to cry when we're tired."

I looked at the Denali tourist magazine in my hand to see where we could go.

On the front, it said, "When we listen to nature, we know what to do."

I smiled.

Thank you, universe. I hear ya!

***

That afternoon, we braved a little walk on a beautiful trail around a lake and chatted to people along the way. The mountain peak was shrouded with clouds and one of the walkers we passed told us that Denali only showed himself to the blessed.

Later that afternoon, we headed on towards the little town where we were going to stay for a few days that was on the base of Denali. On the freeway, Harry saw a sign for the main Denali lookout point and swung the car into the only empty bay he could find. The lookout was full of people and we wedged ourselves into the crowd. Within a moment, a gasp rolled through the onlookers.

"Oh wow, Denali is showing himself to us!" I said.

It was magical, powerful, awesome. Then, just when I thought we had seen the whole mountain, the clouds parted and more of Denali emerged.

An American tourist turned to me and said, "You're the lucky charm! You guys turned up and Denali just came out."

"You guys must be a blessing," said his wife, "We've been here for hours hoping to get a glimpse."

"Oh man, you have no idea how much I needed to get Denali's approval for this insane spiritual quest I've been on," I said openly.

Without even batting an eye at the spiritual quest comment, the guy replied, "Well, you got your blessing right there."

A few moments later, the cloud curtain was pulled closed again and I knew it would be Denali's one and only appearance. Back in the car, all of us were feeling pretty smug.

"Thank you, universe." I said. "Please send one more sign to me to tell me I'm on the right track and doing okay. Maybe a rainbow?"

Three minutes later, Harry nudged me. There in the sky was my rainbow. I roared with laughter and wound down the window.

"Thank you, universe! Thank you sooo much!" I yelled.

That night, I burned my tarot cards in the log cabin fire pit. Here, I needed to follow my inner compass and tune in to nature. Using tarot cards was fine, but I'd been using them as a crutch, and I didn't need them anymore. I handed over to the fire all that was my 36 years. I wrote down my fears and burned them in the fire too. And then I decided it was time to let go of this constant pressure to 'be in service' and 'do the right thing'. I had done all I needed to do and all I could do.

The sun ducked behind Denali in the distance, a river flowed a few feet away, my sacred fire burned strong, and then a raven flew over. I sat in stillness for a while.
Mother Earth, I am a part of this whole.

***

Rebirth

On the morning of my 37th birthday, I woke new.

"There are three things I want today, please, universe. One, to land on Denali and make my birthday offering to the mountain. Two, to have one really nice local beer. Three, to listen to some live music."

I sat in the waiting room for light aircraft flights, ready to accomplish the first of my wishes.

"Sorry, ma'am, it ain't gonna happen today I'm afraid," the helpdesk woman said to me, "Too foggy up there. No one is taking off or landing."

"I'm sorry, but it's my birthday and I've come all the way from the UK to land on Denali today so it has to happen."

She looked at me strangely and reiterated how she really didn't think it *would* happen today. Maybe it would be clear tomorrow, she suggested, but I knew today was it. Like a dog with a bone, which embarrassed Harry no end, I pressed her.

"Seriously, it has to happen today. Is there any way I can get up there?"

Trying to get rid of me, she took my number and promised to call if anything changed.

We headed into town and ate pizza, but I couldn't settle. I called every hour until 6pm and nothing changed, but I refused to believe it wasn't possible. Then something told me to just turn up. We drove back to the tiny airport and – trying to be as unannoying as possible – I asked again…

"Any change?"

Just to appease me, the woman radioed up to the main stations, then looked at me with a surprised smile.

"Well, you might just be in luck. It may be clearing, but don't pin all your hopes…"

Too late! In my head, it was already happening. Then the radio came back.

"We can give it a go."

Before I knew it, I was paying for the flight and signing the waivers as Harry looked on nervously and the woman reminded me that I may end up flying around and coming back down without seeing anything at all.

***

I laughed at myself as the tiny plane took off. I was so used to them now. Such a difference from a few weeks earlier. Up in the air, it was cloudy with clear patches here and there, but nothing really to see. I held on to that tiny glimmer of hope that I would see Denali unveil himself to me just as he had the day before.

Then the pilot's posture changed.

"Erm, you know what? Things are clearing."

He sounded surprised.

A few radio interactions later, the pilot said with a joyful smile, "It looks like we may well be landing on Denali, birthday girl! As you wish. I don't know how you managed it, but we'll be the only plane to do so today!"

EARTH CHAKRA SHAMAN

I laughed, but I'd known we would. I had no doubt that it was Denali who called me all the way from the UK to celebrate my birthday here. Why would he have called without the intention of doing so?

The plane landed on the snow-capped mountain.

"You've got no more than 10 minutes before we have to move again," the pilot said to me as I ran off in the snow looking for somewhere I could do a quick ceremony.

There was nowhere. I was exposed. I had to accept that he was going to see me opening my bag of rocks, laying them on the snow and waving my wand in the air... And I had to accept it quickly!

The ceremony was as brief as it was beautiful. Smiling, I made an offering to Denali of a stone from Lake Titicaca.

"Denali, you called, and I am here. I offer you this stone pendulum, as I surrender my need for divination tools to guide me. I now trust in my own inner compass. As my offering to you to say thank you for guiding me here, I will listen to you. What is my lesson?"

The simple wisdom came. I had picked up a stone on our walk the previous day. Denali guided me that this stone would be a medicine stone – not to go in my mesa yet, but to work with. When the time came, I would know when it was fully transformed into a kuya. Its gift would be 'new beginnings'.

My life was about to see some massive upheaval and change always started by breaking with the chaos of old.

***

Back at the slightly alternative pizza restaurant in town that we had fallen in love with because of its prayer flags and lovely inside-outside eating area, everything was perfect. There was a band playing one of my old favourite songs, "Society" by Eddie Vedder from the movie *Into the Wild*, and it seemed the whole town had come out to be in this moment with me. I plonked down with my beer in my hand and watched the prayer flags dancing in the breeze. The music soundtracked the girls playing with some local kids and Harry looking at me with such awe at the amazing way I'd held my faith and manifested this day into being.

I had the power to create my reality, to be guided by Gaia. The only thing that was ever going to get in the way of having perfect flow was fear and doubt. And I had just let that go.

"To new beginnings..." we toasted.

***

CHAPTER 11

History of our Lands

Exhausted in mind and body, we were embraced into the home of our old friends, Nick and Jayne. We had five days on Vancouver Island to just be, before embarking on a journey through the Rockies to Lake Louise for the final water activation of the calling.

Their house was surrounded by mountains, and night after night, we would sit, watching shooting stars and talking in depth about the world.

As Jayne was a chiropractor who had worked with Indigenous peoples' healing, I found myself asking her many questions, seeking to understand the depths of the intergenerational wound caused by colonization. I felt sick and somewhat paralyzed as she described the darkness behind the church-run residential schools. How, for hundreds of years, indigenous children from the Americas had been taken from their families and their lands and then placed into schools, where they faced physical, mental, and sexual abuse as they were aggressively assimilated into a white culture. She told me it would take about ten generations to heal the intergenerational wound.

I realised that no one just "gets over" this. No culture can "just move on" from this trauma. No child born into this can escape it. As with any unhealed wound, it is passed down from parent to child. And this was huge. It involves lifetimes of healing. This trauma is in the lands. It's in the water. It's in the collective consciousness.

I could see the pain in Jayne's eyes from what she had seen and what she knew of the long path that lay ahead on this healing journey.

I looked over at my own children playing together innocently, and my heart and gut wrenched as the reality began to sink in.

"How can humans become so disconnected and separate that we are willing to do such harm to other humans? To *children*?" Tears of anger, frustration, sadness, and shame burned my eyes. "What could happen to us humans that would lead us to stand aside and allow this harm to happen. Or, even worse, to justify it as acceptable in the name of God?"

I had awoken to a truth that required I put aside the naivety within me, the part of me that only wanted to see the good in the world. I had to accept there was evil in this world, and it was used deliberately in order to gain power. I had to see how easy it was to brainwash humans into ignorance or into blindness. But I also had to believe, beyond all of our ignorance, there is a place within us all where we each will have an opportunity to put right the wrongs and to bring healing to the world.

And now that I knew all this, I could not ignore it. For now, I just had to stay open to learning the uncomfortable truths of the wounds caused and the white privilege that was gained from this and is still gaining from this.

We humans would never truly be at peace while our brothers and sisters of this Earth were suffering. To bring humanity back into right relationship with the Earth and one another was going to take an acknowledgement of the wounding, and then reconciliation, understanding, and deep healing all over the world.

I knew, now more than ever, the people who understand this right relationship with the Earth were the very people who were being wiped out. The indigenous peoples knew of "the way": of not taking more than we need, of caring for our Earth, of caring for the waters, the air, and the trees, and of ensuring a future for our children. This knowing was a threat to industry, to corporations, to civilisation, to money, and to power.

I prayed to Gaia to show me how I could serve in this healing. I stayed open, listened, and was willing to learn and be guided, day by day, with an open heart.

***

World friends

We had a 700-mile road trip to Lake Louise ahead of us , and we were fast running out of money. Nick offered to drive us in his own car.

"It's fine," he assured me. "It has two spare seats in the back."

I smiled as I looked out of the window, watching the way he stacked all our luggage precariously onto the roof of his truck for hours, moving mountains to make sure we could all take this trip.

Finally, all seven of us squeezed into Nick's car and embarked on what was to become a very healing journey through the Canadian Rockies to Lake Louise via Mount Whistler.

In Whistler, we met up with more old friends from our past. It was clear to us that whatever you give, you get back. We had taken many people into our home over the years, and now those doors were open for us as we traveled. We were abundant in friendship, in love. For me, this was the elixir of life.

In the mountains, I savoured my first experience with mountain fairies, little translucent lights that came to me in broad daylight. I'd left the group and followed them to a huge quartz platform. I honoured their request that I share my energy medicine from my mesas; in return, they shared their blessings and told me that I could connect to their medicine any time I needed it for my work on the grid.

***

A rocky road

Leaving Whistler, I squeezed into a tiny seat in the back of Nick's truck and we continued the remaining 600 miles to Lake Louise. Maybe it was the motion of being in the back of the vehicle, maybe it was something the lands were trying to share with me or a past life looking to be healed, but I began to glide into trance and journey beyond the world I was living in. I was slipping into a time I wasn't sure I wanted to be in, but I could not stop it.

I couldn't breathe. I couldn't see. I couldn't move. All was dark. I was on a boat. I was a slave; I was terrified. I was separated from my husband, but I could feel he was alive. He was Harry, but I could not hear or see him. I called for him, but nothing came out of my mouth.

In my own body in the back of the car, I was paralysed. I wanted to reach for the safety of Harry's hand in front of me, but I could not move. I was having a panic attack and he could not help. I sat in motionless silence, trapped between worlds, and silent tears rolled down my face.

Nick chose that moment to open the front window. The air travelled to the back of the car in little wisps, touching my face like trickles of fresh cold water. I began to return to my body and breathe again. Harry turned to look at me.

"You okay, babe?" he said, concerned.

I nodded wiping tears away, trying not to cause a fuss or have anyone else see. Intuitively, Harry knew not to push, squeezed my hand and turned back around.

I took out my mesa and, for the next few hours of the car journey, blew all my fears and prayers for healing the Earth for all the humans who had suffered at the hands of colonizers. I felt the healing warmth of the mountains like a warm embrace and a light around me, and a new sense of safety came to me. I felt I had cleared something big, healed something inside of me and beyond me, into the collective.

The rest of the journey through the Rockies was a sober one. I saw how my own ancient blood lineage was broken, decimated, and forgotten. My connection to my mesa through the Peruvian tradition was the doorway back to the ancient wisdom of the Earth. Who were the shamans, the medicine men and women, the mystics, the healers of the lands I was born on before the Romans came? I had no real connection to the old ways of our ancient Celtic culture. I was raised in a Christian world, and my interest in the mystic was seen as "new age" or witchy, until I stepped onto the shamanic path.

I thought of my Jewish great-grandmother and her Polish-Russian ancestors, back to whom I had no tangible lineage, but I had journeyed into those ancestral lines to connect to the women who had come before me many times and always met with a Siberian Shaman, an ancient grandmother of mine who sort of looked like me. She had told me my gifts of seeing came from her, but she showed me how she was persecuted for her medicine. Were there always stories of persecution in history? Was there ever a time when humans lived in peace?

Along those 600 miles, I thought deeply on these questions. I listened to the mountains and became aware of all the lives that had led me to this point. I felt the Earth, and I knew, in my heart, healing for a new Earth was coming. I had to believe this to be true. To be possible.

***

Lake Louise

On one of the last days in Canada, I stood on the shores of Lake Louise, the sun barely up and the reflection of the mountains in the water. I stood in awe and wonder, delighted by this perfect mirror of sky and mountain on water and for a dizzy moment not knowing which way was up and which way was down. I loved to see the new in the world, to experience something I had never experienced before, and I was overwhelmed with gratitude.

Lake Louise called me to perform the ceremony and asked for one of my medicine stones. It was to be the last offering of the call.

I opened my mesas. Harry and the girls joined me, as I began to anchor all of the medicine to the lands, the lake, and the grid.

Tell me about the Apache Tear in your mesa, Louise, she asked.

On the bank of this great emerald lake, I held the stone in my hand and told her the story.

"Mother Waters, this kuya holds the medicine of 'peace in pain.' My great-grandmother's spirit shared this wisdom with me 18 months ago. She told me that, in pain, there is a space, and in this space, there is peace. The centre of a wound is where transformation happens. I have been using it on my journey through all these sacred places to see the wounds I was blind to.

"Apache Tears hold the stories of the white man's decimation of the Apache tribe in the Americas. It is said that women of the tribe cried tears of grief, which fell to the earth and formed into these dark and strangely shaped stones. All along this journey, I have learned what my ancestors have done through the colonization of lands and the people on those lands, the pain they suffered.

"Along the way, I have blown all my learning into this stone during my morning meditations."

"Mother waters, I see we all were once part of our lands, somewhere. And now it is time for us all to reconnect to our lands, to our Earth, to see the wounds we have created, the wounds passed on to us, the wounds deep within us. We all have to heal. On an individual level and on a global level."

As I had done before, I raised my wand on the shore of Lake Louise and sang songs and spoke words of prayers, then I threw the kuya deep into the lake. In return, she spoke clearly.

You are a portal, Louise.

She showed a vision of me holding the medicine of the earth in my mesas and sang a song into my mind. I had to hold on to this song. I had to try to remember it.

She reminded me of the visions I'd had of fires, dancing, singing, the old way. I saw this way coming back, but first we had to travel through dark times, seeing the death of what was most sacred to us: water, earth and air. We would see these destroyed by our disrespectful way of life. Each human must face their shadow and the shadow of humanity and transform it. We were on the precipice of a great turning, and when the world turned, those rooted in reverence into Gaia would survive. It would be their love and respect for all things that would bring back nature.

Lake Louise blessed us all that morning and it was painful to say goodbye, both to the lake and to Nick and Jane.

That evening, we stayed with another old friend, also named Louise, who happened to be the person who had gifted me the Apache Tear four years earlier as a thank you for some healing I had done for her when her father died. I didn't tell her about the offering I'd made to Lake Louise, not wanting her to feel I had disrespected her gift, but she jumped up from the dinner table with excitement.

"Guess what I have! I need to give this to you."

She pulled out five more Apache Tear stones.

"We keep four here. One for me and one each for my husband and two kids. I always had a spare one, and I feel this is for you."

As our time in Canada came to a close, it felt like everything had come full circle.

***

CHAPTER 12

The Wounded Sole

I was to marry one of my best friends, Claire, and her husband-to-be in front of 100 family and friends who, like us, had driven from England to France for the celebrations. I had a sense of responsibility about me that no one else could understand. I had to keep my energy contained and sacred, and was sensitive in the lead-up, not to mention completely exhausted from traveling halfway across the world only days before.

More and more people arrived at the villa, gathering for the main event, and while the party began days before, like any traditional Irish wedding, I chose to spend time alone in the orchard or overseeing the kids playing in the pool. This withdrawal was unusual for me. I was always the queen of any party. But I had changed. And sometimes I found it hard not being that party girl anymore.

On the day of the wedding, I felt beautiful and connected to the earth from spending the morning barefoot on the chateau grounds. I was in my priestess and called upon Gaia and God to make me an instrument of their peace so I could bring the greatest blessings of love and unity to my friends' marriage. Sunlight beamed through the woodland setting and I looked upon the couple whom I loved dearly. I knew the words I spoke were medicine. I was weaving blessings like a fine tapestry, not just into the couple, uniting them ceremonially, but into all the guests.

When the ceremony was done, I was aware of people watching in awe, having received so much more than they had expected. Gaia herself had come through me and kissed every one of them on the forehead. God had shone his light into their hearts.

The groomsmen, a bunch of mischievous Irish boys, hugged and kissed me like a sister.

"I dunno what you did to enchant this rabble," the groom said, coming over to the group, "but they were hanging off your every word. I've never seen them stay so still and attentive. That was magic."

But that was my job. I held the medicine of the Earth in my mesa. I could not take credit for being a channel of love.

The groomsmen took it upon themselves to see me carried over the gravel patches between the chateau and the gardens where the party was being held.

"Why don't you wear shoes?" they begged.

"I've spent too long walking in shoes and being on aeroplanes. I'm enjoying the connection," I explained.

That evening, I was to perform a fire dance, a tradition among this group of friends. At every wedding, myself and my sisters would spin fire poi to loud beats and woo the guests. There was something magical about stepping barefoot onto the grass holding those familiar balls-on-chains dripping in paraffin.

On the ground was a candle in a glass votive. I dangled my poi over the flame to light them. Great fireballs lit up the ends of the chains and guests oohed and ahhed. The three of us – like fire goddesses – stepped onto the stage. *Whooossshhh* went the sound of the poi, deep and commanding, indicating the fire dance had begun.

The music played, and I danced and swirled, and I felt a long-dormant part of me awaken. I was a Leo. I adored the stage. I loved to wow and woo people, but most of all, I was dancing with my elements, Gaia under my feet, fire all around me in patterns, illuminating the air, awakening the fire as we cut through it. The three of us danced, entranced by the music and motion.

Between tracks, I walked over to collect my second pair of poi, but as I stepped I felt time slow down. The music blurred and I heard myself scream. Then everything sped up again. Suddenly, I was screaming on the floor. It was dark and no one could see what had happened. I thought I had burned my foot, as it was numb with pain, but what I hadn't seen was that the glass votive holding the candle had somehow smashed and left a four-inch shard embedded in my foot when I had stood on it with all my weight. I needed a hospital urgently.

Chaos and confusion erupted in the blackness. No one knew what had happened, but it quickly became apparent that I was the only sober person here.

"You need to get an ambulance quick!" I screamed.

The whole wedding party was gathered around me. Thinking I'd burned myself, they made me put my foot in a bucket of water, but I yelled at them that it was cut. The hotel manager came over, stood motionless for a moment, then told us no ambulance would come out here and walked away. Where was he going? Why wasn't he helping?

"I need to go to hospital," I yelled louder, desperate to get some help.

"It's nothing, Lou. You'll be fine," my friend Pete slurred as he stroked my hair.

Fear went through me as it dawned on me that no one understood the gravity of the situation. Then phone lights began shining down on me and they saw the sheer amount of blood all over me.

Priestess Lou had long gone and I lay on the ground screaming and swearing. Everyone who was drunkenly trying to sort out the situation was making it worse and I needed to take control. Then the groom's brother-in-law David came to my rescue, calm and steady. He kneeled at my foot, gently raised it in the air, and called for a first aid kit.

"I told you to put your bleeding shoes on," he said in his soft voice. "Don't worry. I've got some first aid experience."

"Please, you have to tell them all to leave," I begged.

"Come on you lot. She wants to be left alone. Let us sort this out."

People began to leave my side but hovered a little further away watching. I relaxed my head into Claire's hands, as David wrapped my foot in bandages.

"I'm so sorry I've ruined your wedding," I sobbed apologetically.

"Not at all!" she said, stroking my face, wiping my tears. "We're going to get you sorted. Don't worry."

I could hear the concerned muffled Irish accent of an older man, who was planning what to do.

"An ambulance won't come out here, I've just checked. Someone will have to drive her," he said.

I closed my eyes and surrendered. There was nothing I could do to control this situation. Nothing.

The next moment, three drunk Irish men lifted me up out of Claire's arms, Harry following behind and we wedged ourselves into the smallest car I had ever seen in my entire life. Harry got in on one side of me, David on the other side. I felt the car sink with their weight. David lifted my foot onto his shoulder, his hand gripped around it for dear life to stop any blood loss. One of the uncles who had been making me laugh all day got into the driver's seat. He had a broken arm in a sling. I was confused. His son, who had also had me in stitches all day, and who was not at all sober, got into the passenger seat.

The uncle turned to me and winked.

"I'm the only sober one, so I can drive the wheel, and Olly here can do the gears. We think the hospital is about an hour away."

I felt as if my life had moved into some 1970s comedy show. I wasn't sure if it was the fact I was slightly delirious on adrenalin or the absurdity that I was in this tiny car with four huge men and my leg in the air, but something made me crack up laughing.

"Jesus, Mary and Joseph", I said in my fake Irish accent. "I'm being saved by a one-armed Irish man, and his drunken son! God be with us all."

We flew out of the gates of the chateau and into the long winding lanes of the French Dordogne. The roads got narrower and windier, and yet the car drove faster and faster. Harry was stroking my head, breathing beer into my crown chakra, and I realised just how drunk everyone was and that I was currently in a real-life version of Gran Turismo.

"Guys, slow down!" I shouted without even thinking. "I'm not gonna die of blood loss. Dave has my foot held so tight that I have lost all feeling of my leg! You don't need to drive so fast. I'd rather lose my foot than all of our lives down this fucking crazy lane."

The sense of impending doom left the car, the driver team had been given permission by their precious queen to take it easy, and I felt their panic leave too. Everything was going to be okay.

Ninety minutes and a ridiculous car ride to the hospital later, they parked the car in the ambulance bay and carried me into the hospital like royalty. Harry followed behind amused! With my newly adopted family attempting to speak drunken Irish-accented French to the doctor, he took one look at my foot and sent me straight through to be stitched up.

As the guys reluctantly let me go, I felt a rush of love for them that I could not contain. I was so truly blessed, so loved. I could not have been more grateful for my life.

***

Defiance and derailing

Next morning, I sat on the toilet crying because my foot hurt so much and I couldn't do anything. I didn't even have any crutches!

"Do you think I'm being punished? Do you think I failed Gaia because I didn't do enough work on the lands when we were away?"

"Don't be daft," Harry said, hoisting me off the loo, flushing and helping me hobble to the sink.

A knock came at the door and the groomsmen appeared.

"We've come to take the lady to breakfast," one said grinning.

Cheers went up from the wedding party as the groomsmen carried me down the stairs, like I was their little sister princess on a throne.

"I want a pint of Guinness," I declared over breakfast. The craving was insane, though I hadn't clocked that it was just the iron I needed. As I noticed how badly and how seriously I wanted it, a trigger went off inside me. I wanted to be Party Lou! I was done self-chastising. I was on holiday! No more Earth Chakra Shaman Lou. No more Priestess Lou. No more Little Sister Princess Lou. I wanted to go to the pub and sink a pint and forget all about it.

We drove for a couple of hours to a stunning medieval walled town with five carloads of friends behind us. We parked close to the centre, but I couldn't walk anywhere.

"Fuck, why didn't they give me crutches?" I said, exhausted from hopping just 10 feet and pausing to rest on a wall.

"Let me carry you," Harry said.

"No, I'll do it!" I insisted.

I managed to hop all the way to the town square, where the dreamy sight of cafes all around and people drinking coffee in the sun gave off a relaxed Sunday vibe. I realised I wasn't going to get any Guinness though. *Fuck it. A few beers and I'll be right.*

At the very same second I had that thought, I somehow tripped and slammed my left foot into the ground. My stomach turned as I felt the most disgusting sensation of my stitches bursting open and blood spurting from my bandages, covering the pavement right by where people were eating.

"Harry!" I screamed, taking control and holding my foot in the air for him to take, "Hold it as tight as you can."

I could feel blood pumping out of me. This was different to last night. This was pressure and I knew immediately that it was bad.

A couple on motorbikes pulled up and the woman began running to us when she saw. Realising we were from overseas, she said to me in perfect English, "I'm a nurse. Tell me what happened."

I told her and she understood right away. She took my foot from Harry and examined it, then spoke to her husband in French, instructing him what to do.

"There will be no ambulance, but you need to go to the hospital as a matter of urgency, so the fire brigade are on their way and it will be quick. They'll take good care of you. You are very lucky. God must have wanted me to come to you, because it was unusual for us to come by this way. You would have never made it in time otherwise," she said.

She smiled gently, like my very own guardian angel, telling me that God was on my side and had not cast me off for renouncing my shaman that morning, for wanting to drink alcohol and be a normal person.

The joke was not lost on the doctor, who had seen me carried in by three drunk Irish men just 12 hours earlier, when I arrived now with three bulky French firemen.

***

The gift beyond self-judgment

So, God did not judge, and Gaia was not cross with me, but I judged and I was cross with myself.

Harry carried me out to the orchard and we lay under the stars. We made love, Gaia taking us into her hands and blessing us, and the reiki flowing between us. Then sacred symbols came to me, as we came together. It was like we'd been waiting for months to be alone, finally, and yet the Earth, the stars and the moon were still here holding us.

As we lay in silence, I felt the words of Gaia and could still see the symbols in my mind.

This is your gift from the sacred lands you have walked on, Louise. It contains all the medicine you need. It is time for you to rest and write now. Connect with this symbol. It will be your anchor for what is next to come.

Without breaking the silence, I drew the symbol in the air with my finger, determined to learn it and never forget it. Then I shared it with Harry. And in that moment, I felt like all this was meant to be.

***

CHAPTER 13

Glastonbury & the Heart Chakra

It was mid-September, the time for new beginnings, or so I thought. Yet everything felt heavy and hard. Everything that had been so right was now so wrong! I was stuck in the house on my crutches with seven stitches in the sole of my foot and they felt more like seven stitches in my soul. If I tried to do too much my foot would swell up. In some ways, it was a blessing to slow me down and let me rest, but I sensed it had a deeper meaning, something else was playing out.

Seven stitches for seven chakras of the Earth, I thought to myself.

Somehow, this was a constant reminder that my roots and my soul belonged to the Earth, and this mission was far from over.

As we had agreed earlier in the year, September was supposed to be the time that Jen and I would action our lofty ideas of creating a conscious corporation, taking on staff, training teachers, launching a retreat, creating a new website and publishing our first book. All this was meant to happen by Christmas, and though we had made a start by bringing on board a new team member Lucy, it was making us both feel overwhelmed. Grounding dreams from the ether into reality turned out to be harder than we had imagined. Within a few weeks, Jen decided this path was not for her and made the decision to end our partnership.

Our dreams of changing the world into a utopia were shattered and I was gutted. Far from being the new beginnings I had planned, September was the start of a very long and painful journey of unravelling of our entwined energies – spiritually, soulfully and even potentially legally.

Crestfallen, I sat in my kitchen, staring out of the bifold windows, watching the first leaves drop from the trees and trying to work out how it had come to this. I recalled the prophecy that Angela had given me just before I went to Alaska. The medium had spoken about a friendship ending.

"You don't have a choice in this. The angels are cutting the cords. You must not go back!"

With a strange sense of relief, I realised the message I'd been given all those months earlier was not about my old friend Viv as I had first assumed, but about Jen. This decision was out of my hands, but knowing that did not make the process any less painful.

I thought about the hero's journey that I had learned from Sue at the Storytelling Hut. I recalled how the hero always faced huge challenges. There would be fallouts, enemies, fights, death and rebirth. At the time I'd heard about it, innocent to the journey ahead, I had denied that anything like that would happen to me. I'd thought I was invisible to suffering. Yet it was clear, up to this point in the quest, that every earth chakra brought lessons that came with deep discomfort.

EARTH CHAKRA SHAMAN

Was this a new beginning? A rebirth for the hero of me? Was this pain supposed to take me to my life's next chapter?

***

Reconnection

As I sank into a state of apathy, I could feel the spirit of Jaguar sitting at my feet, nudging me to get outside. Nature is where we all find our peace and where we return back to ourselves when we feel lost in the world. Nature, in other words, is the first step to recovery. Yet sometimes we resist the very thing that heals us. In our humanness, we convince ourselves that it's easier to stay where we are and wallow, avoiding the work we need to do to change, wake up and stand in our personal power.

Choosing to take the reins of our life and steer ourselves the direction our soul is calling takes courage. Sometimes we want to stay in the victim role, hoping someone will come rescue us, but in the end it's better to recognise the sabotage and accept that we will only be at peace when we take responsibility for our own healing and do the work.

"Okay, okay, I'm going," I whispered to Jaguar.

I felt her spirit follow me as I picked up my mesas and hobbled up the steps to my garden where I settled on the grass. I just had to let Mother Earth unravel me. I breathed in the cool air and felt a sense of grief. Tears filled my eyes. Like a child returning to her mother's arms, I let her take me in and rock me as I sobbed quietly into her grassy bosom. I felt a welcome sense of acceptance and calm come over me then, knowing that something beyond me had everything under control. I just had to trust in the universe, even when things were not going the way I had hoped.

Back in my body, my mind was clearer and I began to listen to the lands, to the messages and divine direction of the Earth. She planted words into my mind.

Bring your medicine to the Earth, Louise, and share it with the land. Let the ancient ones feel your growth.

One by one, I took each kuya out of the old Peruvian cloths that held them, recalling the medicine gifts of each. I picked up my Alaskan medicine stone, remembering when Mount Denali had whispered to me that this was the gift of new beginnings. I rubbed it on the sole of my foot.

"Mother Earth..." I asked, "are these the new beginnings: seven stitches and a partnership ending in divorce before it even began?"

I felt my confusion and sense of betrayal like knots in my solar plexus. I was cross with Pachamama for what had happened. I blamed her.

Send your root down, Louise, I felt her call.

As I closed my eyes and brought my inner gaze to the base of my spine, I became aware of my grounding cord, my root to the Earth. I felt it drop deeper and deeper through the many layers, past the rocks and into liquid-but-solid silver spheres of energy. This was the placenta of Mother Earth and my cord was an umbilical cord. I was a child of the Great Mother, being reminded that we had never separated. She loved me unconditionally. She loves us all unconditionally.

I recalled the loving words of Pachamama in the jungle in Peru:

Give it to me, Louise. You don't need to carry this.

Golden energy from Father Sun rained down on me, filling my energy field with a light that helped wash away the hucha, the heaviness. It began to flow down the cord, down into the Earth, where she could do what I could not: return the darkness back to light.

It's time for the ceremony, Louise. You must prepare to return to the heart chakra, came a voice.

This was not the Great Mother speaking to me. This was Mount Shasta. I felt my base chakra vibrate, the realisation that our connection was not distant and ethereal, but ever-present and physical. He was a part of me.

You have a pure heart, Louise. Take your medicine to the heart chakra. Do not underestimate your sacred role on this Earth.

I opened my eyes with a knowing that I had to face the journey ahead. And get out of this funk! I was here to serve the Earth. I had a responsibility to Gaia, to my family, to my community, my students and myself to continue showing up and sharing my medicine. This was going to be a journey of tiny steps and they mainly required me to keep listening to nature's guidance. Mother Earth still had plans for me.

The autumn full moon was calling. Time to head back to Glastonbury to complete the energy work I had started at Mount Shasta and realign my own heart with the heart chakra of Mother Earth.

***

Home is where the heart chakra is

Driving down to Glastonbury, we drove past the ancient megalithic stone circle of Stonehenge and I did as I always did as we passed by at 60 mph. I reached my hands out the window, feeling the cool breeze on my palms, and sent light energy and loving gratitude to the stones and to the lands. The stone circle looked so tiny from the road, but up close on winter and summer solstice you could access the site and touch the giant standing stones. The whole place was as much of a mystery as the pyramids in Egypt. And like the pyramids, I knew the henge was built for reasons yet to be revealed.

As we got closer to Glastonbury, I could feel my excitement of returning. I could see the Tor in the far distance, the huge hill sticking out among the rolling English countryside of Somerset. It was easier to spot with its stone tower on top – St Michael's Tower.

I remembered the first time I had seen the Tor, long before I knew anything about it being the heart chakra. It was the year 2000 and I was watching David Bowie on the Pyramid Stage at Glastonbury Festival as he sang… "We can be heroes just for one night." Harry had lifted me onto his shoulders. And there in the distance behind the glow of the stage stood the Tor. A bolt of energetic lightning went through my body and soul at that moment. At the time, of course, I had zero idea what that feeling was, but I now knew it to be one of the handful of major soul activations that I would receive in my life to awaken codes within me to assist me on my journey. I was never the same after that.

The thought about David Bowie brought a sense of sadness now. He had died earlier in the year and I'd had the strangest response to his death. Apart from deep sorrow, I felt like I'd been abandoned here on Earth.

Driving back to the lands now, I was making more sense of it. During my travels, I had learned of the deep connections to the Seven Sisters star system that was shared by many ancient cultures. This had validated my own connection to the Pleiades. It was like David Bowie *really was* the Starman. He had been here to change the world and now he had returned home. I had yearned to go home too, back to the stars, back to the Seven Sisters. But recently, something had shifted. Earth was my home now. The yearning to leave was less intense. Like Bowie, I too was here to play my part in changing the world.

***

The Isle of Avalon

The Seven Sisters had twinkled down at me seconds after our love-making on the night Avalon was conceived. Right there and then, she beamed down from the stars and landed into my belly. When she was born, her soul called us to take her, not only to the festival at Glastonbury, but to the town. So, with my daughter turning six months old, our annual pilgrimages to the Isle of Avalon began.

Glastonbury is an old English market town, with an abundance of crystal shops and cafes, and a strange, sometimes intense energy. These lands were always healing me in some way, realigning me back to my heart, and that could be pretty full-on. The Tor, the sacred Chalice Well, the white and red springs and the surrounding hills were a pilgrimage site, a place steeped in legend. From magic and dragons, to wizards and witches, to gods and goddesses and the Holy Grail, I was only just getting my head around most of the stories.

When we arrived, Harry went off to his favourite cafe while the girls and I headed over to the goddess temple. As we sat meditating in front of a huge painting of the goddess Brigid, all these questions awakened within me around who we were on these lands before we were Christian. Before religion took hold, these islands were inhabited by the native tribes of Britain, people who worshiped the earth, nature gods and goddesses, the ancestors and the ancient ones.

In Jesus' time, the Isle of Avalon – the Tor – was surrounded by water and was a place for trading. Much like the Vatican today, Glastonbury had its own borders and laws. Jesus is said to have visited Glastonbury many times to learn from the druids. Joseph of Arimathea, a trader and Jesus' uncle, is believed to have brought Jesus' body to Avalon after his crucifixion, along with the chalice from the last supper – the Holy Grail – which remained here to this day at the base of the Tor under the red spring. Legend also had it that Joseph planted his staff on Wearyall Hill where the famous Holy Thorn resided. This was where he built the first church.

Although for a short time, tribespeople and Christian monks were believed to have lived in harmony, respecting each other, learning from each other, but the Roman church, the ultimate power of the time, wiped out all records of the old religions that related to the power of the Earth's wisdom, magic and medicine. Ancient Druid, Pagan and Celtic texts, manuscripts, relics and artifacts were stolen and burned. Any trace of the old ways was soon destroyed.

When the Romans invaded over 2000 years ago, it was the dawn of the Age of Pisces. Now it is the dawn of the Age of Aquarius, and we still feel the trauma of these events in the lands. It takes hundreds, if not thousands of years to wipe out a culture. While destroying records is one way of ridding the peoples of their power, the Earth's wisdom is always within us. It is our intuition. When we listen to the lands, we know what plant medicines we need, we know how to heal ourselves and others.

By the 15th century, the medicine men and women, the healers, the soothsayers, the priestesses, any women deemed 'too beautiful' or who dared to collect herbs in the woods or assist their sisters in childbirth were seen as witches. For hundreds of years, being seen this way had catastrophic consequences. The powers of the time committed mass genocide across the UK and Europe, horrific witch-hunts, burnings, hangings and torture of potentially nine million people, mostly women.

For many years, this had been unbelievable to me, but I had begun to understand that those past lives were within me too. I could feel them now. The memory of what took place is still in the lands of England, and the wound still within all of us who are medicine women today. Hundreds of years on, we still hide our spirituality and our medicine, extinguishing our own power for fear of persecution.

This awareness was calling me to deep healing on all levels. Hurt cultures carry on hurting other cultures. I had seen how we had acted out this very attack on others. What was done to England, England had gone on to do to the rest of the world.

Since returning home, I had come to understand more about the Earth's grid, her ley lines, sometimes called "dragon lines," and I began to see that these lines were how we communicated ancient wisdoms all across the world. It made sense to me that this information would be accessible to all people on the lands all over the world. The ley lines were a huge global information system. The Rainbow Serpent and the Plumed Serpent were a flow of ancient earth wisdom between the Earth chakras.

It seemed to me that the church had calculated ways to claim ancient sacred sites and adopt sacred festivals as their own. The tactic had worked all over the world, uprooting people from their power – their connection to Gaia and the spirit world. Churches were built on the sacred sites to "keep the dragons suppressed," and I had indeed noticed how many religious buildings were clustered around the energy spots that had called to me. I had begun to see that religions had built nearby in order to access the energy lines, stifling the magic and the ancient wisdoms.

Beyond the Earth chakras themselves, it was apparent to me that healing these ley lines was important, too, more so than I could understand at the time. I was only just awakening to how we grow, share, and evolve our Earth consciousness: by walking the ley lines and pilgrimaging to sacred sites.

***

Delivering divine will

As I climbed the Tor later that afternoon, I walked feeling my bare feet on the earth. I felt alive. The lands kissing my scar. Seven stitches for seven chakras. I reminded myself of the sacred connections of Gaia and how I was her servant. Performing shamanic ritual and ceremonies at her request, I walked with purpose, divinity and knowing that I was about to create a great energic completion, an activation for the Earth's grid, a healing, a download of new medicine, of consciousness and a harmony between the heart chakra and the base chakra of the Earth. People would feel this new energy flow. This was shifting the vibration.

Harry and the kids walked beside me, and I knew now that it wasn't just me. It was our union, our energy as divine feminine and divine masculine, the product of our love in our children that was the medicine. I was the Earth Chakra Shaman, returning from her quest to give her medicine, the elixir, to the heartlands, but I was not the only hero in this journey. I was walking this path for my husband, for my children, for my friends and family, for all who had played a part in this journey. Most of all, this was for the rising of the Condor people, the Indigenous people of Earth, to return the heart to balance with divine will from the base chakra.

I looked out across the lands of Somerset on the south side of the Tor and raised my wand in the air. I called in all the energies of the mountains, waters and lands where I had been and placed one of my medicine stones deep into a hole in the ground. My body tingled as I awoke the dragons of the Earth, the Rainbow Serpent and the Plumed Serpent.

"May the earth medicine rise from the base chakra of the Earth, Mount Shasta, to the sacral chakra of the Earth, Lake Titicaca, to the solar plexus of the Earth, Uluru, and into all the hearts of men from the heart chakra of the Earth."

I saw the serpents dance. They moved from Shasta, to Titicaca, to Uluru through my body into the heart chakra of the Earth here on the Glastonbury Tor. The message they had for me came through clearly.

"You are reminding people how to feel their way through this Earth and let go of thinking their way. Trust there is an awakening of the reverence, the aliveness and the wisdom of our Earth in all peoples. Keep walking forward. The quest is not yet over."

***

EARTH CHAKRA SHAMAN

Heart Chakra Meditation & Medicine
Infinite Flow of Love

I call upon the heart chakra of the Earth and the Rainbow Serpent,
my ancestors of these lands
and all who have walked before me
to be with me now as I welcome divine love.
To the ancient lands of Albion and the new Jerusalem,
I bring infinite love and harmony between humans and all sentient beings.

I call upon the true light of Christ consciousness
to bring acceptance and understanding to all humans for each other
and to share one vision of love, peace, freedom for all.

I give my service to the heart chakra of the Earth,
raising consciousness for all humanity

through my own awakening
and the blessing of unconditional love.

I give thanks to those who have been dreaming with heart,
the new Earth,
filled with love and compassion for the children yet to come.

May all humans know the power of the divine love within
and the infinite flow of the heart chakra.
I bring my growth to the grid,
and my will to live a heart-centred life.

***

CHAPTER 14

The Great Pyramids of Giza & the Throat Chakra

"Okay, Harry," I said, "The messages are getting insane. I'm seeing the pyramids and the desert everywhere."

"Me too, babe," he laughed.

"I had dreams of being called by a falcon to come into the desert. And then it changed into my griffin with falcon wings and dolphin eyes. The desert was full of people. I had to take people. The winds called me and said, 'Bring people'."

An old book that I had read when I was 21, *The Alchemist* by Paulo Coelho, was gifted to me the week before and I realised it was all about Egypt. The more I read, the more I realised I had never understood this book the first time around, but now it was speaking to me on all levels. Coelho had written about the desert in Egypt. I knew exactly where we needed to go: The Great Pyramids and an oasis just outside Cairo.

Finally, things began to unfold.

Egypt had seen some very challenging times with its tourism, so flights were cheap and hotels were even cheaper. Before I knew it, the exact amount of money had appeared into my account. There were no questions in my heart and mind this time; this money was for the Earth and this was what I was called to do with it. It was time to activate the throat chakra of the Earth.

***

Pyramid song

We were up at 5am, driving through the city with our guide for the day. It wasn't my cup of tea, this place. Huge, dirty and busy already at 5am!

Even though we'd never left the kids without one of us being with them, there was never a question that Harry and I wouldn't do this together. After all, it was on both our vision boards. We were joined by Adam, an old neighbour who had popped round for a cup of tea a week before we were to leave, and his girlfriend Bex. For some reason beyond our understanding, it felt absolutely correct that they came and they had booked their flights then and there.

Our guide was Gad, a sweet man, passionate about his city and its history. With only three hours' sleep, I was barely awake, but I smiled and listened to him talk as I observed the waking city and let the culture of this land greet me.

We pulled into the carpark of the pyramids and as I climbed out from the back seat, Gad turned to me.

"Excuse me, Louise, I hope you don't mind, but I would like to ask you a question. I feel you have something, an energy. I would like to understand more. I think you are a spiritual person?"

"I am indeed," I smiled at him.

"I would like to ask you many questions. I have seen some things I cannot explain that I think you can help me understand."

I knew immediately that we had the right guide and I thanked the universe in my mind for sending him our way.

We reached the pyramids before the sun had risen. The air was thick, and I wasn't sure if the fog was mist, sand or the morning city smog sitting low in the air. At first, I couldn't even see the ancient forms, but as I walked towards where I knew them to be, leaving the chaos of the awakening city behind, I could *feel* the pyramids, like the ghost of a giant. Then there they were.

The light of the morning sun cut through the haze to create the most delightful beam onto the Great Pyramid. It was not just the pyramid itself but this whole area that met us, opening its veil for us to enter so that we could see it fully. And not see it as something to tick off a list or post on Instagram, but see fully, feel fully these constructions that lay on the throat chakra of the Earth. Countless people have told me how disappointed they were by the pyramids, how they hated Cairo. Now I know what it must be like for a beautiful woman when men only see her for her face and her body, and soon become bored. A man who approaches with reverence, honour and respect will see so much more, because she will let him see her fully, her glorious power and grace, only when he is able to honour it.

Still in awe, I climbed the steps to the Great Pyramid and entered via the steep narrow ascending passageway. I climbed crouching down, the air getting thinner as we went, the smell of ammonia clinging to my throat. Finally, when we reached the chamber, it was a tiny empty room holding nothing other than a stone box, the size of a small human.

The four of us were alone, and we sat down cross-legged and settled into the space. Instantly, I fell into deep meditation.

After a while, I couldn't hold in the simple notes that wanted to flow out of me. I began to sing. Bex, who was a singer, a real singer, joined me. I felt her energy, comfortable with her voice, and it activated my own. I realised why she was here. Allowing the flow to come through us, Bex and I built up an intensity of energy that the men found too much. It was our voices. It was her voice expanding my voice. It was our energy. It all brought about an activation within us, into the pyramid, into the lands, out into the universe. There was a reciprocal flow of energy, a giving and receiving of divine sound. We had the power in our voices to sing around the world, the energy lines shifting within us.

I realised we have all been so smothered into believing we cannot sing, separated from the power of our voices for fear of other people judging us. When I was just six, I had dreams of teaching the world to sing, but already believed I couldn't sing and that it would be impossible. That belief fell away now. Many of us have never been given the freedom to find our own voice, but I saw how true it was that everyone could sing. Everyone should sing! Singing was our divine power.

I squinted into the bright morning light at the smiling toothless man on the gate that we had passed on the way in, who seemed to know something I was yet to understand.

Gad appeared excited as we made our way out.

"You were in the pyramid all alone. That *never* happens! You are very blessed. And I noticed a falcon flew over the pyramid when you were just coming out. This is a very good omen!" he said.

I was in a dream-like state, the intense energy from the activation in the pyramid had me floating and my body was still vibrating and tingling. I held on to Harry to ground myself. I had to sit down on the warm sand. There, I took out my mesa to feel the energy and help process and embed what had just happened in the pyramid. Gad and the others waited patiently as I meditated on the sand dunes overlooking the pyramid complex comprising the three giant pyramids and the Great Sphinx.

I sunk deeper and deeper into meditation. I felt the tied-up camels behind me, on their knees, exhausted, old and abused in their service. My heart ached for them and for not being able to free them from their suffering.

I'm so sorry for what has happened to you, I whispered to them in my mind. *I'm sorry to all the animals of the world. I trust we humans will awaken to the truth that we cannot live in our own harmony if we are harming others, including all beings of the animal kingdom.*

I was greeted by the huge energy of the lands. Divine wisdom was all around me. The message was clear.

Tell people to come. These earth chakra sites are to be honoured and respected. Tell them to come with reverence, with their own internal ceremony, led by their own voice, their own intuition. The pyramids call those who can bring that to this chakra, who are willing to show up in their truth and bring their medicine to activate these lands. When people arrive with openness, the veils will thin for them. These people will not just see a pyramid, a building that still boggles the minds of men. They will see beyond that, the mystic, the power, the connection.

I could have sat for hours, absorbing the warmth of the sand holding me, grounding me, listening for the silence between the moments.

I was falling in love, despite this vast city and its contradictions to these incredible wonders of the world. I revered the pyramids and the truth they held that no human really could ever understand from a place of the mind. Our minds were not conscious enough to believe how it was possible, yet I was at peace with the unknown. No one really knows their truth, how they were built, their mysteries. And yet here, sitting on the lands with them, they felt so familiar, not mysterious at all, but a doorway to my own truth.

***

Feeling more grounded, we were to head off to the Great Sphinx. I had shared with Gad that I was here to make an offering to the lands.

"I know just where you can do this!" he said, visibly delighted to be of service to my work.

As we entered the doorway to the Great Sphinx, Gad indicated a hole in the ground.

"This is an old well where there was once a perfectly preserved statue of King Khufu. We feel it was hidden there during the time of the Persian invasion."

Harry and I stood around the well. All was quiet. Many people before me had made offerings here but this was the first time I was to make an offering in such a public place. It felt right, I decided. There was a certain magnetic energy to this well and I trusted that the medicine would radiate to where it needed.

"Thank you," I said as I threw my medicine stone in, "I bring you the gift of pollination. May the divine gifts of the throat chakra of the Earth be spread like bees carry pollen. And may our new world be rich and abundant."

My heart soared and I found myself once again needing to ground. I found a peaceful space where the sun beamed through a slit in the walls and felt the tears rolling down my face. This place was pure magic.

Afterwards, as I wandered by the feet of the Great Sphinx, Gad found me.

"Did you know you were meditating near what we believe was an ancient altar? I watched you being blessed. Ra, the sun god, shone his light on you."

I was grateful for his insight and interpretation. Never before had anyone fully seen me perform ceremony apart from Harry and the girls, and even they just saw their wife or mum waving a wand in the air looking like the village crazy lady. It was heart-warming to be seen with such reverence.

***

Hours later, in the Egyptian Museum in Cairo, amongst the millions of artefacts, I was transfixed by only one: a full-size statue of a pharaoh in black stone. I could not unlock my eyes or move away. It was as though the statue was holding my energy. And the longer I stayed, the more I left my body. The statue spoke to me, but I could not translate what it was saying in my mind. I was completely taken. Twice Harry tried to come and get me, but I couldn't be moved.

"Louise," Gad called from the entranceway, his voice unhooking me. "You know why you're here, don't you?"

"I have no idea, but he has some sort of hold on me," I said.

"This is the statue of the king I told you about, King Khufu, the statue that was found in the well where you threw your stone!"

***

Together in the desert

Fifteen kilometres from Cairo, we passed through Sakkara on our way out to the desert and visited an incredible complex of tombs, burial chambers and pyramids, believed to be the very first ones built.

Again, I stood in awe, knowing that this place would play a bigger part in the journey that lay ahead of me.

"Look, there's alabaster in this sand. This pyramid was once covered in it. I feel you should take some. I know you like stones," Gad said to me, with a knowing look, holding out a handful of glistening white chunks.

I did not know how important these stones and this gesture would be in the year ahead, but I took the alabaster gratefully.

We reached the edge of the desert where Etman, our Bedouin guide, greeted us and took over the job of leading us. Dressed in his white desert robes, red headscarf and a smile that could light up the desert on a dark night, I knew him instantly from a memory of playing with him as a child, but not in this lifetime. Etman welcomed us, seeming shy to me, and this made me conscious that I wasn't sure what protocol to follow. Until now, I had been keeping my shoulders covered at all times out of respect for Islam, and I assumed that similar respect applied with the Bedouin men and women.

After talking to our driver Ayman, Etman asked if we could take him with us to the desert too, as he had never left Cairo before or visited the desert.

"Yes, of course," I said, shocked that Ayman had never been outside the city, even though he was older than I was. Ashamed for my privilege I didn't want to be seen as anything other than equal, but I wasn't equal. It was very apparent that I was a tourist here.

Etman raced the Jeep over the sand dunes, letting loose in front of us for the first time, but always watching Ayman like a big brother, caring for him on this first trip out of Cairo. Playfully riding the dunes and spinning the vehicle fast, we all found joy in Ayman's joy. His laughter, innocence and childlike wonder was infectious. *I am with good people*, I thought to myself, as I felt love for a stranger, who was instantly a brother. This was my happy place, being with people who truly cared for each other.

When we reached a hut in the middle of the desert, I wanted nothing more than to do nothing. It was pure peace out here. Etman took his time over everything, even making our food and drinks with care, and we spent a delicious number of hours settling in. I took my mesa to a dune overlooking the camp, not wanting to flaunt any of my shamanic paraphernalia, in case it was offensive to his culture. Harry sat behind me, with his arms around me, stroking my hair and loving me, enjoying the nothingness as I played with my medicine stones and listened to the stillness of the desert. Occasionally, Etman would appear and smile at us and I started to feel that I didn't need to hide from him what I was doing.

Then, in the peace, the meaning of the message fully sunk in. I had to bring people here, I realised. I was here because I had to bring people back, to return, to lead a group.

We ate and I mused over the fascinating cross-section of heritages sitting here at this dinner table in the middle of the desert. Adam, my friend had Indian and white parentage; Bex, Jamaican and white; both had Jewish grandmothers like myself; Etman was Bedouin and Ayman was Egyptian; I was a mix of Celtic and Jewish, and Harry had English lineage through and through on both sides. One thing seemed plain to me though. Something had brought us all here together. We were all children of Mother Earth.

I could see that Etman preferred to be out in the desert than at home. He was not a man to stay in the oasis for long. Beyond our obvious cultural differences, I felt like he had the same energy as me. There were few people in the world I felt had that same essence. And despite our lack of exchange in words, I felt sure he sensed something too. I knew we were both indigo starseed children on the same mission: unity of the Earth.

"Sleep here tonight," Etman invited us, showing us the spare sleeping bags.

The peacefulness of the desert and the closeness of our group felt wonderful and I didn't want it to end.

"Aww, Etman, I would love to but we can't. We fly home tomorrow morning."

"Then we must leave the desert before the sun sets," he said sadly.

"I don't want to go! I don't want to go!" I said into Harry's chest, hiding the tears.

"I know, I know, but we'll be back. You know that, babe," Harry reassured me.

Etman looked at us warmly.

"The desert loves you, Louise. You will come here again."

We had returned to the oasis and were making our way to leave, when Etman turned to me and tried to formulate the English words to express his heart.

"What is it that you believe, Louise?"

He looked concerned, but I sensed he needed to know more about the energy we shared. I knew he saw in me something that he knew was within him too. I held my hand to his heart.

"That your God is my God. That all the gods are one god. That God is here in our hearts. God is love. God is alive in the desert, the trees, the water and the earth. And God's love heals us. We can feel it everywhere. It's just love," I answered.

He smiled, maybe with relief, maybe with knowing.

"This is good. This is very good," he said smiling broadly and seeming deeply connected with my answer.

"We will miss you. The desert is your home, Louise. Come back to your home."

***

LOUISE CARRON HARRIS

Throat Chakra Prayer
Courage to Live in Truth

It is the air that I breathe
and the songs that I sing
that cast out the dark in the night.
It's the harsh words that I share,
the untruths that I bear
that keeps me caged in a fright.
So I call upon courage
and the throat chakra knowledge
to awaken the sound of my soul.
For it is my truth that I will live,
and my heart that will forgive
that reminds me I am love and I am whole.
I invoke divine light
on the throat chakra site.
The spirit message that's so strong.
She calls for us now
to join together somehow
and unify our ancient soul song.

CHAPTER 15

The Show Must Go On

*I*t was a year to the day that I had been in Uluru and spring was returning back to the lands after a long hard winter in my soul. So much had happened since the beginning of my call that I couldn't understand how it had gone so wrong. Yet, I heard whispers from my eagle that nothing *had* gone wrong, that I must honour what had happened and remember the wider picture.

Jen and I were going through a brutal separation and I felt a deep sense of injustice, like a caged lion, wrongly accused, wrongly judged, sad and scared. I fell into a cave, hiding. The prospect of a legal dispute hanging over my head had me feeling utter shame in having got myself into such a situation.

Scotland called me during a reiki healing in which I was flying over lochs. These lakes were calling me to activate the Scottish waters and were somehow connected to Alaska. I had to come to the lochs right away, they called. And yet, I was done. I was angry with Gaia and I didn't want to serve her anymore. I wanted to stop working, stop serving, stop teaching, and hide.

Harry would not let me, reminding me I had responsibility to my assistant Lucy who had been living and working with us since September, trying to keep some sort of business afloat for all my students and community. My people needed me. They needed me to overcome this, to be positive, safe, magical, their warrior, their light. I needed to cut it out. No one liked broken Lou!

So, when Avalon came in from the garden with a small green crystal angel that I had been given five years before, I had mixed feelings of blessings and brokenness.

"Mummy, I found your angel in the mud. The sun was glimmering on it, so I dug it up, but now she is all dirty and white, and she has no head."

I recalled when I found her broken years before. It had wobbled me to see her that way, so I put her in an offering to the fire and sent her back to the Earth in the embers. Now here was Avalon, holding it in her hand.

Seeing it again now frightened me. I saw myself in that broken angel. I didn't want to be her, but in many ways I was. I had lost my head! I took the angel from Avalon and placed it on my altar. *Why have you come back to me, little angel? I thought I'd sent you home.*

The following morning, I felt guided to clean and cleanse my healing room. As I was pouring crystal chips from a glass vase, thousands of them, I saw among the rose quartz the perfect tiny head of my angel, no bigger than a pea and exactly the same green.

I sat with the two pieces and closed my eyes.

"What does this mean?" I asked the angel.

She showed me how, since my 37th birthday, I had been going through a transformation, beginning with a process of dismembering all that I had become. This was the symbolic death I had experienced at Denali. Now I had to stop trying to reinstate the cords between Jen and me. I had to let her go, for they weren't to be in my next chapter.

Like the angel, I had been through the fires of transformation. Like her, I had been buried, lost, left in the dark. Like her, I had lost my head.

And like her, I had thought myself powerless, unable to fly. It had been a long time since I'd felt my own wings.

Yet she was never lost, just as I was never lost. She was always where she needed to be. And in my life, I knew it was the same. Despite everything, people had shown up, delivering messages.

Now the angel had returned looking very different. She reminded me of my strength, determination, sense of knowing, discernment and wisdom. She was back where she belonged, transformed. The *dis*membering had ended, and it was time to begin the *re*membering of who I am.

The angel wanted to be my new kuya, because she was here to teach me about discernment and not giving away my power. Where I was going, she told me, I would require respect for my own power; the most loving thing I could do was to honour it so that others could learn to honour their own.

She reminded me of a past-life vision I'd had a year earlier, where I was one of 12 chosen to anchor the light, each of us holding a sacred spell. We stood on a huge grid and I was given a box holding the ultimate power of protection. But I was told by an old hag that I was unworthy of protecting the sacred box, too young and inexperienced. I was told it would be better off with her so I handed it over to her and everything went horribly wrong for the future of the Earth.

She showed me that this was the lesson I needed, but I knew it was not one I would learn overnight. Few inductions into wisdom happen overnight. Often, we must tread the same path a few times, before we alchemise it into reality.

My mom called a few days later and suggested we go away as a family for the Easter holidays – her treat! She had noticed I'd been low over the past few months and I smiled that inner knowing that something was unfolding when she suggested going to the Secret Coast in Scotland.

Within an hour, one of my best friends Beck called out of the blue and invited us to stay with her in the Lake District, which would mean spending a week with my family, then driving down to spend Easter weekend with friends, my soul family, the people who loved me, knew me, and accepted me despite my weird mystic ways.

I felt a sense of happiness that I had not felt in months, just like the angel had told me to seek out. Life was looking up. I was back in service!

***

Everyday miracles

Driving through Scotland was like entering nature's womb. The lonely rolling road went effortlessly deeper and deeper into the hills, the mountains, sacred lands towards the Secret Coast. I welcomed the familiar feeling of coming home, even though this part of Scotland was somewhere I had not been in this lifetime.

Reiki travelled through my hands into Harry's, music played songs from our America trip, and tears rolled down my face as the views became increasingly beautiful, even in the dull March fogs. Pale grey skies, dusty brown heather and vibrant green trees with buds on the cusp of blooming pushed the sadness out of me and I found my centre.

All of sudden, the car jolted and the engine slowed, as if all power was draining from it. Slowly, we pulled over, turned off the engine, and started it again. It crawled a short way, struggling to get past 20 miles per hour, then coasted into a valley and ground to a halt.

"Well, I can think of worse places to break down," I said as I surveyed the gentle movement of waters on a loch surrounded by stony beaches and mountains.

Harry reckoned that this was Lock Fyne. There was no signal here, of course, no one around, and only a tiny little house far in the distance in the hills. Fussing, we tried all the things – turning the heated seats off, turning the radio off – but there was no power getting to the engine.

"Okay, calm down, everyone," I insisted as the kids shouted in the back and Harry swore. "There is something more to this, guys."

Just like he had in America, Harry let me lead for a moment, knowing there was nothing much he could do but surrender to me and the only way I knew, the mystic.

I opened my mesa. As if it was calling me, there was a kuya that wanted to work with this issue: the medicine stone of Christ consciousness. I held it in my hands and it led me to the medicine.

"Harry," I said seriously, looking him in the eye, "blow all your fears into the kuya, all the blocks, all the stress. It's time you honour all that you've been carrying, so you can let it go."

Overriding his usual awkwardness, he took it without questioning, even though he sometimes felt a bit silly doing this stuff.

And so, we sat there, with nothing else to do other than to blow the pressure of the past few months. A stillness came over all of us. The girls sat quietly in the back as Harry and I allowed all the stuck energy to be seen and gave it time to be acknowledged. I looked beyond my own hurt and confusion and realised the pressure that my family had been under, what all of this had done to them. I closed my eyes, welcoming with gratitude the healing that was happening to us all, and there was Jesus, right there, smiling at me.

Come and perform ceremony here on your return home, Louise.

It had been a long time since I had seen him so present. I opened my eyes and, with a sense of mischief, announced to the car what Jesus had asked.

"Okay, no probs," Harry said without judgment, which was insightful.

Of all the mystic work I'd done, he struggled most with accepting anything that involved Jesus as a guide.

"We'd better see if we can get up this hill first, then call your parents to tow us to the cottage or something."

Harry turned the key in the ignition and the car sprung back to life, as if nothing had ever been wrong.

"What?!" I cried with laughter, "We must say thank you, Jesus!"

"Thank you, Jesus," Harry played along, voicing the last thing I ever expected to come out of his mouth.

EARTH CHAKRA SHAMAN

***

The views from the cottage over the waters were mystical in every way. The clouds parted by icy winds to reveal blue skies and rainbows that warmed my heart. Although I felt disturbed by the tree-felling we saw everywhere, reminding me that everything we consume has a price, walks over the hills to explore secret beaches with my family was the tonic I hadn't realised I needed.

I was sitting in the pub posting photos on my Instagram, when someone on there messaged me to say that we were in their neck of the woods and felt compelled to tell me about an ancient woodland they thought we should visit. Mere hours later, we followed the thread and climbed through Puck's Glen, touching and singing to the wise old trees and ancient waters. I cried meeting them. I was not sure I had ever met trees so old. Further and further we walked, thinking we knew where we were going, and before long the four of us were blissfully lost deep in the woods.

Gaia sang through me a melody that she had seeded in my heart at Lake Louise. I had not felt this sense of deep contentment that I am in divine service to the Earth since walking up the Glastonbury Tor the previous autumn. I had almost forgotten that feeling of knowing I am doing exactly what I was sent to Earth to do. Then the trees spoke lyrics that I could not grasp as they flew through my mind. *Damn, I need to train myself better to remember these images,* I thought. I asked the trees to help me see their message and the song began to stick...

The rivers and the rain are calling. The fire and the flames are dancing. The wind in the air is whispering. The trees are calling us back home. For we are one tribe. We are one.

The wisdom of the Earth is whispering. Echoing the message of our song. Voices of one people singing. Unity returns to the Earth. For we are one tribe. We are one.

It was as though all the rivers, all the mountains and all the trees I had ever connected to were all here in this message, in this medicine song, and I knew I had to bring the medicine of the Earth and that song to the people. I was determined to hold onto the words by singing them over and over in my head as we walked. The green lands were seeping into my soul and I was floating down the glen in a state of oneness, reverence and unity. Holding Harry's hand, I felt the flow of energy between us from our hearts.

Come to the seat and share your medicine, Louise, the trees whispered as we made our way down, down, down.

And there, at the end of glen, was indeed a large piece of slate made into a seat. As with all ceremonies now, I brought out my wand, which I had felt the need to bring because of the synergies. Being tipped off by a random woman on Instagram was enough of a nudge to tell me this was a call to service. I let Gaia guide me, setting aside my ego. The girls watched me smiling. Harry, too, was looking on with love. The prayer became a spell…

For all whom sit upon this seat together, may they feel true love and unity, may all fears be transformed into faith and all doubt into love, if that is what they desire.

I saw ghosts of couples parted sitting on the seat and then coming together as they walked away. My heart overflowed. It was all I had ever wanted to see in the world: people coming together in unity, love and joy. I felt the ceremonies were part of weaving together again the wounds of disconnectedness in the world that were separating humans from each other.

As I got up to leave, the trees sent another nudge to turn around and take my gift. There on the ground was a huge stone, bigger than my hand, in the shape of a heart. *Wow!* I picked him up, the dark grey slate shining almost iridescent as the sun glimmered through the canopy.

"You are beautiful. You are so big I can't possibly accept you!"

But I felt the nudge.

Take him. He is your gift and will serve you well.

Overwhelmed at the size and sense that he was too special for me, too much, I held him close to my heart and had a feeling that he truly belonged to this ancient glen, that he was special to the fairy folk. Not bearing to imagine him stuck in my house away from this magic, I promised we would work together and then I'd return him.

"One day, Puck, I will bring you back to this glen, return you home to your family, and you will hold the medicine of the earth chakras to share with your people, so we can awaken into a new world."

I had no real understanding of my words, but he did.

***

When the car began to limp again, we were still about 10 miles from Loch Fyne where Jesus had called us to perform ceremony. I remained calm, pulled out my mesa and played with my kuyas, running my hand over them. *Which one of you can help me find out what's wrong?* I wondered. The kuya from Egypt, the one that held 'faith', came to me. I held it and blew the hucha that was in my body into the medicine stone, then gazed out the window while I waited, trying to remain faithful that we were where we needed to be.

The going was slow, but the car got us to the edge of the loch, eventually, and I was convinced it would be fine once I had performed the ceremony. However, a fearful energy meant neither Harry nor the kids felt like getting out of the car with me to be part of the ceremony. I had to go this one alone.

The waters lapped close to my feet, the sound deep, heavy and grounded. These waters knew this place and welcomed me here. I raised my arms in the air and the mist of the loch fell onto the crystal of my wand. Prayers flowed and I made the offering of a kuya that I had been gifted by the shaman at a ceremony by a waterfall in the jungle near Machu Picchu, the same day I had released the salamander. That shaman had gifted me the 'star keeper rites' and this was the medicine of the kuya. It had travelled with me to all the waters: from Titicaca to San Luis, Shasta, Yukon and Lake Louise.

The ancient light energy was sent out to the waters and I made the connection. I let the cold come into my body, resisting the urge to leave and get back to my family. I stayed a little longer than was comfortable, the cold wet mist on my face and hands sending shivers into my bones.

Then a heron flew overhead, affirming I was on the right path. I was so happy to see her.

"Thank you," I whispered.

The car did not fire up as I had expected, and we had no choice other than to crawl over the mountain roads at 25 mph for an hour until we reached Loch Lomond with the intention of calling the AA and getting towed home. As we got into town, anger took hold of me and I opened up my mesa and picked up my Christ consciousness kuya again.

"I've come all the way to bloody Scotland and done what you wanted. I always do what you want! Now I want you to get us to the Lake District and then home safe as planned!" I said.

As before, I got Harry to blow his fear into the stone and instantly the car took off like a rocket! It went 25 mph to 70 mph in seconds!

I laughed hysterically with a mix of both shock and expectation.

"It's a miracle a real miracle! Thank you Jesus. Oi, Harry say thank you to Jesus" I joked.

"Thank you, Jesus!" Harry replied with a smile.

The whole way to the Lakes, I could see Harry's logical mind ticking over, trying to figure out how this miracle car malarkey could have happened.

"Look, babe, I get it. You want to make sense of the miracle, but can you just enjoy it and accept it now for what it is – something reminding us to hold faith? We are not victims to the universe. We can command the energy when it's in alignment with our purpose," I said – more to remind myself than to tell him.

We did indeed comand the car to work so we could enjoy our break away, and it did get us home safe, just. The engine began to fail one mile from home and its destination after our trip, was the scrap yard!

***

CHAPTER 16

Third Eye Chakra Magical Mystery Tour

The summer came and there was a sense of waiting for something to happen.

"Babe, I look at you and see you've lost your passion. You don't seem to care about getting out there and getting work," I said to Harry one morning.

I could see on his face he didn't welcome this challenge, but it was my truth and I could not go on ignoring it.

"I'm fed up with leading. You're not doing things for fear of what others will think of you. You're not finding the courage to pick up the phone and call your old clients. I need you to take control and get a handle on things, Harry. Take responsibility."

He didn't say anything and stared forward at his computer. I heard blame in my voice and I caught it.

"Fuck, Harry, I'm sorry. I'm projecting onto you. I need to step up too. I need to do all the things I am telling you to do. Fuck, babe, I'm lost as well. What I see in you is in me."

Still Harry didn't say anything. He just stood up and left the house. And he didn't come back for hours. This had never happened before, not like this. I had brought the shadow to the surface for us both.

I knew Harry blamed me in some ways for him losing business while we travelled the world. Now here I was talking about shutting my business down to start afresh and just become a writer. Harry felt I had given away my power and wasn't showing up because I was scared of what people thought. And I felt the same about him. We were both licking our wounds and hiding from the world! He had to shift... and I had to shift too.

When Harry returned later, I was in the kitchen making dinner when he grabbed me from behind, spun me around and hugged me so tightly.

"Lou, I spend my entire life worrying about what people will think. I'm desperately shy. I tell the girls off for making noise in a coffee shop assuming it will upset someone. I say yes to you and everyone else just to make life easy. And this is not doing me or anyone any favours. I don't want to be this way anymore. I'm stopping myself from growing out of fear! You're right."

I didn't need to be right. I just needed him to see that we both needed to grow up. We had to stop waiting for things to happen for us and take charge of our lives. I knew he had digested all I'd said, because he was no longer being defensive, but contemplative. And I knew this had happened because I'd owned my side of the road too. I wasn't blaming. I was sharing what I saw and admitting my part in it. And Harry had truly seen that I was not in this for conflict or for winning. I was in this for growth.

That night I dreamed a big dream, where Archangel Gabriel was calling me, showing me that he lived through King Arthur. He told me I must come to him. In my dream, I was in a museum, but running out of time, trying to find a church down a cobbled street. There was a king with herbs and a huge plinth but a missing statue. Adam who had come to Egypt with us was there. He was Archangel Gabriel's brother and he was telling me I had to go to Shaftesbury.

I awoke with that same sense of deep knowing that I had to go. And I had to go right away.

***

The divine duo

Harry was already up and working when I woke. I stood in the doorway of his office in his pyjamas.

"I've had a really big dream, babe. I don't fully understand it, but it was a call to Shaftesbury. I need to go, but you don't need to come with me. I don't want to stand between you and your work. I'm aware that yesterday you said you always just say yes to me for an easy life and I respect that you have gone all around the world with me. So you don't need to come, but I do need to go. Either today or tomorrow," I told him.

Harry paused and said genuinely, "I want to come with you. I really do. Is there any way we can go tomorrow morning so I can work on this today and tonight?"

I was desperate to go right away, but knew it was right that he came, so I agreed. We decided to make it a mini holiday for the girls, and it popped into my mind that we could go to the Avebury stone circle on the way. Harry smiled his warm calm smile, the one he gave when he was about to honour my call even though he didn't understand, and suggested we take the camper.

"We can set off at 6am and get to Avebury for sunrise, then head to Shaftesbury so you can do your thing, then camp at Glastonbury. We haven't been away all summer and the girls will love it," he said.

I couldn't believe how willing and supportive he was being. I was so grateful for him, for everything we were, for his open heart, for his open mind, for his trust in me. Even though my thing wasn't his thing, he *wanted* to come. And on some level, I sensed that he had always known beyond mind, beyond ego, that actually this *was* his thing.

***

Shaftesbury adventure

I had never been to Shaftesbury, nor did I have any idea how this activation was going to take place. All I knew was that it was about an hour from Glastonbury and I felt the pull to go there after. I didn't know what it looked like or where I needed to go in the town. I looked it up, searching for the church I had seen in my dream and found out that there was an old abbey, which had been built in 888 AD. I touched my necklace, in which was engraved the angel number 888, the number of prosperity and abundance. I knew exactly where we needed to go.

When I told Harry, he laughed and kissed my forehead then went back to his work. I was back to being that innocent child again, guided by wonder, excitement and joy, moment to moment. I had missed her. I had missed her so much.

Next morning, we loaded the van at 6am. We were going on an adventure and it was exciting. I'd packed my wand and mesas, and wondered what kuya I would need to offer, but something was telling me that I wouldn't be required to share my medicine stones with this activation; that I could do this another way. The energy around this call felt different, maybe because this chakra was unusual in that it moved in accordance with the change of aeon. The chakra would only reside on my lands for a few more decades until the Age of Aquarius was fully anchored. Something told me to check the moon charts before we left.

"Oh my God, no wonder we had a crazy blow-up yesterday. Today is a full moon solar eclipse!"

"Of-fucking-course it is!" Harry replied, catching my vibe.

I wandered into my healing room to check all the windows before leaving and reality went into slow motion. Something made me look at the huge pile of stones I had now collected in this room, and I picked up the alabaster from Sakkara in Egypt, recalling the moment when I knew that these white stones would be important for some unknown point in the future. I was surprised to see I had some left, as I thought I had given it all away in medicine pouches during the shamanic courses I'd run. It seemed it was time for these two remaining pieces to do their work and I shoved them in the back pocket of my jeans. Then I noticed my despacho boxes, full of sweets, rice, coloured shells, candles and various bits that I used to make offerings to the Earth.

"Okay, universe, I hear you. Despacho ceremony at Avebury it is!"

EARTH CHAKRA SHAMAN

Before we fired up our camper, I took one last look out at the garden and was urged to take cuttings from the bay trees and sage bushes. Without any real knowing why, I had learned to follow the nudges of intuition.

Our bright orange VW camper, rusty and temperamental from his 47 years, started without a cough or splutter. The kids curled up in the back, wrapped in blankets, hiding their sleepy faces from the morning chill. I went into third gear to tackle the hill out of the village and whispered to the van, "Get us there and back safely, Sunny Nesta."

I felt so present in the warmth of just being, not thinking, watching the moment as it unfolded, listening to the girls giggling, observing the beauty of the passing trees. I sensed the Divine guiding us and felt a deep connection to all, even our old van.

We made great time getting to Avebury stone circle but realised when we arrived that we didn't have any cash for the car park. We chanced it, somehow knowing we wouldn't get a ticket. We were on a mission after all. The pathways of ease to our destination were open.

Wrapped up in waterproof trousers and raincoats, we wandered into the huge field of ancient stone rings. Harry squeezed my hand. He felt the ancientness of this huge Neolithic henge too. Unlike Stonehenge, we could go up to the stones and touch them. From previous visits, we each had our own favourite stones, so for a while, we wandered off, giving each other space to place our heads on them, speak with them and be in stillness to feel their energy. I loved to just listen and sing back the songs they would put into my mind.

I found a place in the middle of the circle against one of the smaller stones and began to create a despacho offering to Mother Earth. In my box, there were my bay leaves, sweets, sugar and all sorts of nuts and beans. I created a small circle of beautiful patterns and blew all my love and gratitude into the elements of the world, for animals, food and family to honour the energy of the lands. I completed the small circle by covering it with the sage from my garden and then remembered the alabaster in my pocket. I took a piece out, broke it into two, and put one half in the centre of the offering. The offering was subtle. True shamanic medicine would be invisible to anyone passing by. People could walk right past without even knowing the medicine brewing within. That evening, when the tourists had gone and only the druids and fairy spirits were about, maybe the birds and the animals would be enticed by the sweetness of it and have their own full moon feast.

On our drive to Shaftesbury, I was awash with love and blessings as the sun broke through the morning drizzle, bringing blue skies and warmth. I was touched by the pure beauty of England's rolling hills, our own sacred lands, and became deeply aware of how ideal the moment was. The sun now shining, tunes playing, kids laughing and Harry looking at me in *that* way with love and pride, our little orange van tootled through the lanes with ease, ravens, kestrels and kites following us. Everything was perfectly perfect. All was as it was meant to be. And all was well.

***

Let your dreams guide you to Gaia's call

Shaftesbury was the most English town I had ever seen. From the top of a hill, we looked down on beautiful cobble streets, just like the ones I'd seen in my dream. Outside the old abbey ruins was a sundial and a view of the sweeping English countryside of Somerset, Dorset and the Cotswolds. It was sacred here. I could feel that.

I wondered if I was to do a despacho earth offering here too, like I had in Avebury. The inner guidance said to go into the abbey. In the entrance, my heart fluttered again. It was exactly like walking into the small museum that I had also seen in my dream. I tried to process the symbolism. This place was the same in so many ways, not the layout, but the *feel*. It felt so right to be here on every level and I was over-awed.

I approached the two friendly-looking older ladies at the information desk.

"Hi there, I was wondering if you could help me?"

They seemed warm and open, so I continued.

"I had a dream about this place. There was a king with herbs in his hands like medicine."

One of the ladies smiled and told me that the abbey had been built by King Alfred the Great. He had gifted it to his daughter, who became the first ever abbess. The abbey was known for growing herbs for medicine.

"If you take an audio guide, it will show you around the infamous herb garden," she suggested.

As if I was floating in the dream itself, I opened the door to the old abbey ruins, now a stunning walled garden. Everything was alive! Leaving Harry and the girls to their own devices, I listened to the voice through my headphones, talking all about the herbs. In front of me grew more varieties than I could imagine, and above them, a huge statue of a king, identical to the one in my dream, that took my breath away.

The king's face was gentle and beautiful, like my grandfather's. I felt instant love. This was King Alfred the Great, not King Arthur, but I knew there would be a connection I didn't yet understand. I didn't need to figure anything out. I could feel his energy. He was a good king, a protector, who carried the same energy as King Arthur and Angel Gabriel, from my dream. I wondered if these men were incarnations of each other. How else could it be possible that they were all coming up in my dream together? Though I could not work it out, I reminded myself that my mind was not as old as my soul.

I wandered the garden, drawn towards an old stone cross that would have once been the altar of the abbey before it had been burned down by Henry VIII's Church of England. As I approached, something on the audio made my ears prick up.

"The centre of this stone cross was once filled with alabaster but was removed for research purposes."

My heart leapt. Oh my God! I reached again for the alabaster in my back pocket. I held a piece in my hands and knelt at the cross, my head bowed and my mesas in front of me.

"I fly blindly on the wings of the Divine. Earth's whispers lead me in time to the oath that I align. Great Spirit, Gaia, I come in service with a gift to activate the third eye chakra on this full moon solar eclipse. I feel you here right now and I bring this offering from Egypt, so your energy can radiate into the cosmos, activating the field that will bring a higher level of consciousness to all on Earth. I give thanks."

I wanted to place the alabaster in the centre of the cross, but I would have looked too conspicuous. There was fear within me. *What if I am seen? What if I get caught doing something I shouldn't? What if I don't leave it in the right place or the gardener moves it?*

This felt so big. The familiar feeling of responsibility fell into the mix. *I will fail my mission. I will get this wrong.* I had to deliver the gift to the third eye chakra of the Earth, not with fear but with the same childlike innocence, wonder, reverence and love I had met all the earth chakras. This was my superpower. This was why I was called.

I found a crack in the stone's base and placed the offering inside of it. Feeling the movement of the Earth and the sacredness of the moment, I gave thanks again and prayed for a while. Little did I know, this activation was far from complete and entwined with other lands. There would be more to come.

High on life, I floated back out of the abbey, content to hold hands with Harry, watch the girls playing and wander the cobble streets, knowing I had been here before many lifetimes ago.

***

Aquarian aeon activation

"I can't believe I brought that alabaster," I mused, as we parked up in the campsite at Glastonbury that afternoon. "Alabaster must be some sort of activating crystal or something. If it covered the Pyramids, surely it's some form of communication to the stars, like the crystal you get in a crystal radio."

"You're probably right, babe," Harry answered, unquestioningly.

I lay on the grass for a while, my heart open as I listened to the girls chatting away to our new campsite neighbours, smiling at the bliss all around. I felt Harry lie down next to me and slip his hand into mine. I opened my eyes and turned my head to look at his beautiful face. I gasped. All around us were dragonflies.

"The gift of transformation, flow and rebirth," I whispered in reverence for the miracle.

The evening sun beamed down on us as we walked up the side of the Tor. There was a festival vibe in the air as we passed people meditating on rocks and couples cuddled up in their own space. We headed towards the sound of drums coming from the top. Everyone was anticipating a beautiful solar eclipse this evening, and later there would be a full supermoon. *How much more magical can this get?* I thought inwardly.

I found a ledge on the west side of the Tor, looking out to the setting sun, and chuckled to myself at my blissful innocence that had not known it was happening. Once again, divine guidance had led me to where I needed to be, when I needed to be there. There was no 'figuring it out'. How wonderful to know that something bigger than me was in charge. The less my mind knew, or my ego thought it knew, the more the Divine could flow through me, doing work from a much higher place. I was merely the instrument. The vessel of the Divine.

Under the eclipse, I made my offerings to the lands with a despacho, bringing sweets, beans, rice, each a representation of my gratitude for the work I had been called to do, for the Earth, for humanity, for a new level of consciousness. I added the last sprigs of sage from the garden onto the despacho and then remembered I had another piece of alabaster, from the one I had broken in half. I placed this in the middle too.

As I did, the world began to spin inside me. I felt my energy vibrate. The sounds of the drums were taking me into the mystic. I was expansive and could feel the energy of all the sacred places I had been, all the chakras awakening. As if I had plugged into some great grid, they recognised me and their energies ran to me, their energies meeting together and rushing up my roots into my belly. The sounds of the didgeridoo were playing somewhere on the Tor now, a remembrance of a distant world and a reminder that I was anchored. Uluru, Shasta, Machu Picchu and Lake Titicaca, Denali, the Great Pyramids all vibrated into my soul.

I felt the Rainbow Serpent rise, coming into my body and flowing into my head. Her eyes became my eyes. *Oh my God. This is what it has all been about. It's all connected. And Lake Louise said I am the portal.* Here, finally, I knew what she meant. Through my own eyes, I looked out to the lands and a grid of sorts: a triangle between Shaftesbury, Glastonbury and Avebury, a holy trinity. I believed the alabaster in each location was communicating each with the others, activating energy, acting as some sort of connection of the energy flow between the sites, through me, and into the grid to fully activate the third eye chakra.

I felt movement and the third eye chakra of the Earth shifted, shook almost. The energy could flow more freely. A new activation had taken place for both the heart and the third eye chakra of the Earth. This unity had been bonded.

It was beyond my mind's understanding. I was a mortal in my body, but my immortal soul had no doubt what she was doing. I rejoiced in the knowing, honouring the wonder with my tears. I had never really understood what I was doing, yet dutifully showed up to do whatever was required at the time. I had always done what Gaia, God, the universe, the guides had asked. I wept at the blessing, the magic and the joy, then thanked the lands, feeling the solar eclipse come to a close.

***

Oracle confirmation

Bella was off running around the tower, and when we wandered to the other side of the Tor and found her on the south-facing opening, she was looking at the ground and talking to an old man in a high-viz jacket who was holding a can of cider. From first glance, I could not quite work him out. His face was friendly enough, he was a little drunk, and overall, he seemed harmless, though clearly bemused by my little girl asking him a stream of questions.

On the ground were thousands of flying ants and they appeared to be dying.

"What's happened to them?" Bella asked.

"I've been coming here for years and I've never seen such a thing," the guy replied.

"Will they die?"

"I don't know. I sense they have lost their natural path somehow," he said.

"Why don't they fly where they need to go?" Bella persisted.

"I don't know, but there is a portal to another world right where we're standing, so maybe that's how they got lost. They say if you spin around and around and around, you can go through the gates to the other world right in this very spot," he grinned.

Curious at the sight and at Bella striking up a conversation with this stranger, I knew I had to speak to him too.

"Hey, I'm her mum," I introduced myself. "She loves chatting to anyone!"

"Ah, she's alright," he smiled.

"Do you come here a lot?" I asked, looking to get beyond Bella's questioning.

"Yeah, I live not far from here. I used to live in the cottage at the bottom of the Tor, but it can be a bit intense living right in the centre, y'know?"

"Yeah, I get that," I replied. "We come here a lot, when she calls us. We've just come from Shaftesbury. Do you know much about that area?"

Some part of me felt he would have answers for me or something to share that explained what it was I was doing. I longed to talk with someone who understood what I was doing, share my stories, find answers to the mystery of my missions.

"No, love, never been myself."

Disappointment hung over me, as I noticed I was still searching for a father figure to take me under his wing, share his wisdom and tell me how proud of me he was. I had got myself all the way around the planet. I knew what I was doing, even if I didn't fully understand it in my mind. And yet that old wound still came up.

"What did you do over in Shaftesbury? Is it as beautiful there as it is here?" I could sense he wanted to move on from the awkward conversation and was just being polite.

"Well, I work with the earth chakras. Do you know much about them?"

It was still strange for me to articulate it, but then I saw the man's face turn from awkward-yet-polite to warm-and-interested.

"Come with me," he said.

I followed him to a huge group of people, the ones playing the drums and the didgeridoo.

"These are my friends," he said indicating the crowd and passing me his can, "Here hold this."

He began rummaging through his bag. As I waited to see what he was doing, I took in the people around. They smiled and greeted us, and one got up to give me a hug! They were my kind of people, I decided, young and old, all colours, all ages.

"Thanks so much for your music," I said to the didgeridoo man. "It was beautiful when I was meditating. I could feel Australia with me and I'm so grateful for that."

"Great to know it's appreciated," he replied.

The high-viz guy got back up from his bag holding a pack of cards, which he started shuffling. I could see the white cards had fine delicate golden line drawings on them.

"They wanted to come here today. I had no idea why. They're really old. Twenty years ago, when I lived in the cottage, someone put them through my door. I haven't picked them up for years but for some reason I did today," he said. "They're worth a fortune now. They don't make them anymore. First of the oracle cards. Not like the ones you get these days. Last I looked, you could only buy this set on eBay for £500," he chuckled.

He stopped shuffling, pulled a card and handed it to me.

"This is for you," he said grinning. "This is why they wanted to come here today."

It was old indeed. Nothing like oracle cards today. The white card had what looked like a golden hand-drawn picture of the Earth with criss cross lines and circles joining them up like a grid. Underneath the image, in bold golden letters, it said:

LEY LINES (POWER SPOTS REACTIVATED)

My heart beat hard as I flipped the card back over and read the short paragraph in golden writing. There was my answer in golden writing.

"The Earth is waking up! I join with others in using my powers of awareness to reactive light centres around the planet."

In total shock, I just stared at him.

"I knew you were a messenger. I knew it," I said at last, when I found my words.

I was so paralysed that I couldn't even throw my arms around him like I wanted to. I read the card again, aloud this time.

"Oh my God! This means there are others like me!" I sang, delighted and relieved that I was not alone. "Do you mind if I take a photo?"

"Keep it. It's yours."

"I can't keep it! Your deck is worth so much money! It's so rare," I insisted.

"It's never about money, love. I was guided to bring it today. It's for you! I'm glad you got the answers you were looking for," he replied.

My heart swelled and I hugged him tight. When I let him go, he looked down at the girls and fanned the pack for them.

"Now then, I think you need one too."

I was overwhelmed by his generosity. Harry put his arm around me, enjoying the usual mystical weirdness unfolding.

Bella took a card with a picture of stars on a blue background that said:

STAR CHILD (SEED)

Her description read, "I am here from the stars to birth a new planet into light."

Then Avalon picked a card with an angel on it:

ANGELICA (ANGELIC REALM)

Her explanation said simply, "I move into the angelic realm. I acknowledge who I am on this plane."

The girls were delighted and I could not have put it more perfectly myself. We thanked him and went to leave, but he looked at Harry, like all men looked at Harry, with love and respect.

"I feel you must take one too, mate."

The card he pulled for Harry had the words:

WHITE LIGHT (END OF THE TUNNEL)

The words of his card said, "The purest white light I have ever seen now shines before me. My heart desires with all of its being to join with the light. We become one!"

As we hugged more and began to say our goodbyes, the older man turned to the girls.

"Make sure you run barefoot down the Tor to connect with the Earth."

Then I watched as the girls whipped off their shoes and floated down the grassy banks of the heart chakra of the Earth.

***

Third-Eye Activation
Innocence & Inner-Sense, Intuition & Knowing

I call upon the sacred union,
the cauldron and the cross,
this Gaia symbol codes
crystalline-embossed.

I call upon the eagle and the condor,
the Spirit and the Science.
Aquarian Age, awaken.
Divinity is of this essence.
The shaston-glaston marriage:
the structure and the flow.

May I always follow intuition
to give, receive and grow.
Whispers from the grounds of Gaia
and God and Heaven above,

EARTH CHAKRA SHAMAN

Jesus, Mary, Arthur and Guinevere,
herbs and medicine of love.

May the blessing of the third eye chakra
open up my knowing,
whisper me back home
and water the love I am sowing.

***

CHAPTER 17

Listen to your Spirit Guides

The King's reminder

*L*ucy was the most unlikely of reiki students. She had only learned because I had suggested that she did the training to understand the energy before working for me. Lucy had a logical mind and would try to 'figure out' the reiki energy. She was private about her connection and reluctant to share with anyone outside of our community that she could do reiki. She would joke about it being weird and crazy, saying it wasn't really her thing, but I knew, and she knew I knew, that she was more connected to source and visions than she liked to admit.

So, it was unusual when, one Wednesday night, she asked to practice doing a reiki attunement on me. It was a sporadic idea on her part and the idea made me smile. Maybe it was an inner nudge to be a messenger or maybe she really did want to practice her attunement skills.

As soon as Lucy laid her hands on my shoulders, I felt myself ask the reiki to take me into worlds I loved and for completion of my peace with Jen. And then I felt myself sink into deep surrender, no longer the teacher, but the receiver. This energy was different and flowed into me fast, sinking me deeply and quickly.

I saw gold and red light everywhere and became conscious of two male energies behind Lucy. She moved to the front of my body, putting master reiki symbols into my third eye, that activated the passing on of the reiki gift from one person to another. Then I went beyond this world.

The King regarded me from his chair, a small thin desk between us, as if I was in his office. Jesus stood behind him, which confused me. I could not understand their ranking. Who was more important? Were they one? Who was he? The energy was so powerful, maybe this was God himself?

I could see the King was frustrated with me for not doing what I was meant to do, and I was sorry. I felt like a daughter who had disappointed her father. Though I kept apologising, he loved me and was not judging me, but I could feel that he wanted me to succeed in my mission. His frustration was with my wallowing and lack of self-respect, for dwelling on Jen and missing my opportunities and gifts. And I still had not produced the book he required of me.

I begged the King to help me, but he wanted me to learn how to help myself and didn't want to bail me out. He showed me that I was meant to navigate this issue with Jen myself and that I had been wasting time trying to reconnect bonds that had been severed.

"Please, father, release what is holding me back. Please can you help me."

The King indicated his difficulty in having to do this for me.

Louise, you should by now be able to release this yourself. I am now forced to do this for you, because you have not been able to get there yourself.

Looking at me with a non-judgmental yet stern expression, he wrote on two pieces of paper. He threw them across the desk towards me. On the paper was a wish or command, some sort of magic spell that he had done. It released something inside of me that meant I could now access what I needed to get my first book going, while the other was all I would need to be in service to the call of activating the Earth's grid going forward.

Remember you are special, Louise. That is the energy that brought you here. Knowing you are all special is what powers your wonder, the wonder with which you must write the book. This book will change thousands of lives.

With the King's departing words echoing in my mind, I was back in the healing room and Lucy looked shocked. Before I could say anything, she was desperate to tell me her experience.

"There was a king and he's really pissed off with you, Lou!"

"Yeah, I know. He talked to me," I replied.

"You have to write this book," Lucy said.

And we both sat in dumbfounded silence. I was ready to write my first book.

***

Having lunch in the kitchen a few days later, I heard Lucy's laughter from the next room. She was on the phone to someone. Her laugh made me smile. She had become a good friend to Harry and me over the last year, while she'd been living at our home to help out, but she was also so willing to learn and tell me straight-up what I needed to hear. She walked into the room, beaming.

"Soooo... your king has been to see my mum!"

"Your mum?" I repeated, frowning. I had never met Lucy's mum but I was sure she had no idea what I did. Lucy didn't tend to share with her any of the batshit crazy that went on in our world.

"Yep, she just called to say that a king came to her in a dream. He was cross and wanted you to write a book."

"Shit!" I laughed, slightly unnerved. "Did you tell her about our visions before he came to her?"

"God no! Why would I do that?"

I laughed. Nothing surprised me anymore, but I also took his nudge seriously. I had to keep my promise of writing. I had to show up, stop hiding. It was time for me to rise and take my place. How could I empower others to rise up in their own unique soul service if I was not doing so myself?

I found myself in a semi-unconscious state, pulling on my trainers. Before I knew it, I was running alongside the waters of my own land, the river. The rain began. Huge raindrops fell on my face, reminding me of the rains in the jungle in Peru, and as it dripped down my neck, I recalled the rains at the Yukon river.

I had to write this first book of my personal awakening, the journey of healing oneself, before I could even begin to tell the stories of healing the Earth Chakras. I ran and ran and ran. I felt strong. I had never felt such fierceness before. I ran off the victim in me. I ran fast and hard, in time to a drumbeat in my chest. I ran to awaken the warrior within. Lion ran alongside me. Jaguar ran with us too. My guides were present, though not moving, almost a hologram in front of me. They indicated solely that I was not alone. They just wanted me to say yes, to resume my rightful place in the order of things.

Time to say goodbye to human chains, the crucifixion of myself, the entrapment of my own mind. I had to be brave enough to show up. To dance the dance with the Divine and trust she would guide me.

***

The beginning of the end

"I need to go to Glastonbury. I need to write. I have to start my book and keep my promise to the King," I said to Harry, as I returned from the river, soaked from head to toe and covered in mud.

"Go, babe. Do what you need to do," Harry said, supporting this shift in me.

When I arrived in Glastonbury, I realised I'd been in such a tizz that I'd forgotten my bags, so I had to buy a new dress. Buying new clothes was not something I did very often at all, but this dress was like a new beginnings dress – long and floaty – and I loved it. I was changing. I was stepping into worthiness.

For three days, I sat in the corner of a cafe drinking herbal tea and eating only one raw meal a day to keep my body and mind clean. I watched the locals of the town meeting and greeting each other. And I did what I had promised. I began to write.

I wanted to teach how anything was possible, about love, about divine union, about awakening to the magic and the wonder. There was always a process, but sometimes we had to navigate the dark times to get the wisdom. I wanted to inspire people to have the commitment and courage to show up for something beyond the conditioned self, to welcome ego deaths and learn to dance with the universe. It was about having to honour the hard times and the great times and show up even when it could mean failure and rejection. It was in this realisation that I began to listen to myself. I had to write the first book before I could write about the earth chakras, because we don't get called until we have done the inner work. And I want people to be called. I want the whole world to be listening to their divine special unique soul purpose and have the courage to walk it.

On my final day in Glastonbury, there was a glow across the Tor. I looked up and recalled the words of the old man we'd met who had pulled oracle cards for us and told the girls to always go there barefoot. I pulled off my boots, hitched up my dress, slung my laptop bag over my shoulder and hiked up the Tor with more ferocity than past visits. I climbed with power and certainty, a smile so big I could not contain it.

As I climbed the west side, I was not once breathless. It was as if something was lifting me. I scrambled up the slope by the side of the steps, and as I got closer to the top, words of a new song came through my mind. I spoke to them aloud.

> *I am a wild woman. I cannot be tamed.*
> *I am the Divine Mother. My love is not contained.*
> *I am the writer, the wisdom of my soul.*
> *I am the listener that sees me whole.*
> *I am the rivers that guide me to gold.*

I am the wind whispering truths untold.
I am the earth that nurtures and grows.
I am the fire shining in the shadows.
I am the birds bringing messages and wonder.
I am the friend reaching out when I fall under.
I am the mountain that calls my name.
I am the consciousness that ignites my flame.
I am the goddess that brings compassion.
I am the love and that is my passion.

Tears from the wind had dried on my face when I got to the top and I was now breathless, but excited. I had forgotten how I loved to feel this way, without a care in the world, bare arms, bare feet, the wind blowing my hair. Wild! I stood overlooking Somerset, these lands I loved so much, and stretched my arms wide to send love to them, knowing that near where I stood was the veil of worlds I could not see but knew were part of me. Behind that veil were my guides, working with me to help me complete this mission.

A woman came up to me and said how beautiful and happy I looked. She offered to take my photo. I was delighted.

"I would love to capture this moment, actually. Thanks!"

This was the lion returning to her heart lands and regaining her roar. Ready for the next part of her quest.

***

CHAPTER 18

Leading a Sacred Journey to Egypt

Any pilgrimage, I had begun to understand, was a journey not just over the land on which we travel, but into ourselves. The gift comes from the challenges within and without, from getting to that place, and from how we overcome and grow. It is our growth that we bring to the sacred sites. When we arrive, there is a shift within us. We have evolved. We hold a code. We gift our growth to the grid, the great grid of Gaia, her interconnected web, the energetic structure of her immortal energy.

At Mount Shasta, I was told that a shaman takes people on a pilgrimage to a place of power. It is the shaman who transfers the power of that place to those on the journey; this is part of the shamanic healing. From direct experience, I knew any human could turn up to a sacred site. Whether the life force opened to that human was another matter. This is why some people rock up at sacred mountains and climb them with no understanding of the sacredness of the lands on which they walk. They do not vibrate on the same level of consciousness. Their integrity is out of sync with the place. A shaman can meet the energy where it is.

On the other hand, I deeply believe it is our own consciousness, reverence and understanding of reciprocity, of giving our gifts and then being open to receive that opens the veil and the medicine of the lands. This is not unique to sacred lands, but my destiny was to bring people back to the earth chakras to be part of the activations so they could share their medicine with the lands and receive its blessing.

The chakras felt like an information point to me, somewhere we would download our human lessons and growth like an upgrade on a universal computer. The more we visited these sites with reciprocal reverence, the more it felt that the chakras were expanding and that we humans were expanding. This was what the Age of Aquarius was about: expansion of consciousness, communication and connection to the earth and each other.

***

Discernment and responsibility

The pressure of planning the Egypt trip was one thing, but the responsibility of ensuring my group of 10 students were safe and happy and their experience transformational was quite another! I had done all I needed to do as far as hotels, tours and guides were concerned. I had organised the vision quest in the desert with my brother Etman. I knew I could handle the responsibility to lead people. However, a couple of weeks before we were due to leave, I got a call from my guy on the ground, Nicolas.

"Lou, yesterday 50 men were led into the Oasis in the Western Desert. They were ambushed and have all been killed. The whole area is closed and we're on high alert all over Egypt," he said solemnly.

My heart sank in sadness for Egypt, for the lives lost and for the Earth. On top of the sadness, there was fear in me. The ambush had happened not far from where our three-night desert retreat was due to take place.

For the next few days, Nicolas and I played with all sorts of ideas, including moving the whole trip to other parts of Egypt. Even that came with blocks, though. All the deserts in Egypt were closed. Every retreat centre shut down. All the roads across the county on red alert. And no tourists were allowed to go anywhere. The only option seemed to be visiting the pyramids then staying in hotels by the Red Sea, but that was so touristy and this was not a holiday. This was a sacred journey.

The more I meditated on it, the more I knew something was unfolding that I did not yet know. I could trust in the flow, but my greatest fear was letting down the group and not being of best service to them. Could *they* trust in the flow as much as I did?

I put it to the group and we talked. I was honest and vulnerable with them, sharing that there was now no plan or anything set in place, and offered a full refund to anyone who didn't want to go. Every one of them said they trusted in the flow and they trusted in me, which was the beautiful boost I needed to remember to trust in myself too.

Five days before departure, Nicolas called. He had been with Etman and the Bedouin guys, figuring out a way forward.

"Hey Lou, here's the latest. Etman and the tribe know these deserts. They say the attack was not on tourists. It was a government attack. Yes, the deserts are still closed, but they have said they will assure your safety and still want you to come. They will set up camp a little closer to the oasis, but far enough out that you are still in your own space."

"Do you really think this is the *responsible* thing to do?" logical Harry asked when I hung up the phone. "Taking your group to a place of terrorist attacks, making yourself vulnerable in the middle of the desert..."

I went back to the group with the new information to see how they felt about the options, offering for them to stay in a hotel close to the oasis if they didn't feel comfortable camping. They opted to make the decision when we got there.

All of us had nightmares of being attacked, being hooded, being dragged off in the night, bundled into vehicles, raped, tortured, never to see our families again. I surrendered. If that really was to be my destiny, I would face it, but I felt it wasn't going to go like that. I knew this was fear, my mind pulling together images that I had collected over the years from news snippets. I knew in my soul it was right. I knew we had to go. I knew this was where we were being called. Everything on paper said no, but my heart whispered yes. And I trusted that whisper.

***

Before I left, I received my new shamanic drum in the post and a book called *Earth Chakras* by Robert Coon that I'd bought on his website. Robert Coon was the man who had brought the concept of earth chakras to the world, and though I could not understand much of his website, other than confirming the seven chakra sites, I knew this phenomenon to be true, even without his validation because I'd been called to them. Still, I wanted to learn from him. Before buying the book, I tried to track him down, knowing I learned better directly from people, but had found no trace.

I flicked through the book now, as I packed for Egypt, and saw something called an 'activation calendar' spread over the pages where the author had listed a handful of important dates over the coming 50 years to do activations. I flicked to the page for the year 2017. There were only two dates on it. One had been back in May. And the other was in a few days from now... 11:11:17, the date I would lead my group to the pyramids.

My heart lit up. Until now, I'd danced with the fear that I was leading my group to their death, but the book fell into my hands at just the right time to help me hold faith! Everything was going to be okay and this was the validation I had been seeking, something in black and white telling me it was right.

More than anything, I loved the statement printed under the date:

"New laws and principles of the aeon of the immortal child take root and expand through the world."

I understood what this meant, not on an intellectual level, but what it meant for me. I was the epitome of the immortal child and always had been. I was the one who would play and dance, act carefree and see the world with wonder... The immortal child was still alive in me. And it was her energy that I would bring to Egypt, to the throat chakra of the Earth.

***

Pyramid problems

Lucy and I arrived in Cairo a day before the group, so I could ground into the chaos of the city, deal with my heartache and helplessness at the terrible abuse of camels and donkeys, the litter, the dirt and the pollution around the pyramids, yet also honour the vibration and aliveness. The human energy that 21 million people bring as they reside at the throat chakra of the Earth cannot be underestimated!

After a few conversations with locals, we found ourselves with an Egyptian temple healer, a wise old Egyptian man with the deepest voice that almost sang as he spoke. This was a dude who'd refined the throat chakra energy!

He understood the work I had been doing on the Earth and talked about being called to Stonehenge. My eyes lit up as he mentioned it and I knew I had to give him the piece of bluestone that my aunt had been told to send me a year before in a dream. (Bluestone being the same stone as Stonehenge.) He invited us to return for a healing with the group once they arrived.

The next morning, when all of us had gathered, we went back to see him. When we got there, the man told me he'd been guided to give me a huge piece of alabaster from an old altar in the most sacred place in Egypt. It was so powerful that I knew instantly it would play an important role in my work one day, perhaps a key to unlock answers around my journey in the future.

***

Later that morning, the group ate breakfast on a balcony overlooking the pyramids. We joined together in meditation and bonded over stories of what had brought us all together to this point. The group was as wonderful as I had hoped and I felt this experience was going to be big.

As early as 10am, I became aware of coach loads of school kids already arriving and the site getting busy. It looked like chaos, queues for miles. Nothing like the stillness I had experienced the first time I came.

"How cool would it be if we got to the pyramids at 11:11 on 11/11?" one of the group said.

"Okay, guys, I think we need to let that expectation go," I laughed, hiding my disappointment, pointing to the crowds below.

Trust in the flow, Lou. We'll be where we need to be when we need to be there, I reminded myself silently.

When Gad, the wise guide I'd had on my first trip, didn't turn up, I grew concerned. Especially when I saw the young whippersnapper who had come in his place. He was not wise and his energy was not grounded. Irritated, I knew he was the sort of guide who would hustle us into sales and not understand the spiritual call. I felt a deep responsibility to my group to provide the experience I had promised, but equally I had to trust that he had shown up for a reason.

The guide came into the complex with us, as was the law, and though I would have preferred him not to be there, I had to accept what would unfold. When I asked him to honour our silence, he had no idea what to make of the request and spoke all the way to the pyramid. The irritation in me was increasing. This was going to be a great lesson indeed!

***

At the entrance of the Great Pyramid of Giza, the guards refused to let us take in our mesas or my wand. I was surprised. I had taken everything with me the year before. The energy felt edgy, certainly a different vibe this time.

Our guide – the irritating one – came over to look after everything while we went into the pyramid. I gave him a huge smile now and let go whatever it was that had been bothering me. He was just trying to do his job, as I was, and I felt a flicker of a bond between us.

As we stepped across the threshold, one of my group checked her watch and told us, to our delight, that it was indeed 11:11. We made our way up to the King's Chamber. This was nothing like my first visit. The tiny chamber room was filled to the brim with tourists. However, we were now in a place of accepting. We enjoyed the experience. And we sang and laughed and pinched ourselves that we were in the actual pyramid! We stood with our backs against the walls in silence feeling the energy move through us.

We held hands, I closed my eyes and let the energy spin inside of my body, when I opened them again I looked at the faces of my group, these beautiful people, these shamans, healers and magical humans had such groundedness too. And this was just the beginning. I felt blessed beyond blessed.

I witnessed the energy change in the throat chakra of each member of the group. Our presence, our very being there, vibrated through my body into the earth. Tears rolled down my face. It felt like we were preparing for the journey ahead.

Exiting the pyramid, we were all exhausted by the huge energy download and needed to sit and ground. We gathered in a circle to process, but our guide was agitated and didn't want us to sit down. He pulled me aside.

"Louise, the guards told me you were meditating in the pyramid. You must not do that," he stressed.

"We were just singing and feeling the energy. What's wrong with that?" I asked.

"You can't meditate in the Great Pyramid. The guards don't like it!" he replied.

"It wasn't an issue when I came last time," I reiterated.

The guide wanted to take us out of the complex and go to the papyrus paper makers, a classic tourist trap, where guides made sales commissions.

"No!" I insisted, "We're here to see the other pyramids and the Sphinx. We need to sit and process the energy."

We were head to head. He was everything about Egypt that I despised – constant hustle, constant selling, control and refusing to take no for an answer. The temple healer had warned us of this and explained that the hustlers would distract us from our purpose. He had told us to ensure we stayed focused on our mission and for the group to go and meditate by the second pyramid, which I was determined to do.

I called Nicolas to complain. I had to ensure that my group could enjoy this time. Subsequently, he called the guide and told him to do what we wanted.

"Miss, if you want to meditate, we can go behind the second pyramid and sit there," he suggested.

I invited him to join us and he said he might, but when we got to the second pyramid, he left us to chill. Sitting here was amazing. There were no crowds at this pyramid, just peace, and it felt like the pyramid was pulling down all the frantic energy around us. A few of us took the opportunity to open our mesas and play with our stones, feeling the stillness.

Right then, a car pulled up and four policemen with guns came over.

"What are you doing? No meditation, no meditation, no meditation!"

Initially, I was frightened but then a familiar feeling came over me, like a mother who needs to stay calm and controlled when her child has fallen over.

The police made us walk back to the car park, where more police came to tell off our guide. I felt a bubble of fear building around the group and began to work on the heavy energy of the situation sending it down into the earth. A tangible calmness came over the situation. From nowhere, a policeman said, "There is nothing to worry about. You can take your group back to the car and leave the site with your guide."

***

When I told him about it later, Nicolas had never heard of such things happening.

"They like to sell the pyramids to spiritual groups for more money. They try to get £10,000 for a private viewing," he told me.

This was all about money? Wow! I felt fine about it, though, like everything was perfect and that we'd all learned to speak our truth. An adventure in itself! We had been glad to leave there, to eat a mammoth lunch and to head on to Sakkara to meet Gad, our original guide.

I was pleased to see him again and we were blessed to go into some ancient tombs that are not often open to the public. Gad was like an excited child when he saw a famous archaeologist, his hero and old teacher, coming out of the tombs.

"I can't believe he was here right at this time," Gad said, shocked.

"That's the universe, Gad!" I laughed.

We walked the long corridor of tombs, each unique and huge. The energy was so intense that one of our group decided not go in, but I was pulled down that corridor, drawn to one of the huge granite tombs. I could not move from it, and nor could Gad, and I became aware of a dream I had had the year before of being caught in a tomb and stuck between worlds. In the dream, I had been placed in the tomb alive, and had to breathe so that I did not panic and so that I could pass through the worlds effortlessly. I shared this vision with Gad now and he told me he'd also had dreams about these tombs and of being in other lifetimes. For a brief moment, we were frozen in time together, in front of this tomb, as if this particular one – out of all 20 or so tombs down there – was pulling us into its energy.

***

The Egyptian experience is different for everyone. It awakens something in each of us. And for me, it was awakening the inner child of wonder and miracles.

As we wandered around this pyramid, I talked to the group about the alabaster you could find here in the sand and how I had gifted it to the third eye chakra. But now I couldn't find any! I joked about how I had to let go of finding it and let it find me, saying this journey was teaching me so much about detachment, allowing the flow, yet also knowing when to act. As I made the comment about letting the alabaster come to me, I kicked at the sand playfully and a huge piece landed on my foot. We could not stop laughing. I was back to being intoxicated with the synergies, drunk on the wonder, awake and alive in my divine purpose. I was exactly where I was meant to be and it felt so good!

It wasn't all good all the time though. When we made our way out to the desert, it was dark and there was traffic bumper to bumper. To top it off, our bus was pulled over for a random check by police. As soon as they banged on the window, a tension came over everyone on board, another moment reminding us how far we were from our comfortable suburban lifestyles. With what had happened to us back at the pyramids as well as the killings in the desert a few weeks earlier, we had to honour the fear within all of us.

***

Desert dreaming

Seeing Etman's face was like returning home. He greeted me with open arms and embraced me like a sister. This man was my brother. He brought the protector energy and the divine masculine. It reminded me how important it was to have the balance. Harry had assured me that he knew Etman would keep us all safe and I knew this to be true.

"Welcome home, my sister. The desert has missed you."

His English had come on so much in a year! As we chatted, all my fears melted away. I knew his love and warmth would envelop the group.

EARTH CHAKRA SHAMAN

Shortly after we met Etman, the group climbed into Jeeps and drove across the night desert to our camp. From a distance, our 11 little tents, arranged in a circle, looked like lanterns lit up in a magical scene. Next to this was a huge marquee-style tent, where the Bedouin brothers cooked and slept.

The energy was delicious around the fire, and we chilled out on pillows and blankets in rich oranges and reds, surrounded by candles. The last of our fear was blown away by the desert breeze and we came home into the twinkling desert magic.

***

Overnight, I dreamed of the worlds beneath the pyramids, of other lives and of activations throughout my body. I had imagined it would be special sleeping in the desert, but this was a night of pure insight into the unseen realms.

Waking in the desert was as much a dream as sleeping there. Such stillness, not a sound, not even an aeroplane. How had we built our world so high that we could not even find peace in the night skies back home? Here, there was nothing... and how I craved nothing!

On our desert adventures that day, there were certain patches of the desert where – evidently to us – murders had taken place. A few of us could clear the spirits and set them free. This was what we could give back. That night, back at camp, I gave each of the group an attunement with the earth chakra symbols that had been gifted to me in France, representing both Gaia and God. Drumming into the dark sand dunes in ceremony was truly beautiful and far-out mystical, even for the most grounded members.

On the second day, we woke early for our vision quest and drove for hours in silence to some giant ancient mangrove caves, from a time when the Sahara Desert was under the sea. At the site, I knew I had to let each person have their own experience. In my own experience, I could feel each one of them, though not see them, but I was aware that I could commune with them if needed. I spoke with the desert and the four directions, and then I knew each member of the group was safe, and that the Bedouin brothers were patrolling the site and knew where each person was. For the next five hours, we opened ourselves up to the visions and wisdoms of the desert.

It was a powerful experience, overlooking the desert, holding space in my own little cave, that was shaped like a vagina! My entire body vibrated, like a power spot of energy, almost shaking from the intensity. My heart held so much love and peace that it was on the brink of combustion! I grounded, letting the rocks hold my body, feeling the support of the cave as I supported the sacred energy for my group.

When I looked up, I noticed a 40-foot rock overhanging the cave, which looked like the perfect face of an Egyptian goddess or Queen Nefertiti. Her long neck, cheekbones and the curve of her forehead and crown told me that she was the Queen, the stepmother of Tutankhamun, whose images I loved, though I knew little about her. Nevertheless, I knew her to be a strong representation of the divine feminine. Here, sitting in this vagina-shaped cave, looked upon by the divine feminine, I felt the power!

For a moment, strong visions came to me and I was unable to stop them. My spirit guides reassured me I was safe to receive and that my group was safe. I was taken into a membrane, as if through a birthing canal, where I was greeted by my celestial parents. I could not see their faces but I knew their energy. I had met that energy before, when I had first seen a past lifetime on a golden planet. My celestial parents embraced me and told me I needed to control my telepathy. I needed to be aware of what I was sending out. When I was ready, a teacher would come to help me with this; my galactic telepathy would grow more, but I must learn how to control it.

That afternoon, the group sat in silence and we broke our fast together. I could not give enough thanks for the sacredness of the moment, as I looked around the group, each person touched deeply by this place. Onwards, we drove to a magical lake for a sunset swim. This lake had called my soul and now I was here. Music played from the Jeeps and golden light surrounded me. I became lost in dance, in love, in laughter and in the freedom of the group as they played and swam in the waters. *We are the immortal children*, I thought, and when the Bedouin guys joined in, I realised we had now become one.

***

Universal energy of one

"Hey Malika!" Etman caught my attention.

The other Bedouin brothers had nicknamed us all, which was an endearing and beautiful gesture of acceptance.

"Show me what you do, Louise," Etman said. "I want to know and understand it, please. Can I have the same blessing as you gave everyone last night?"

"Are you sure, Etman? This is not part of your religion. I would be honoured, but I want to respect your beliefs," I responded.

I knew he had no idea what we did, but I had seen that he knew his soul. And he had recognised the same in me the first day we met.

"Yes, I understand, Malika, please show me."

We gathered around the fire that evening, with drums and song, and practiced giving and receiving the energy. The fire glowed on us as Etman closed his eyes and I lifted his hands and placed the symbols on his crown, third eye and palms. When I brought down the light of God and Gaia, his body began to vibrate, and when he opened his eyes again, they were glistening with tears. Forehead to forehead, we sat for a moment, feeling the energy blessing us both.

"Thank you, Malika, my sister," he smiled.

The energy pulsated through his palms into balls of light between his hands, and he transformed in my eyes to my six-year-old brother being shown magic for the first time. Everything in him changed. While his mind tried to process with logic what he could feel, he just gazed at me in shock.

***

That evening, it was as if all my childhood dreams came true and the most magical night of my life emerged. Other brothers learned how to send and receive energy with each other. They were mind-blown by the love and gentleness of it all. The Bedouin are relatively tactile with each other and extended those hugs to us too. As a tactile person myself, I love it when people will meet me with the same purity. The group became like a bundle of baby chicks in a nest, our nest being the desert, and we were held in the palm of Gaia's hands. She encapsulated us, holding us safely as we experienced unity under the same stars, breathing the same air, warmed by the same fire, the same water flowing through our bodies.

We sang and drummed and laughed and drank peppermint tea for hours and hours, all of us together, forehead to forehead, hand to hand, heart to heart, united. Energy flowing between us, flowing through our hands to each other.

As our desert party began to exhaust us, I lay by the fire looking up at the galaxy with tears rolling down my face. This was the world I had always wanted.

"Lou, what is that?" a distant dream voice called from the other side of the fire.

I looked up to see red lights dashing around in the sky.

"I don't know, but they are beautiful," I answered.

I watched in awe as the red galactic orbs danced in the night sky. Tiredness came over me, my eyes began to close.

"Lou, I love you," the voice called.

"I love you too, Lou," Simon called.

"I love you too, Malika," Etman said.

And one by one, like something from the Waltons, voices popped up to say "I love you" to each other, using our Egypt nicknames.

"Thank you, Gaia. Thank you, God," I whispered. "Now I truly have found my unwavering faith in you."

***

CHAPTER 19

Show Up for your Purpose

Back at home, back in my everyday reality, the mountains called again from my sleep.

Louise, it's time to write and honour your journey.

Clear as day I heard it and my eyes pinged open. No amount of negotiation was going to allow me to stay in my warm bed. I had no doubt it was Illimani, the mountain that first woke me from my sleep and called me to Peru. I felt how far I had come.

Louise, you have been guided to the earth chakras all over the world, taught to collect energy medicine to assist you on the quests ahead, and know what it is to share it with others. Medicine has been created within you. As you walk the path of wisdom, you must teach it now through your writing.

I stirred my sleepy body, letting the message of the mountain settle into my being.

Your medicine is for those who are remembering there is meaning to life beyond the material world. It is for those who realise they have a purpose and can reclaim their personal power. It is for those who know deeply that they must become the change they wish to see in the world. Those who take the journey – not just to the lands but within their own heart – will transform through their dreams. They will learn beyond ego and their transformations will be miraculous. Those with pure-hearted intentions will become the hands reaching out into the darkness for others.

I had to get up. I had been commanded by my mountain. These miracles happened to me because I would share them. It was time to begin writing.

Uluru came through then. I felt the solar plexus of the Earth awakening deep within my body. Recalling the connection I felt as I touched the red sandy cave walls, I heard her speak:

The energetic pull from my core will awaken the power inside you to manifest the dreams I have placed into your mind. Your threads have been connected to me since the day you were born into this body. Your soul carries the same essence as mine. I have been with you throughout your life, but you cannot know a stranger who is watching you from the other side. It is not until your cross and meet me that we can begin to converse. I see and feel all of you.

As she spoke, I wrote under the low bedside light.

Here on the red lands I have my own energy lines. Paths walked became crevices of the medicine. The people walked this medicine deep into the layers. Their bliss will become yours. And yours will become theirs. I am the heart of Australia. My people feed me with their honour and respect. We work together, bringing the energy of life to all the lands. The flow of my love connects to all other places near and far.

Coming to me was a gift to the Earth and to yourself. You carry my medicine now and can bring people to me. Like all beings, I too have a soul that loves to connect. I carry sadness and pain too. Yet when people come, I sing with joy, with the sound of celebration, because I awaken more. I can make anything possible for you. Speak with me and honour me, and I can make your dreams awaken in the hearts of all.

Dance upon the Earth, Louise, and sing my song. Show others how to do this too. Say yes in your heart and let me guide you. You are so loved by so many. We are here to help you. You are a channel for all the lands, Louise. You speak the language of the earth. Your family is protected and will serve in their own unique way. Your love of each other, the Earth and your life will be the inspiration for others to hear their own call.

I got up, made a cup of tea, lit a candle, opened my mesas in front of my laptop, and began writing the story of the call, the story that led to my quest, from the very beginning. I wrote and wrote about how this all came to pass. *The Awakening of the Western Woman* was coming into being.

That morning on the school run, three cars drove past with 888 on the number plate, a heron flew over, a client booked in a block of one-to-one mentoring sessions, enough to put down the deposit for my editor. Huge shifts had happened. I shut down my old website, Lucy got a job offer at an awesome company, and we agreed she would live with us rent-free for another four months, so we were square on what I owed her. Harry received a regular contract with a new client, which meant I could get my head down and write. This was the way things worked. I knew that now. When you let go of something and follow with the universe's nudges, when you are in divine service only, the universe provides.

***

The next call

I had known for over a year that this call would come. And six months earlier, it had dawned on me that I had activated six out of the seven earth chakras and my ego delighted in it! *I am so special, the chosen one, the Earth Chakra Shaman.* One day, I would be called to Tibet to Mount Kailash, the holiest mountain in the world to the Buddhists, the Bon and the Hindus. I winced at my ego's rush of excitement with deep awareness, calmed myself down with compassion and reminded my ego to step down.

The earth chakras don't call our egos. They call our spirits. We don't 'just go' to the earth chakras to say we've been. We go because we are called. That is the medicine.

Until then, I had a bigger mission: writing my first book! In early winter of 2018, I found myself in the writing cave. And the deeper I went into writing, the more I could feel a shift inside of me, realising how far I had come in my journey before I was even called to the earth chakras, how much Harry had supported me as my spiritual connection rose, and how he had feared me flying too far from him, not wanting me to change. And yet, I *had* changed. As I wrote, I could join the dots and it all made so much more sense. Wow! I had done so much work. I could see now why I had been called.

At first, it wasn't Kailash that I felt calling, but Mount Everest, even though I didn't know that Everest was in Tibet.

It began with the usual nudges. Driving past the village green, I flicked radio stations and landed on someone talking about her trip to Everest. Walking round the village, I saw the name Everest pop up on a sign. And while I knew that every device I owned, from my phone to my Sonos, was listening to everything I said or typed, I knew the images that began to pop up on my social media feeds and in random emails were no coincidence. But I was confused. Why were they all pointing to Everest? Surely Kailash was where I was supposed to go?

I looked it up on a map and realised Everest was in Tibet *and* Nepal. That's when I knew I would be going. It was affirmed the next day when Harry called me into his office to show me that a load of DJs were planning the greatest party in the world on Everest to raise money for the earthquake in Nepal. A matter of hours later, a tour company I'd signed up with the year before emailed to say they were doing a 15-day Mount Kailash and Everest tour in May 2018.

White-faced in trepidation and joy, I knew what was required of me. And I loved nothing more than clear messages from the universe.

"Harry, Kailash is happening and I have to go to Everest as well."

Maybe he had known it was coming, because he was unfazed.

"Okay, when do you need to go?" he asked.

Surprised by his ease, I replied, "I suppose in May. There's a 15-day trip at the end of the month."

"Maybe I'll have enough by then to pay for you to go," he offered.

EARTH CHAKRA SHAMAN

What? I couldn't quite believe what he was saying. Harry was willing to pay for this call? Harry? The same Harry who didn't trust the call until I manifested huge amounts of money for it. The same Harry whose heart I broke telling him my calling was bigger than him. The same Harry who had watched me rise and fall, who had seen so much mystic but still was a man of science, who loved me so much, but hated it when I left the family nest. This call had turned our world and our family inside out!

We left the conversation there. It was only January, after all, and I had a book to write.

***

The next few months I noticed a subtle energy change in Harry. Whenever I mentioned going to Tibet, he closed down. I had put all my money into editing costs for the book, so I was now kind of relying on Harry paying for me to get there. He had never made such an offer before. Our money was always *our* money with no divide. But this one rested on him.

I could feel the avoidance was fear on his part. The reality of going to Tibet was not like hopping over to Peru with a group of people who already knew me, and it wasn't like going to a Western country. I would be in the hands of people he didn't know with no phone contact. He had done his research and knew more about entering Tibet than I did. I was still riding high on the wings of the universe with unwavering faith. If I was in service, the universe would protect me and I would be fine. I had experienced this. But Harry, although watching from the sidelines, did not know the direct communication with the universe, the mountains, the waters, the spirit guides. He had seen miracles first hand, yes, but never had that direct call. He had not been on the journey that taught unwavering faith, building it block by block over years.

May arrived and we had not spoken about Tibet in three weeks. I was due to go, but nothing was booked. Unacknowledged, the issue lingered and we carried on as normal. I wrote in my journal every night clearing the fear, trusting I would be where I needed to be, and hoping he would see my strength and not fear losing me.

***

Harry's warrior steps up

We headed into London for a gig. Spring was here and we wandered through Hyde Park laughing and giggling together. I had a pint at the gig, just to keep Harry feeling like he wasn't drinking alone, but he drank a lot more than usual.

As we left, it was clear we were on different wavelengths. I was sad for both of us and it was another reminder to Harry of what he had lost – those magical nights when we would stay up until sunrise drinking, dancing and chatting about all sorts of crap, laughing away the hours just the two of us. Party Lou had left the building years ago, but he still grieved for her, no matter how much fun we had, even when we went to gigs or danced all night at drum and bass clubs. It just could not fill the gap of his wild wife, who would always ensure an entertaining evening of mayhem and debauchery!

On the train home, I chatted away to a couple, who it transpired were from Nepal.

"Oh that's so exciting. I'll be going to Nepal in a few weeks on my way to Tibet," I told them with delight.

Harry turned from the conversation.

"I'd like to see how you're going to get there," he said under his breath with an energy I'd never experienced in him.

My heart sank and I pretended not to hear as I continued talking to the man about his home. At the train station, we got into the car and Harry chattered away as if nothing had happened, but I had closed down, remaining just polite enough so as not to cause drama. I needed to process. I didn't want to be angry. I understood why he was being this way. But I also had to let go of any expectations. More so, I had to release the frustration that it always had to be someone else who got me where I needed to go. I didn't want to be indebted to anyone, least of all Harry, so why could I not just earn enough money to get myself there?

On cue, later that night, Avalon woke with a headache and I climbed into bed with her, giving her reiki and welcoming the excuse to not sleep next to Harry.

It was as if Harry knew but didn't. The next morning, he nipped out with Bella and let me and Avalon sleep in. When he got back, I was up and in the kitchen making coffee. Our eyes met and then I saw he had a plant in his hand.

"I got this for you. It's a dragon plant," he said.

"Why did you get that?" I answered coolly.

"Just had a feeling you needed cheering up, after being up with Avalon all night," he said.

He moved to put his arm around me but sensed my energy was off. Not cold, not hot. I wasn't angry or sad. I was simply detached.

"What's up, babe?" he looked at me concerned.

"Do you remember what you said to me last night?" I asked.

"No, what?"

He seemed genuinely not to know, so I told him what had happened and what he had said. His face fell.

"Oh my God, Lou. I'm so sorry. I'm so sorry," he wrapped me in his arms fully now, holding me tight as if he was frightened of letting go.

"Let's go buy the tickets now. I'm sorry. That was a dickhead thing to do."

"I don't want you to buy my tickets out of guilt, Harry. I don't want you to feel like you have a duty. We know the money will always come."

"Oh Lou, babe, I've just been so scared. I've been trying to ignore it, putting my head in the sand. You know what I'm like. I don't want you to go but I know you have to. I can't protect you from here and I'm so scared of losing you. I know you know you're going to be fine, but it's hard for me to feel that faith that you feel. I do understand, though, babe. I really do."

I was crying by now, witnessing Harry's warrior rising. He had been courageous enough to apologise, willing to see his whole self, even his shadow. He had been unafraid of it and had compassion and understanding in doing so. *Of course, Harry had to be the one to send me to the final earth chakra,* I thought.

It was beautiful to see how this was all part of the divine story, including Harry overcoming his fear of anything happening to me. It was *his* faith in my work that was sending me. That was the energy. It wasn't just my own consciousness, my own growth that I used as medicine to activate the earth chakras. It was Harry's. And Jen's. And

James'. And Josephine's. And that of all the people who played a role in my journey. We all had a part in this great gift of awakening the new earth grid.

In that moment, I felt it. I knew I would have to give up my most precious kuya, my very first medicine stone, the heart stone. Harry had picked it up on a beach and given it to me when he was just 18 years old. It became one of my first medicine stones, and possibly the most potent. It was safe to say it was my favourite. I was fully attached to it, but I knew that was why Kailash was asking it from me. It held the gift of presence, but also the gift of Harry and me. It held the medicine of our transformation, our love, our unity.

A few hours later, Harry received a letter with some unexpected inheritance from a late uncle. It was exactly how much he had given to me for my trip to Tibet. That is the flow right there. When we give and receive without attachment, we are reminded that money is just energy and that energy is God manifested. We show up to give God through us and we always get back what we give and more.

***

Harry and Lou 2.0

When we woke on the Saturday morning before I was due to leave for Kailash, we found ourselves in the strange situation of being in an empty house. The kids, now 7 and 11, were out at a sleepover and scout camp weekend. It was weird. Our kids had a social life beyond us now. Lucy had moved out a month before, which was like losing a teenage daughter, although we loved it when we heard her key in the lock when she came home for occasional dinners. It was also unusual to have free time. We always had places to go, work to do, people to see. With no plans, no guilt, and no need for a babysitter, this was pure freedom! We had a whole day to ourselves and a bit of spare cash to go and enjoy it. This was a whole new experience in itself.

I sat at the breakfast bar, searching for a playlist to put on, while Harry made us coffee and breakfast. This was his domain now. Since Peru, he had claimed the kitchen in the mornings. He would serve the girls whatever they wished and I was relegated to the bar stools, which had impacted my number of morning dance-offs! We pondered over coffee what to do with the day, feeling like kids again ourselves.

"Let's have another baby," Harry joked, grabbing me by the waist, pulling me close and kissing my forehead.

"Erm, no way, mofo! How about we drive into the city and see where the universe takes us?" I suggested.

"How about we pretend to make a baby and then head into town?" he said lifting me from my stool and carrying me upstairs.

After all these years, he still fancies me, I thought. *I could be fat and haggard and covered in spots and he would still love me. In fact, I've been all of those over these past 20 years!*

We drove into the city, my hand in his, and I drank in his occasional glances at me. I played DJ and turned up the tunes as we flew down the motorway in the spring sunshine.

The city grew and buildings began to surround us. I felt what I always felt as we entered the London bubble – love. We had been in and out of the city a lot over the last week, going to gigs. We parked up not far from the river near Borough market.

"What do you wanna do, babe?" Harry asked.

"Whatever we do, I want vegan food, a pint of vegan ale and some vegan chocolate cake at some point today!"

Summer was coming and that vibe was tangible, despite the slight chill in the air. It felt so good to be out, walking hand in hand down the back streets of London Bridge. On one corner, we saw an old guy in a wheelchair, his hair a mess, his clothes tangled. Resting on the front of his chair was a full catheter bag of urine and he looked like he was struggling with the fly on his trousers. I wasn't sure where he had come from, but he looked like he could do with a hand. Before I could offer, Harry was off. He walked right up to the guy.

"You alright, mate? Do you need some help there?"

"Nah, I'm alright, I think," the man beamed, clearly happy that someone had come over to talk to him.

"Okay then, mate. You take care of yourself and have a good day," Harry said.

"And you, mate."

As we carried on walking, I squeezed Harry's hand.

"Seriously, babe, that was beautiful. You didn't think twice about helping that man with something deeply private. You just acted on your instincts without fear. It was an honour to see that human connection and that man appreciated you seeing him too," I said.

Harry was more courageous now. He had never been the one to go out of his way to check in with a stranger until the moment I had just witnessed. He was usually too afraid of getting it wrong and upsetting someone. Usually, I was the one to approach strangers, going up to homeless people for hugs and banter. He liked to stay out of the way, plagued by an inherited worry that I could offend people with my openness. This change in him lit something in my heart.

Courageous brave warriors weren't about the big fight, but about showing up in any situation.

In a cobbled courtyard in London Bridge, we stumbled upon a mini market, where pop-up stalls sold trendy local beer and vegan food, and vintage clothes and antiques. A couple moved just in time for us to take their space on a bench in the sun, next to a sound system playing some epic tunes. We sat listening to the music, eating and drinking exactly what I'd wanted, and people-watching in pure joy. When we finished, Harry wrapped me in a hug and pulled my head back towards him to kiss me lovingly. There was nowhere to be. Just here. In this moment. Forgotten was the fear that in two days I would be flying to Nepal and not be back in his arms for nearly a month.

***

CHAPTER 20

Growth & Challenge in Kathmandu

I sat on the floor, nervously packing and unpacking hiking gear, base layers, warm clothes, cool clothes, my sleeping bag, a filtration straw and my mesas. This was a journey that I was not at all prepared for. In the end, it was last-minute and barely organised. I hadn't even got my Chinese visa for Tibet. I would have to wait in Nepal for six days and apply for one there. I had also been warned over and over again that it's not a given that I would make it; that the Chinese didn't like people going to Tibet; that they decline most visa applications! I was so far out of my comfort zone. Even Sue had told me she knew many people who had tried to enter Tibet and failed.

"It will be interesting to see if you get there," she mused aloud, leaving a seed of doubt for me to play with over and over. Would I water it with fear or choose to see this as truly sacred, a journey only for the chosen few?

I didn't know much about the history of the area, other than the Chinese Communist regime had invaded Tibet in the 1950s. When I was seven or eight, I'd seen news clips of monks being beaten and I had an image in my mind of people trying to get across Tibetan borders, so I knew no one could enter or leave Tibet at will. However, back then I had no idea what or where Tibet was.

Yet there was an imprint on my soul, as if the universe had shown me long ago that I would be one of those souls who would try to enter. I had been warned that the Chinese government would use anything as an excuse to not let you in, so had purposely avoided going via China. I had no desire whatsoever to go to mainland China. Indeed, it scared me, because I didn't know much about the culture there. I had seen Chinese tourists, though, and I had profound pre-judgment about what I would experience.

Take alabaster, I heard as I packed.

I knew I had none, other than a medicine stone that the Egyptian temple healer had given me, which I felt wasn't to be offered at Kailash. I had given my last four pieces to my friend Jamie. Something told me to just ask him.

"Dude, I need your help. I leave for Nepal this evening and have to take some alabaster, but I've run out! You're the only person I know who has some. I would never normally do this but please could I take a piece of yours with me for an offering? It's crucial in the activation I need to do."

"I'm not home, babe, and not due back until later tonight. I'm so sorry!"

"No worries. That's cool. It is what it is…. It will work out as it needs to."

And so the fear of failure began…

***

As we ate our final family dinner around the table, I focused on all the things the girls had to look forward to while I was away – play dates, parties. The icing on the cake was Harry doing something he would never have done without going through so much personal growth; he was taking the girls away to Ibiza for four days on his own! We chatted and laughed, trying to hold it together. I wanted to bottle this moment and take it with me. I had been all around the world, but never wanted to be anywhere more than here in my kitchen with my family. This was where I was happiest.

For as long as we could, we all held off saying what was really on our minds. As the reality started sinking in, Bella went quiet, then Avalon, then me, until we could ignore it no more. Bella broke first.

"Mummy, I'm going to miss you so much!" she said, letting tears fall down her face.

Avalon came over and hid her face in my arms, her little sobs trembling into my arms. Bella's wet cheeks pressed against my belly, as I stroked her hair. The dam burst and too many tears that I had been holding back now flowed from my eyes. Harry wrapped his arms around us all and there we stayed for what would never be long enough.

Just then, the doorbell rang and I opened it to see Jamie holding out a piece of alabaster.

"I knew I had to get it to you somehow."

***

Welcome to crazy Kathmandu

A wave of dirty heat hit my face as I climbed off the plane in Nepal. Already, the energy was intense. Sweaty, crazy, frantic and adorable in every way, it was completely unfamiliar to me, not like landing in Peru. It opened up my innocence and curiosity.

I had made it. I had got my connecting flight and overcame all my dyslexic fears of immigration forms and visas. I was super proud of myself, at 38 years old, experiencing solo travel and doing okay. This was huge for me. And now I was sitting in the back of a family car, a man called Raj, his wife and their little girl all smiling at me, taking me back to their homestay.

The city made me laugh. I could see six people on a motorbike, including two kids hanging off the front. *Is this normal in Kathmandu?* Turns out it was!

It was a city of cars, dust, litter, dirt, too many people, and local street shops that sold everything from bottles of fizzy drinks and snacks to batteries and random household stuff. All the shops seemed to sell the same crap. *How many plastic buckets and bottles of Coke does one city need?* I wondered. There were half-dead cows roaming the streets, weaving between the car chaos, all winging it to get across the junction. I had a headache and felt bemused in one way, but joyful in another. I knew I had to curb my eco hippy ego and accept it all as it was. Sure, this was not my kind of city. Anything but. I had no idea where the romance of Kathmandu others spoke of came from, but there was *something...* something about it was going to make me and break me.

In time, we reached the homestay and I was relieved to see a patch of grass. Then on being shown my room, the view made me cry. Trees! So many trees! Maybe the only trees in this city! And every morning, I would wake up to the monkey temple right there outside my window.

"Thank you, universe."

My visa guy Kamal came around to the hostel within 10 minutes of my arrival. When he looked at the passport photos I had brought, which I thought adhered to the strict Chinese rules, he shook his head.

"We need to get these photos redone. You are showing teeth."

"But I have goofy teeth!" I said, flabbergasted. "One pokes out. It's hard not to show them!"

He did not laugh with me.

"They will not let you in," he said. "Seriously. And you can see your necklace a bit. They will find all excuses not to let you in. We need to go now and find somewhere to get your photo done. We only have half an hour."

He seemed agitated now.

Before I knew it, I was on the back of a motorbike, without a helmet, with a man I had known for a couple of minutes, flying along those insane roads, past the shops I had judged... *If Harry could see me now, he would be so worried*, I thought to myself. And yet I felt so fucking alive, exhilarated as the dirt hit my face and smog hit my lungs. I knew this was just a cosmic joke to get me into the Kathmandu vibe.

Inside one of those strange shops that sold everything was a guy with a camera and I dutifully did what these two men wanted. I was a little more chilled than they were, but I realised this was serious. I was not going to get into Tibet unless this photo was perfect in every way. I had never done anything with perfection in my life!

Back at the homestay, we went to my room to fill in the visa form and the pressure was on. My brain went into full dyslexic overload. I just could not do this form. Kamal could see I was struggling. Softly, he took the pen.

"Why don't I do this for you, Louise?" he offered.

I didn't want him to see my tears of relief and gratitude, because I didn't have the language to explain why, but maybe we didn't need words.

***

The Bon shaman and the Hindu swami

I clung to the rooftop veranda of the homestay looking out at the view across Kathmandu, like a child holding on to her mother's apron strings, afraid of the world beyond here. Now that I had unpacked and called home, there was nothing left to do but leave the hostel. I was not ready to face Kathmandu on my own. When I'd asked, I'd been told there would be a tour of the city on Sunday, but today was Friday. So, I was here on my own until then. I had no idea how to use a map, another dyslexic hurdle of mine. I couldn't even use Google Maps. My brain went left. My legs went right. The arrows never made sense and I ended up going in circles. At home, this was comical. Here, not so much! I sat in the swing chair, watching the city like a TV show that I was unsure I even wanted to watch.

A few hours later, the owner of the homestay returned and we had a chat. Raj said he knew of a shaman and was happy to take me to meet him! He was a Hindu himself, and nervous of the shaman, but he had been told the shaman was good.

Though Kathmandu was so vast that it took hours to cross, we walked only five minutes up the dusty street before we reached the building. It looked like an incomplete block of concrete apartments, with concrete steps, and a dark room at the top with no door, no window, just a small frame.

Entering the darkness, I could make out a large altar on top of which were gods I didn't recognise. The shaman, sitting cross-legged on a chair, had the appearance of a tiny buddha-like fellow. He was about my age and wore a yellow tracksuit. I could feel he was like me. He didn't need to wear regalia. He did not need to impress anyone. He had no need to smile either, since he was not here to make pleasantries.

He beckoned me to sit in front of him, which I did, while Raj sat anxiously by the door.

"Meditate," he commanded.

I closed my eyes, somehow completely at peace in this strange cold concrete room. Yes, it sounds like a great beginning for some twisted horror movie, but I accepted all that was and felt a shift and a new energy around me. Falling deeper into meditation with the heartbeat of his drum, I slipped through many doorways, in and out, looking and seeking. I sunk into visions, into darkness, the only thought being how amazed I was that my body stayed so still and so upright for so long.

I felt my body being sprayed with water and something else, but I stayed in meditation until the drum stopped and I knew it was time to open my eyes. The shaman told Raj to tell me that my energy was too scattered. I was ashamed that he saw me like that and my ego wanted him to see otherwise. But the shaman said I needed to rest, that I was tired and lost.

Raj and the shaman continued their conversation. I heard Raj mention Kailash and the shaman repeated the word Kailash with a new tone in his voice. Almost…

impressed? *Now he sees I'm special,* I thought, as a part of me still wanted to be accepted by those seemingly more powerful people. Then I laughed to myself, realising the shadow of that thought. I needed to accept the seemingly more powerful part of me, not project that onto others.

"He would like to teach you," Raj told me. "Come back and stay with him. In seven days, he will teach you how to sit in the fire."

The shaman took out his phone and showed me videos of his people in their regalia, singing, drumming. It was beautiful and familiar, but then he showed me an exorcism that had been performed right where I was standing. In the video, I saw this whole room on fire and a woman screaming! It was the old way, the shamanism I was yet to touch, and it frightened me.

Part of me was curious though. Maybe one day I would come back and learn the old ways. *But do I need to?* I asked myself. I had brought people back from the darkest depths of their human journey, from grief and psychosis, suicide and spiritual attack, and I was able to extract spirits and entities with love. Or maybe I was yet to meet something that dark?

As we walked back to the homestay, I asked myself, *do I really need to learn how to sit in the fire?* My ego wanted to say yes. But my soul said no.

***

I'm done with this crazy

In three days in Kathmandu, I had got myself lost and almost run over more times than I could count. I had come close to being conned too many times as well. I had learned the hard way that if I smiled at strangers as I usually did, it was met with confusion or I was opening myself to a sales pitch. Still, I was proud of myself for exploring so much of the world on my own without Harry. I was 38 years old and learning about travelling 20 years after I'd once hoped I would. I was doing it. It wasn't amazing. I didn't love it. I'd rather have been around the kitchen table at home with my family, listening to music and drinking tea. Nevertheless, I was growing inside.

After coming to terms with broken donkeys being dragged along on ropes, seeing a plastic-filled river, navigating a five-lane bridge with no pedestrian footpath and crossing a road where the traffic never stopped nor gave way to humans, I had made friends, lots of them. Most were 15 years younger than me, but somehow I felt these kids were like me. In the evenings, we would sit for hours, chatting and learning. They asked me so many questions and I agreed to teach reiki to some of them.

I had been out and about, seen all the temples, and loved how Hinduism and Buddhism warped and weaved into each other in this city. I had honoured my first teacher from ten years before, a Buddhist monk, who in his later years became ordained as a Hindu yogi. In all of this, my meditation practice became scattered and nowhere near as good as I wanted it to be. I no longer meditated twice a day for 45 minutes to an hour. Instead, in Kathmandu, I had been grabbing 5, 10 or 20 minutes here and there.

Fear crept back in. *What if my energy is too scattered? What if my energy is not clear enough to reach Kailash? What if this is the gateway, the cleansing journey I must take before I'm allowed into Tibet?*

I lay in my room beside myself. I was done with this city now. No temple was a sacred temple to me. Each one was a place of money, bartering and dogma. I wanted to go home to my family.

I journeyed with my main spirit guide, Xakier trying to gather my energy. A new power animal came to me, the owl. He would help me speak with the spirits. Xakier took me into a circle of people, then kissed me on my cheeks and forehead, like you do with a child. Indeed, I felt like a child.

When I came round, I knew I needed to see a healer, someone of my own energy. In no time, I found someone on the internet and took a punt at it. I needed reiki and booked in with a swami and reiki teacher out in the mountains. Somehow I managed to walk out of town on my own, crossing a fallen drainpipe that acted as a bridge over the polluted river, then found myself a safe cab to take me to the mountains.

It was far and the driver was unsure, but he was kind and committed! And an hour out of the city, when the roads were no longer roads, he still drove me all the way into the forest. The driver spoke a little English and we swapped stories of our kids. He told me he had never been in the mountains before and pointed at the view. A few times, we stopped the car and both got out to take in the view, breathing the clean air.

Eventually, the driver called the swami to get better directions and we found ourselves at a grand house overlooking the dense trees. He insisted on waiting for me, telling me I would never get another taxi out here. I knocked on the ornate wooden door and was instantly greeted by an old woman in a bright orange sari. She was half my height, twice my width, and had a welcoming smile that she delivered with her arms open wide. I returned her smile and she pulled me right into her and held me tight. I burst into tears and sobbed like a child coming home to her mama. The relief! I had needed a hug, to be touched, to be welcomed into a home.

The woman held me until she felt a calmness enter me. She brushed the tears from my face and then led me to the swami. Swami Basu was a man a little older than me, dressed in a white and orange kaftan. Without words, he gently took my arm and guided me into a massive room with chiffon drapes dancing in the breeze around floor-to-ceiling windows. From here, I could see the rainforest, soothing me with whispers of welcome, safety and knowing.

All the tears fell and I had no idea why they needed to come, as Basu sat me down in a chair and listened to my struggle with Kathmandu. In time, he lay me gently on the floor, placed his hands on my energy and sent me deep into the peace and healing I needed so much. This was what I did for others. It had been a long time since anyone could hold space for me in this way.

Warm blues and purples appeared, and Kailash called to me from the distance, reminding me to let go of the incessant worry of not being good enough or doing the right thing.

Just bring your joy, Louise, the mountain said.

I woke up an hour and a half later with a peace I had not felt since arriving in Kathmandu. We sat outside drinking tea, watching the trees of the jungle. The air was so much cleaner here. Down below, I could see mama and the driver sitting together drinking their own tea and laughing.

"Louise, this city is too much for your energy. It is why I live up here in the mountains. Even here, the force of the city makes its way up from time to time. I want you to forgive yourself. You carry so much unnecessary burden," Basu said.

I welled up. So much had happened these past few years. In my human mind, I didn't really know what had happened. It was impossible to process all of it and I was still weighed down with grief.

"Tell me, Louise, why is it you carry such responsibility on your shoulders? When you have such good karma in your energy, why do you worry so much?"

I began to cry again now, because he could see me, and with compassion too. I told him about the journey I had taken and where I was going. When I mentioned that I was going to Kailash, his eyes lit up like the shaman's had a week before. I could see Kailash really was the holy mountain that welcomed only a chosen few. And I was going.

"It is important that you maintain your good energy now before you go. Would you like me to take you to see Kathmandu through my eyes? I will show you how to see the city so it does not overwhelm you so much and so you can remember that Kathmandu is like the mud from where the lotus flower grows."

"Oh yes please!" I grinned. This was all so divine.

"Tomorrow, we will ride together and I will show you what you need so you are ready for your quest. I will collect you on my motorbike at 8am!" Basu promised.

Mama hugged me for an eternity, with no words, just chuckles and love, and all the way back to Kathmandu, the taxi driver talked about how special the place was. He told me how he'd felt the trees were alive as he'd sat drinking.

His face was peaceful and dreamy. I wondered what mama had put in his tea!

***

The mud from where the lotus flower grows

Once again, I was flying through Kathmandu, without a helmet, with a man I barely knew and loving every moment! When I was a kid, my dad and his mates rode motorbikes and I knew how to relax into it. I observed how Basu moved with the flow. We never stopped. We were always flying through the insane traffic. We should have been dead, but instead, bikes, cars, cows and children would move just in time. I had utter faith in him and his faith in the flow.

This is like life in the flow, I thought. *If we just keep trusting that the perceived blocks will dissolve, our faith in ourselves, in the Divine, and in the action we take will remove them.*

Tucked away at the far end of the city on the edge of a golf course was Basu's guru's resting place. We climbed over what appeared to be a waste dump, litter and mud up to our knees, before reaching an access point between old ancient tree roots. We hiked and hiked until we were greeted by an old man in a woodland area that housed some huts, a true hideaway, a slice of paradise.

Right away, Basu told the man I was going to Kailash, and the man reached for my hand and held it firmly, smiling into my eyes.

"Kailash, good karma, good karma," he said and then let my hand go.

Basu smiled and told me that the man was the last student of the late Shivapuri Baba, a Hindu mystic that lived for 193 years and possibly the first Indian holy man invited to meet Queen Victoria. He had been invited back 18 times, then after Queen Victoria had died, Shivapuri Baba had spent three years in the USA with Theodore Roosevelt, then travelled the world to Mexico, Peru, Australia... He had travelled 25,000 miles, 80% of which on foot, inspiring leaders with his holy wisdom. Shivapuri Baba was known for answering questions with simple idioms and spent his last years right here where I was standing.

"Those who saw him received a sense of inner peace and realisation."

Basu took me into a shrine of Shivapuri Baba and pointed where to sit.

"We will meditate," he said.

Fear washed over me. What if I was expected to meditate for hours? I had no idea, but I took a breath and surrendered to what was. I went deep quick and there he was – Baba the Mystic himself teaching me a mantra. It flowed through my mind.

"God is light. I am the light."

Over and over it echoed, seeding into my subconscious, reminding me of my divinity.

In my meditation, Baba sat next to me on a swinging chair. With curiosity and compassion, he looked at me and posed a question.

"What is your medicine and your mission, Louise?"

I found it hard to describe and began to belly-laugh. He laughed and laughed with me! He was playful and wise.

"Louise, it's simple. Connect to the grid. The energy is within you always. You are the holder of this medicine."

EARTH CHAKRA SHAMAN

As Baba and I swung in our chairs, I felt Jesus, my very first guide Gupta, Xakier, Archangel Gabriel and even Archangel Michael with me. All my guides together, loving me so much. I returned to the big blue crystal, where six years before Jesus had first come to me in meditation and asked me to make my oath to him. As I reached the crystal, I could feel myself releasing all that no longer served me, the fears, the sadness. I felt forgiveness for my teachers Josephine and James, for Jen and for myself and all I had done to create these situations, the roles I had played in the drama. I had karma to mend, stuff I needed to let go before Kailash. I continued releasing this energy into the crystal, knowing I was doing this so that I could meet Kailash with a pure heart, with clean intentions.

My hands on the crystal, I spoke within the vision.

I release the past. It no longer serves me to look back. I walk forward creating good karma for myself and others. I walk forward knowing my integrity in all I do, all I say and all I am. I ask God's light within me to always show me my shadows, so I may amend my behaviours and remain always in line with my true path. I see God in each and every person from this day forward. I walk as a master, a teacher, a shaman, a healer, as heaven on this Earth. I will for this life and forever more be in service to bringing peace within so that there is peace on Earth. I will hold that energy for others to change through my presence.

I came back to the day with a smiling expression. The anchors of my past were sweetness, innocence and speaking nicely to power. Now I held power of my own. And in doing so, I would show others how to hold theirs too.

***

CHAPTER 21

Kailash & the Crown Chakra

*P*assport in one hand, visa in the other, more than anything I was holding a sense of achievement, not just for the fact I had the actual paperwork I needed for this rare golden ticket, but for having got myself from one foreign country to another without Harry to be there to wave me goodbye or help me with the flight transfer. I had been on one adventure already and was about to embark on my quest. For a moment, a thought flickered across my mind that I was flying *ever further* away from Harry and the girls. My stomach sunk a little, but I pulled myself together and pivoted the thought to one of achievement. *Oh my God, I've managed to get myself three plane rides away from home on my bloody own!* I felt myself smile through my heart, stomach and soul.

"No!" shouted the Chinese man on the door, one step before passport control. He looked at me sternly. There was a fold line through my visa. He scowled at it, then at me. I looked at him bemused, half-deciding what role to play. The innocent child? The victim? The 'please don't be mad with me, I'm sorry I didn't know' nice girl? No, I had tried being nice and vulnerable and sweet in too many situations. Instead, I faced up to him. I looked him in the eyes with no emotion and I trusted he would give it back to me. I stood there with my energy telling him I knew he was going to hand my visa over and everything was going to proceed. He hesitated. He didn't know what to do. Then his energy changed. It was a face-off.

The man became a petulant child, slamming around, playing the game. I was unwavering, refusing to accept what were clearly bully tactics. I knew my visa was fine. I would not believe that there was a problem just because it was folded. He threw it back at me and refused to make eye contact.

I breathed again, plugged in my headphones, and made my way through to the gate where I waited a few hours to board.

As we took flight, I saw the *actual Himalayas* sprawling beneath me. They were incredible – so vast and not quite real. I felt like I was watching it on TV. How could I ever in a million years be going to the Himalayas? People like me didn't go to places like this.

Yet my wonder was disrupted by my culture shock and the sheer number of men surrounding me who were hacking loogies. The sound of snot hitting the back of their throats made me heave. I was triggered and I turned up the music even louder, but it was not helping. I had always been so accepting of people and not much really bothered me, but this did. This really did. I used every mindfulness and conscious awareness tool I knew to come to peace with the noise of slurping snot. *The flight is only an hour and a half. It's fine*, I told myself. This was an opportunity to practice acceptance. I breathed and I practiced and it seemed to be working.

Then I was distracted again. A flight attendant spoke over the tannoy. I was excited. We were close! I could feel Tibet beneath me. Lhasa, the capital, was below us somewhere. Tears filled my eyes, realising how far I had come to get here.

"This flight will not be landing in Lhasa today. It will be redirected to Chengdu," she said.

That was it. Nothing more, nothing less. I could hear Sue's voice, "I know many people who have tried to get into Tibet over the years and there was always something that stopped them. It will be interesting to see if you make it."

Lost in my thoughts and assumptions, there were no English speakers around me to ask. I wanted to revert to my little girl again, to have someone come and rescue me!

Fear of failure came in too. I was not pure enough to go to Kailash. What was going on?! I needed to pull myself together because the people next to me were cool as a cucumber. I had a silent subtle cry, wiped my tears and blew my nose. Then I remembered that I'd been told it was rude to blow your nose in China. That's why they must hack their loogies! I was amused by the thought.

Another old story popped up. What if I am being punished for not having done enough work while in Nepal? I hadn't given any offerings to the lands, no sacred stones, no ceremony, nothing. But I hadn't been called to do any of that. I thought back to all the people I had met in the homestay. I had attuned them to reiki, taught them meditation, sat for hours listening to them, helping them process their own lives, but also learning from the wise kids of the future. They had been in awe and it had been reciprocal. I gave to Nepal, maybe not to the lands, but in service to people.

I breathed and tried to understand the spiritual meaning of this manifestation. I was on a flight to China where I had never wanted to go in the first place. Why had I never wanted to go to China? Ah yes, I avoided coming into Tibet this way through fear of not being able to get through a Chinese airport because of the signs, the words, the letters, the language.

Maybe this is my lesson, I thought. *Maybe I have to face the fear of Chinese airports. God, where will we go? I have no idea what will happen next!*

I put my thoughts aside and noticed how the energy of the flight was actually wonderful. People were chilled and accepting. Maybe they all meditated a lot!

I got up to go to the bathroom to wash my face. On the way back, I found a group of friendly Americans whom I had met in Kathmandu. They had befriended me in a cafe on my fourth day in the city. Instantly, I had known the universe was sending them to me. The eight of them had climbed Kailash fifteen times together. They were filming their journey and trying to get a monk back into Tibet. Their advice about climbing Kailash had been invaluable. I would not have picked up half the shit I would need had I not met them. One lady had taken me to a pharmacy herself to buy all the vitamins and homeopathic remedies that would help with altitude sickness, headaches and exhaustion. I hadn't even realised how high I would be going or how massive a journey it was until I met them. They had prepared me in mind, body and spirit. It was delightful to see them here on the flight.

"Hey Lou, so good to see you. Turns out we all made it then!" Tom the group leader chuckled as he climbed out of his seat to embrace me. He was a huge handsome guy in his mid-sixties.

"Hey Lou, are you alright?" his wife said smiling up at us.

I loved that they remembered my name and spoke with such familiarity. I tried to be a grown-up and not to fall for the appeal of the loving arms of this mother and father figure.

"It's so good to see you guys!" I said with tears in my eyes. "I don't really understand what happened. Where are we going and why are we going there? Do you know?"

"They won't give us any information either, so hold out. We'll all get there."

I smiled. I wasn't alone.

***

Chengdu

I looked out of the window and centred myself as I watched us leave behind the Himalayas and head towards the city of Chengdu. Breathing, breathing, breathing, I took pen to paper and found my connection back to the universe, the place beyond mind, where my love, trust and connection was always to be found. I wrote and I wrote.

I knew now God had a greater plan for me and for all of us on this plane. Peace followed as I tuned into what was really going on. I began to sense there was someone on the plane who I was meant to connect with: maybe a guru or teacher or maybe I was here for someone else.

EARTH CHAKRA SHAMAN

***

On landing, I overheard the flight attendant say that it was due to high winds that we could not land in Lhasa and she didn't know when we would return. It could be tomorrow or the next day, but there were no guarantees when.

I allowed a few tears of uncertainty to fall. I knew I had to trust, really trust, but I also had to feel the feels. Only two hours ago, I had been crying with overwhelm at the realisation I was going to Tibet. Now I was crying because I had no idea if I was going to Tibet at all. If I did make it, would my guide and group have already left for the 16-day journey through the Himalayas to Kailash? And if they had not left, would I have the time required to acclimatise in Lhasa, which was 3,500 feet above sea level, in order to prevent altitude sickness for the rest of the journey?

I found myself being ushered through a slick and simple process and onto a bus heading to an airport hotel, where we would have a bed and some food and where we would wait it out until they could find flights to put us on over the next few days. All at no cost! The Americans had been taken on a different shuttle to a different hotel, and most other people on this bus were much older than me, so I sat down next to a guy who looked about my age.

Leon was Swiss and could speak enough English to converse with me. Within a few minutes and to his own great surprise, he opened up and told me all about himself. He had been with his wife for many years and was taking some time to solo travel.

"You are waiting for your baby to come?" I said, knowing.

I couldn't help but feel it and these insights about people tended to fall out of my mouth without thinking. His eyes opened wide.

"Yes, but sadly it has not happened yet," he said, "I feel I have been unravelling something since I got to Nepal. I was told I would meet a shaman on my journey to help me."

"I'm a shaman, Leon," I said. "I can help you."

I smiled, unsurprised at this perfectly planned set up! He seemed unsurprised too as I showed him the notes I'd made on the flight about how I knew I was landing in China for someone else.

"I felt that too," he smiled softly. "That is why I was not worried about coming. I knew I was going to meet someone."

Leon was sweet and gentle. I offered him a healing once we'd settled in the hotel.

"Yes, of course," he said, willing to do anything to help his baby come.

In the queue in the hotel lobby, a woman also around the same age as me, who looked like a laid-back hippy traveller, tapped me on the shoulder.

"Hey, I'm Anna. They will make us all share rooms. I've done this before. Wanna buddy up with me before they put us with someone we don't want to be with?"

The moment she asked I fell in love with her confident smile and easy-going energy. We were instant best friends and roomies, getting to know each other fast. She was German, but had lived in Chile for years. I had missed this sort of deep conversation and connection in recent weeks. And when I told her Leon would come to our room for a healing, she was totally unfazed.

The dining room was full of people who had come off that plane and I found myself in a magical moment, surrounded by the most amazing people. Anna, Leon and I sat at a table with three other guys who brought laughter, joy and inspiration. Strouse was a 72-year-old Greek man with limited English, but who managed to tell me he had climbed to 800 metres on Everest. He was quiet yet funny. I loved him instantly. Then there was Jesus, a 65-year-old mischievous and energetic Spanish-Columbian man. He had me laughing in no time. We spoke the same joyful language of dancing and jokes, despite the limitation of our words.

So, here I was with a Greek, a Spanish-Colombian, a German-Chilean and a Swiss. And we met in English with laughter. I felt blessings rain down. All *would* be well after all.

Apart from Leon, it turned out we were all going to Kailash, and though we would travel with different tour guides, our dates were similar. Everyone seemed impressed that I would be going to Everest afterwards too. Strouse told me not to worry about the altitude or not having enough time in Lhasa.

"You can't stop it. If it's going to get you, it will get you, any time, any age, even if you have acclimatised. God willing, we'll all be good."

It was a relief to know I wasn't alone in my dilemma.

Leon came to our room for an hour after dinner and I passed on a blessing and healing, working as I was guided. He was shocked, but grateful and happy. Anna watched in awe from bed as she listened to what I was telling him. She felt the divine energy too that would bring him a baby in 12 months' time. Afterwards, she asked me about my quest, and we lay in our beds chatting like sisters until the early hours.

"This pilgrimage to Kailash is my purpose, the activation is for the people, for consciousness and for the Earth. Kailash will bestow me with medicine so I can share it with others. But you know, I sense that Everest is a gift just for me."

***

Get to Tibet

The 6am flight was fully booked by the time we got to the desk at the airport, but Anna, Jesus, Strouse, Leon and myself were all put on the last few seats of the 11am flight, the final flight for the day. Many people behind us would not be flying to Lhasa until tomorrow. It felt like divine flow indeed.

We looked for coffee but nowhere was open. A young Chinese man and his wife came up to us and said they could take us somewhere. I hated KFC, the place he took us, but the guy was so sweet that I overrode my judgment, silently vowing to never spend my money in places that supported unethical and cruel food production. He ordered coffee for us, but the restaurant only accepted cash or WeChat, an app where you could pay on your phone, so the couple insisted they paid for all our coffees. Being here in China was transforming my preconceived ideas of the country and opening my eyes to the uncovered racism within me.

We sat in the deserted airport with our coffees, Jesus playing music on his speakers. Aretha Franklin came on and Jesus offered me his hand to dance. In no time, we were whirling around the airport like hyper children and I cried with slightly manic laughter, excitement and exhaustion. Watching in amusement were the Buddhist monks who had arrived with the Americans. And I am sure the universe was watching too. Everything aligned, the energy clear, we were ready to bring our joy to Mount Kailash.

***

I was greeted by my Tibetan guide Gelsen at the airport. He was about my age, sweet and concerned about how I was. He told me not to worry. Three others in the group had also just landed, having been delayed in Nepal. We were a day behind schedule, so we were going to go straight to a monastery. Excited to meet who I would be traveling with, I flung my bags in the boot of our minivan and jumped in. There was an English couple Tom and Erin, in their late twenties, who had come with their friend Jim. They were teachers in China, and had come to Tibet on a bit of a whim. They had some holiday to use and money to spend. They didn't know much about Kailash but fancied going to Everest, so they'd booked the tour last minute. There was a Malaysian man Jag and his sweet and quiet Chinese wife Suzi, who both spoke a little English and told me that Jag was Hindu and this was his once-in-a-lifetime pilgrimage to Kailash.

In truth, I was somewhat disappointed in my group. I missed the fun-loving, excitable, open and laid-back nature of my friends from Chengdu. It was clear I didn't quite belong and there was certainly no common ground. It was not like being sat on the back of the bus with my shaman friends in Peru that's for sure. Erin was very guarded with me and it was hard to escape the feeling that she eye-rolled every time I spoke. I got clear signs that she wasn't overly comfortable with my friendliness and certainly didn't like me chatting with her boyfriend. All of a sudden very alone on my quest, I overrode the feeling of being disliked and continued the getting-to-know-you conversations. After all, we were about to sit in this van together for 10 hours every day for the next 14 days. And I began to see this was part of the bigger plan.

As we drove to the first of many monasteries, I could already feel the altitude squeezing my head. Passing through the Lhasa city all I could see out of the window of the minivan were designer shops and high-rise buildings. My heart sank. What is this place? I thought I was going to see ancient Tibet.

"I have to inform you that our car is tracked and wired to the Chinese government. They listen always and there are things I am not allowed to tell you, but I will do my best to answer your questions," Gelsen said.

I let this information sit with me. Reminding myself, Tibet belonged to China now. It was time to drop any expectations of how this trip was going to be, to come from a place of learning and non-judgment, and to know that everything was teaching me.

***

Old Lhasa, New China

Even in the peaceful streets of old Lhasa, where our hotel was, we had to go through checkpoints, bag checks and X-ray machines. Here, there were worn buildings, narrow streets, flags, monasteries, shops filled with beautiful Tibetan items (some genuine, some Chinese replicas).

I witnessed Tibetans of all ages prostrating: praying, sliding onto their bellies, then sliding back up onto their feet. They did this – a practice called *kora* – all the way around the pathways that circled their sacred sites for good karma. The kora circulated the main temple in Lhasa. Most of these people would prostrate the entire way around three times, a distance of a few kilometres, saying the mantra "om mani padme hum" with every move. Not every Tibetan prostrated, though. Many walked around the sacred sites, whispering the mantra under their breath, some spinning prayer wheels, but witnessing hundreds of people prostrating was still an incredible and humbling sight.

As I turned the corner into a beautiful town square, I was faced with masses of young armed soldiers in riot gear holding shields. But there was no trouble anywhere. Just peace. Yet these boy-soldiers were doing what they needed to do, following orders of intimidation. It was a juxtaposition that baffled my mind, but that I knew I had to accept. They were just humans doing what they were told. This was China now.

I asked the three teachers, Erin, Tom and James if I could come to dinner with them, knowing I was not ready to navigate my way on my own yet. They looked perplexed at my request and I was perplexed that they would not invite me. Were we not adventuring to Kailash together, soon to be friends? How could they say no?

"Look guys, I'd totally appreciate tagging along, if that's okay with you. I don't speak Chinese and I'm useless with a map. To be honest, I'm feeling a little nervous and to make things worse, I'm vegan and afraid of starving or eating something I may regret!" I joked.

They all spoke amazing Chinese and helped me find something to eat. I was so grateful for their company. Recognising I had just crashed their dinner time, I didn't take their initial aloofness too personally and they soon began to warm up to me.

***

Later that night, after an hour of sleep, I woke feeling suffocated. I calmed myself with slow breaths, staying present, giving myself a reality check that I was not dying.

"This is my body adjusting to the altitude," I assured myself.

I opened my mesa and clung to my heart-shaped kuya, wishing I didn't have to give it to Kailash. I loved this medicine stone. It was my favourite, and for a moment, I tried convincing myself that I didn't need to offer it. I was kidding myself. I knew I would. I had said I would.

The next day, the altitude sickness lurked in my head, my body and my mind. I drank water by the gallon, but still felt dehydrated. Gelsen cared for me tenderly. Suzi, the Chinese girl, was suffering terribly and had not left her room, except to go to the hospital in the night where she'd been on a drip.

For the next 24 hours, we went from monastery to monastery. Although deeply beautiful, it was clear what was left of Tibetan culture since the Chinese invasion some 50 years before was a mere shell of the divine power it once held. Now the Chinese government owned the monasteries. Everything was controlled, even the young monks had been trained by the Chinese, the ancient Tibetan ways washed away. Gelsen shared that I was seeing what 'they' wanted me to see. I felt the depth of his grief, for the loss of his culture, for his will to hold onto the last threads of his ancestry before the truth was finally rewritten by their conquerors.

***

The road to Kailash

The four-day journey to Kailash would be long and arduous: 10 hours a day in the minivan with stop-offs along the way to various monasteries. Slowly, I found myself accepting my group and my group accepting me. I let go of expectations of deep conversations about consciousness and spirituality, personal growth and awareness, earth grids, magic and manifesting, and simply learned to be comfortable in the silence and in the presence of these strangers.

This new way of being for me was part of my lesson on this journey, not being the leader, the teacher, the wise woman, the mother, wife, friend, or healer. And I certainly was not seen as any kind of earth chakra shaman. I was just Louise, part of Gelsen's group on the road to Kailash.

As we ascended through the mountains, I could not deny that I was struggling with the Chinese invasion. Even in the highest mountains, all signs of old Tibet had been wiped out. It was startling to see empty high-rise cities built in the middle of nowhere contrasting with the vast Himalayan peaks. Car parks filled with JCBs but no one around. *Wow, the Chinese really do love to build*, I thought. It was like they couldn't stop themselves.

I had to come to peace with these empty Himalayan cities. I had to see the shadow I was projecting on to 'the Chinese' – my own country's shadow. The English had done exactly the same – 'conquering' – and I had seen with my own eyes how we in the West had wiped out ancient cultures during colonization. I had to see this to heal within me the shame of my own ancestry.

We drove for days through the Himalayas. The road was extremely rocky until we reached the freeway. One of my judgments about the Chinese was their need to build. And yet right now, I was grateful for those long smooth roads, imagining the pilgrimage to Kailash before tarmac. Even with the gates and constant police checkpoints, I was glad for this road!

We zigzagged up the mountain pass and stopped to stretch our legs at 4,700 metres and take in the breathtaking view of holy Yamdrok Lake's turquoise waters. Here's where I needed to make my first offering, I felt. As the others ate and rested at the side of the lake, I sat at the water's edge on my own taking in the clean air. It felt sacred as I opened up my mesa and I knew it was time to lay the headless angel to rest, to let that healing be passed to others. The angel of discernment kuya flew from my hands into the sacred lake. I let her go into the waters, and blessed myself and all who had walked this journey with me so far.

We drove on through magnificent valleys, exquisite villages and past holy Mount Nyenchen Khangsar, where I witnessed the effect of climate change on this melting glacier. We stopped at more monasteries and were fed salted yak milk. I didn't want to refuse gifts because of my veganism, which would not be understood here in the mountains. Within three sips, however, my stomach churned. I could not!

We stayed in Chinese hotels in the random cities that appeared out of nowhere and ate in traditional family-run restaurants with cloth doors, smelly wooden furniture, questionable cleanliness and no toilets. Every day, I ate the only vegan option I could find: rice and chilli oil for lunch and rice noodles for dinner. At least, I thought it was vegan. I didn't ask too much. It was all about survival up here!

Instead of sewage, there were dumping areas in the middle of the village or on the side of roads, where dead dogs and other literal shit from the villages rotted. At best, it was rewilding, but it wasn't only the places where we had to go that proved challenging. 'Going in nature' was exhausting full stop. The altitude made us all feel like our bodies were heavy as a lead weight. Finding the breath just to walk to a spot was enough, but I was not prepared for how hard it would feel to pull my leggings up and down.

By now, six days in, I rather liked my group. We had bonded over our toilet stops and I shared my pharmacy of oils and homeopathic tablets. However, what I loved most was having the time to be in my own headspace. I watched stunning views of the mountains pass, occasionally seeing nomads whose lifestyle remained close to their soul. And I spent a lot of time in meditation, going inwards, journaling, shamanic journeying with my spirit guides, gaining deeper wisdom. I had never had this amount of time to *just be*. Life back home was a whirlwind from morning to night. Here, it was just me, the mountains, my spirit helpers, pen and paper.

We are getting close to Kailash. I sense a new energy will come to me, a new level of understanding. I can see the mountain that is opposite Kailash and I feel her almost like a wife. Gurla Mandhata, the female mountain that overlooks Lake Manasarovar. Oh this holy lake! I cannot wait to meet her at the end of the journey. I can feel her power like she is welcoming me home.

She tells me the prayer and the mantra will be the final part of the healing. My ability to contain this energy will be my gift. This is beautiful and I can feel something big is happening, although I am taking it all in my stride. There is neither excitement nor fear – I am in a state of neutrality. This is unusual for me. I prefer to be excited.

***

We drove into Darchen, once a small traditional Tibetan village since made commercial for pilgrims with its mix of Tibetan and Chinese guesthouses and restaurants. The town was heaving with thousands of Tibetan people and it was clear that it was under constant surveillance by the government, more so than others.

It was cold, dark and now snowing, and I was hungry beyond hungry, but there was a problem, a huge problem. Our pre-booked guest house had been given to Tibetan pilgrims. Gelsen was furious.

Every guest house in the town was booked, so we ate in a busy Tibetan restaurant, waiting for Gelsen to return with news. Two hours later, he came to fetch us. He had managed to get us two rooms in a hotel, but we would all have to share! He handed us the keys.

As we entered the hotel, which was clearly the most expensive hotel in the village, but by our standards would be no more than a one-star, I smiled at the manager, but he shouted at us and blocked the door. We showed him our keys, but he refused to let us in because we were not Tibetan; we were tourists and he did not want tourists.

Gelsen and the hotel manager argued, and the fight was insane. Then Gelsen began to run and the manager ran too. The hotel manager brought the police and Gelsen brought the military, who turned up in massive trucks to sort their quarrel. It was like a scene from a movie, as we all huddled freezing in our van, observing this curious scene from the window. Within the hour, police were ushering us into our room. The manager of the hotel looked deeply unhappy at having his hand forced and poor Gelsen was still running around like crazy because he was yet to do all the official check-ins that the authorities required. If he missed the deadline, he would not have the paperwork to take us up the mountain.

He made it with two minutes to go. The universe was on our side.

***

The first day of the Kailash kora

Kailash was mystical for all who came here on spiritual pilgrimages. Jain, Bon, Hindus and Buddhists all came. Some said Kailash was the birthplace of Shiva. Some believed Kailash to be the Earth's *axis mundi*, the connection between heaven and Earth, between the physical and spiritual worlds, the celestial centre. Whatever their ideas about Kailash, one thing was for sure. It was shrouded in wonder.

I had done my best not to be infused by others' beliefs, but even back in Nepal people had talked about Kailash being a manmade pyramid, like those in Egypt, holding the same energy as the Great Pyramids in Giza. The owners of the homestay in Nepal had told me that it had a lot of alien activity around it, which intrigued me. Some said that 'other beings' lived there. Some said sages lived there. And no one had ever summited the strange peak.

It was also said that whoever climbed Kailash would age 10 years; their hair and nails would grow and they would be gifted wisdom on their climb.

"So, I'm trading wrinkles for wisdom, hey Kailash? Let's do this!" I said to the mountain.

I had not really understood the importance of the timing until we'd arrived the night before, but it turned out we'd come into Darchen ahead of the holiest day of the year for Tibetans. Now I understood why the hotel manager didn't want tourists in his rooms, when there were so many Tibetan people here for *their* most sacred ceremony. I felt how Gelsen had been torn. He loved his people but he was also our guide and had to ensure our safety.

Saga Dewa was the most holy festival for Tibetans. Many only make this pilgrimage to Mount Kailash once in their life, if ever. Gelsen had explained it as the raising of the prayer flags and a foreseeing of the future. And it was why there were so many people in town.

It seemed the universe always took me to the places I needed on the most magical dates. Yet again, I could never have planned this with my mind. In addition to it being Saga Dewa, it was the second full moon of May, a blue moon, a powerful energy indeed for the sacred festival, and an indication that this was exactly where I was meant to be.

EARTH CHAKRA SHAMAN

We rose early, leaving behind the security of the van and setting out on foot. I had a small backpack for the three days, which contained two heavy mesas, a journal, three full water bottles, a handful of base layers and waterproofs, and a sleeping bag. It weighed more than anyone else's because of my mesas. I had carried these bags of heavy stones around the whole world with me, but I had never actually climbed a mountain 5,000 metres above sea level with them. And I was unable to breathe due to altitude as it was!

We left the village and ascended the narrow path up the mountain. I was bone tired. Walking was like wading through mud and I was exhausted in minutes.

The effect of the altitude on my body was insane. It was suffering from a lack of its usual fresh organic greens too; I had eaten nothing but white rice for a week. As I thought this, I was passed by a pregnant woman prostrating up the mountain followed by what looked to be her grandmother and grandfather! In awe of these three Tibetans belly-sliding up and down, and knowing they were going to do that for the next three days, up and around this mountain, I could hardly moan about my all-rice diet. From now, I promised myself, I would keep my head up and my mind focused on the moment, seeing abundance, not lack. After all, I was walking upright on my legs. I had much to be grateful for!

The morning sun began to creep through the clouds and warm my third eye. Tears welled, as I looked around and saw myself as part of this tiny ant trail of humans, up the mountain path. Reality awakened within me. I was on my quest to circle the holiest mountain on Earth!

Gelsen repeated how blessed we were to be doing the kora with so many Tibetan people, that this was a truly unique day, the most magical of the calendar.

"I can see why you were brought here at this time, Louise," he said to me. "You never see so many Tibetans. This is a blessing for you."

Noticing my energy shift with wonder, I observed the beauty of this culture, the traditional dresses, the layers and layers of long black skirts with colourful pinafores on top, the smiles like sunshine. The women reminded me of those I had met in Peru, who could scale slopes like mountain goats. And here I was puffing and panting away, leaning on my walking sticks.

In two hours, we made it to the flag-raising festival in the basin. We had to move through hordes of armed Chinese military who were putting a damper on things, but I tried to be grateful for them, since they'd been responsible for getting me a bed for the night!

Seas and seas of people sat around the mountain, looking down on a huge 25-foot pole in the ground. The old flags were being removed ceremonially and new flags were being attached.

I sat on my own, sticking out like a sore thumb, but trying to hide from the police, who had prohibited tourists from the festival and told us to move on. In true shaman style, I knew how to make myself invisible to them, even in my bright neon walking gear! I huddled among the thousands of Tibetan families, among children, babies, and even older grandparents, all meeting and greeting each other with warmth and love, sharing food and flasks of salty yak milk, laughing and celebrating.

Although I was alone, I was included in their celebrations. Grandparents sent young children over to offer me food that I swallowed dutifully. I smiled through a grimace, trying to wash down the strange pieces of food with water. Sweet or savoury, meat or veg, I couldn't tell. It was a taste beyond anything I could ever palate, but I had come here to learn about Tibetan culture, I reminded myself. The smells and tastes were insanely different here. I recalled the smell of burning lard candles in the monasteries, wondering if I would ever get it out of my nostrils!

The longer I sat, the more I could feel the energy of these people, of Kailash, of this ceremony. This was their Mecca, a once-in-a-lifetime opportunity. Coming to Kailash was not easy even for Tibetans and we were all blessed beyond blessed to be here. That gratitude was like a golden light, a gift to the Earth. I realised that these people were holding a sacred energy for all of us on Earth. Every day, they prayed for us, for the freedom of all people, for the cleaning of karma. Their purity, love, joy and laughter was rare on the Earth now. Yet they brought that to Kailash, anchoring peaceful energy deep into the Earth as they walked the kora both of the flag pole ceremony and the mountain.

When the kora began, what felt like thousands of Tibetans passed me and smiled. Naturally, we reached out our hands to each other, catching eyes, holding, shaking, kissing, and blessing each other on our way. My heart burst. I was part of this, of them. The light of the blessings shone from my centre all the way out into the universe. I was accepted and loved by these people. We moved around the mountain as one, weaving in and out of each other along the path. I was never far from my group members, but we didn't walk together, which was nice.

Within a few hours, the crowds dispersed – Tibetan people were fast on their feet and their bellies! – and as the people thinned out ahead, I became aware of the nature surrounding me. Pure beauty. Stillness of water and rocks and sky. Greys, blues and browns calming my every unsteady step.

I reflected on the message Kailash had given me when I was in Nepal.

Bring your joy, Louise.

***

Crown chakra activation

It was a sacred moment, when I got my first glimpse of that strange pyramid peak of Kailash. Indeed, it was eerie, not of this world, and commanded my reverence. Within moments of seeing it, I had fallen to my knees sobbing tears that I did not understand. I was a part of this mountain and it was a part of me. I knew I had to make my offering of the heart stone in this very moment. It was time for me and my beautiful kuya, my favourite medicine stone, to part ways.

I scrambled off the path to a quiet spot and unraveled my mesa. I took the kuya in my hand and breathed into it all that was in me: my love, my gratitude, my wishes for a peaceful Earth, my vision of utopia where all beings, humans, animals, plants, trees and waters were free.

"Mount Kailash, I have come a long way to bring you what you asked of me. I have transformed along the way. Here, I bring love, unity and presence. I bring all the medicine of my transformation of the earth chakra journey, the darkness that I alchemised into gold and all the wisdom of all the Earth from all her sacred lands. I pray. *Om mani padme hum.* May all beings be free. May the world be blessed with love and light."

EARTH CHAKRA SHAMAN

I cried as I buried it, creating a stone tower on top and carefully praying into each rock I placed. Something deep inside overrode my already exhausted body and pulled me into oneness. In my silence, I listened to Kailash.

With this gift of deep connection to the energy of Mother Earth and Great Spirit, you walk the sacred path of purpose as a protector of all sentient beings, of Mother Earth and her waters. You awaken love in each moment, bringing harmony, joy, peace and connection to all your brothers and sisters, the mountain spoke.

With this gift, connect, understand and transcend all parts of yourself. Shine your authentic light bright so others can find theirs as they walk the path of integrity. The more you connect to this energy, the deeper your understanding will be of your inner and outer worlds, and the power of this energy will transcend you.

I activated the chakra and it activated me. I felt like I had been powered-up, gifted a few extra bars on my body's battery! Behind the blue skies, the moon was completing its fullness, everything was divinely aligned.

"Thank you, Kailash," I whispered.

***

I found myself looking at the ground for the next few hours, desperately seeking a new heart-shaped stone, until I heard my guide whisper into my mind:

Louise, do not seek a new stone. It will appear when you least expect it. You cannot will the sacred gifts to come to you. Await your gift with grace and stay present as you walk with Kailash.

Grace, I'm afraid to say, was not entirely forthcoming. I caught up with Jim, . In a moment alone together, I saw he was a sweet kid, deeper than he allowed people to see or maybe allowed himself to see, and I began to see a different side to him when we were not with Tom and Erin. We began to talk a little deeper about our experience of the journey we had had so far. Both of us had been deeply touched by the festival, the mountain and the people and I welcomed the reverence in how we spoke.

The monastery where we were to sleep that night was a place unlike any I had seen. Behind the grand white walls tucked into the side of the mountain were corridors of concrete rooms with no windows. In our room, six old beds were pushed together. On entering, I felt completely overwhelmed by the cold and dark.

I was tired and it was getting late, but somehow it was still light outside. Time seemed to move fast then slow and I was disoriented. Tom and Erin arrived alive and fresh-faced, but Suzi was struggling with the hike, and she and Jag were way behind with Gelsen.

"Chinese people don't walk anywhere. The girls are so precious. They don't do anything outdoors. I don't even know why she came," Erin bitched.

It had been a long time since I had been around people who talked this way about others, but I knew not to react. Anyone who has to put others down is hiding their own inadequacies, after all.

As I lay on my rickety old bed, my body shook with cold and it was as if I was losing myself. I became unaware of the group around me, and I could see a tunnel getting narrower and narrower.

"Louise, you have to move," Jim said, stirring me.

His concern for me pulled me back.

"But I'm so so cold," I muttered.

"Get outside. You need to get in the sun," he said.

"There's sun?" I asked.

It was so dark in here, but surely the sun had gone by now. Jim pulled me up. I didn't want to move and my head was spinning. Then I remembered that altitude sickness killed people. People died on this mountain. It was more real than I had understood, but I was going to be stronger. I must move. I forced myself outside and there was the sun. *How is it still up?* I thought. But here it was.

I stood with my mouth open and eyes closed, letting the evening sun breathe me back to life, recalling the moments when the shaman in Peru had taught us to 'eat the sun', to bring the rays into our mouths, chew and swallow. That lesson all the way from Lake Titicaca was my only survival.

Jim shook me again. Not one for physical contact, I knew this was big for him.

"How are you feeling, Lou?" he asked.

I opened my eyes. I needed to stay present. I realised how very easy it would be right now to choose to fall down dark walls or be intoxicated with the light.

"Better," I answered.

Jim stood alongside me, awkward but dutiful, and we stayed there for a while. When we returned, Suzi and Jag had arrived. She was my hero, Suzi. She had never really done anything in nature. She had come so far, and I loved her for it. And I loved her smile even though I knew it hid her pain.

Erin, Tom and Jim teamed up, not letting me get away with not eating, but I couldn't manage more than a nibble.

Jim handed me a bottle of Coke, which I would never drink normally.

"Drink it," he insisted. "You'll feel better."

Oh my God! It was the best thing I had ever tasted in my life! I fell asleep in the strange bed, pressed against the cold wall. I missed Harry so much. I missed the way he could pull my entire body into the cocoon of his. I missed his kisses and his touch, but I could not go there. I was safe and that was as much as I needed to know.

Remembering Kailash was teaching me all I needed to learn, I fell asleep.

***

Seeing angels

There were only eggs for breakfast and I could not make myself eat one. Even if the chickens had been happy, I just couldn't. I forced down a bite of protein bar and some peppermint tea, changed my knickers inside my sleeping bag, wiped my face with a wet wipe, and went outside with Erin to brush my teeth and face the disgusting holes in the ground!

There is a reason why insurance is so expensive when you climb Kailash. If you get sick, you have to be helicoptered out. I had seen this happen already and had no intention of going down that way.

I am strong and I am here because I am meant to be here, I reminded myself as we ascended higher and higher that day. I knew my body was on its last bar of battery. I had barely eaten and I was warding off altitude sickness with sheer mind power.

Constant tears burned my eyes, tears that held the energy of all the exhaustion, the overwhelm at what I was doing, the power of the mountain, the kindness of the people. And a little bit of fear. My body had never felt like this. My mind was all I had to be strong now.

Although walking on his own, Jim was holding back and checking in on me regularly. I, however, seemed to be doing much better than Suzi, who was far behind us on the climb. I stayed focused, listening to music to keep me moving, but the road never ended. Just when I thought we had come to the top of the highest point that we could climb, I saw another level and the path stretching upwards. For miles and miles, I ascended. It went on and on to 5,600 metres. And now snow began to fall! It was so hot when it was sunny. And so so cold when it was not.

As I climbed to the next brow, my heart hurt. I needed a hug, to fall into someone, to feel a connection. It had been oh-so long since anyone had really held me. In that moment, I prayed for help.

"Kailash, I'm lost. I need support. Please help me."

I pulled my head up from looking down at the ground where it had been for hours and saw a miracle. Standing a few meters away from me was my Chengdu detour buddy Anna. She said nothing as I took my last step onto the ledge. She just grabbed my hand and pulled me up into her embrace. I sobbed and sobbed and sobbed, letting all the need to be strong flow out of me. I allowed myself to be human and be loved. I knew she was the angel who would pull me quite literally back from the edge!

When our long hug was over, Anna and I moved into the tea tent rest stop, or rather a traditional kitted out marquee filled to the brim with hundreds of people. The tent was a hub of magic and joy. Everyone sat around on carpets and sofas, laughing, smiling, getting hot water and resting from their hell of a hard climb. Then I heard that cheeky giggle...

"Jesus!"

I threw my arms around him, feeling like myself again with friends around me. I had not felt like this with my group the whole time we'd been in the mountains, but this gang were my vibe, even if we'd only spent 12 hours together in China! I realised I was an affectionate human. I needed love and connection to thrive. And as much as I had sort of bonded with Gelsen and the others, they didn't get me. It was hard to have deep conversations and I was not their vibration. Yet the universe had thrown us together for a reason. I had learned what it meant to be humble.

Topped up on love from Anna and Jesus, it was time to move on. The next climb was to be the hardest I would ever experience. I waved goodbye to Anna who set off ahead of me, knowing in my heart that this was to be the last time I would see her in this lifetime. The world was a big place and we all had our missions, but we touch each other's hearts and lives along the way. We are all human angels and I will never forget how she showed up for me. The occasional Tibetan man or woman would come close and touch me too, a hand here and a smile there as if God was recharging my once near-depleted power pack. Their love filled my heart and made me cry harder as the long path went on and on and on and on...

***

It was time to make the summit. I lingered far behind Tom, Erin and Jim, walking tiny steps, as the mountain got steeper and steeper.

The altitude sickness hit me on a whole new level, not enough to take me completely, but enough to make itself known. It dominated and it could win if I let it. I would not let myself entertain the idea that I was weak. Instead, I focused on the other energies I could feel. The energy was intense, not just in my body, but cosmically. I could feel so much. I was purging here, not just for me, but for everyone on the Earth. This pain I was going through was growth, the mud, the shit, the letting go. Whatever this suffering, I was purging for humanity. Whatever the reward, I was gifting it to the grid. I tried not to be sick, occasionally apologising to the stones that I had to spit on. I was leaning so far into my walking poles by the time I reached the summit I could not lift my face to the snowy wind to see the view.

Staring at the ground, I knew I had to stop. There was something I needed to do up here. Somehow, I had reached the summit alone and cried tears of abject exhaustion. I stood here shaking, then raised my head to see an eerie yet beautiful sight in the fog. I could not see one single rock for 500 metres that wasn't covered underneath years and years of bright-coloured prayer flags that had been placed by pilgrims who had reached this spot. The energy was as powerful as I had felt. Kailash was fully open to me now, showing me how far I had come.

I have to find the alabaster, I thought, and willed myself to get my bag off my back. *I have to make the offering right now*. It was as if I was moving in slow motion, my body like a space suit, my head spinning and disoriented. Yet somehow, I managed to get my mesas open, find the alabaster and blow all of my soul into it.

There were no spoken prayers, only fleeting intentions in mind, but they were enough. I knew that. My intention was so clear and pure, that no words could have done justice to this final activation for the seventh chakra of the Earth.

I threw it with all my might, into the depths of the prayer flags and my heart knew I had given my all. There was nothing left of me to give.

***

It was all of a blur how I made it two hours on my own to the next rest spot or how I came to be lying under layers of stinky yak blankets with an oxygen mask on my face. Four old Tibetan men smoked roll-up cigarettes nearby, watching over me with concern, trying to coax me into eating with sign language. I couldn't bear the thought of food, but found myself transported to being with my mom as a child eating semolina. If I had semolina, I would have eaten it, but the offerings of noodles or rice or chocolate made my stomach churn.

Then one of the men had an idea. He passed me a dish of freshly ground barley flour, mixed with water and some sugar, and spoon-fed it to me. My eyes widened in pure delight and shock. This was *exactly* like the semolina I was dreaming about, simple medicine right from the lands. Had I called it in or did Kailash place that thought in my mind to feed my body and soul?

Gelsen turned up and was so happy to see me alive that he came and sat by me, then gave me a massive hug, which was not really his style!

"Suzi is far behind and I must wait for her. She may have to go down the mountain on a truck, so you must carry on on your own," he explained. "The path is flat and straight to the monastery, where you must go and meet the group. It will take you about five hours, but it will get dark in four and a half, so you must not stop, okay? Eat more, drink more and then you must leave quickly."

I nodded at his instructions, drank a bottle of Coke and thanked my Tibetan guardian angels profusely before going for a wee and realising it took all of my energy to pull my pants back up. I breathed. *Four hours until dark. Fuck me! Okay, I can do this!*

***

Kailash walks me home

An hour into the long walk and I was fully aware of how alone I was. I had passed nobody but a prostrating woman and it felt like everyone else had come through here hours ago. The walk was stunning, and flat like Gelsen had said, for which I was grateful. On the occasional slight incline, I could feel intensely how weak I now was, but retained my awareness that this was something I had to experience. I wanted to really truly feel it. I had refused to let altitude sickness take me fully. I was a warrior. And I was on my way!

I talked to my guides, the river and the mountains, and they spoke insights that I couldn't remember but felt profound and beautiful at the time. I was part of nature and nature was a part of me. I held wisdom that I had never known and I prayed that this wisdom would stay inside me.

I thought about Harry and the girls. I missed them all so much. I missed being a mum, dancing in the kitchen, doing the school run, eating dinner together every night. I missed Harry's heavy arms on my belly and snuggling with whatever child climbed into bed that night. I missed seeing clients. I missed teaching. I missed feeling loved by everyone. But I was here. On my own in the Himalayas. On the most sacred mountain in the world. And Kailash was walking me home.

I heard wild dogs and knew I must be careful. I had heard that someone had been bitten the week before and could see one far in the distance, so I called in my jaguar power animal and she walked by my side. I felt safer and stronger with my jaguar there.

I sang songs that came from the earth, words I didn't even know, as if the mountains, the rivers and Gaia herself were singing through me, like she had before. I felt fear rise and fall. And I even feared that I would be vulnerable and attract attack if I let fear in, so I sang more and I sang louder. I felt myself rise out of fear and into faith.

"I am here on a quest. I am safe and protected," I chanted.

I knew then that any encounter with wild dogs would be my journey too. I would cross that bridge if I came to it, but for now, I would sing. I would expand my energy and walk these lands like I was part of them. I carried on along the lonely pathway, each step sinking me deeper into commune with the earth.

Deeper and deeper I went into Gaia as the sun set and dusk enveloped me. I had no idea how far the monastery was but I couldn't see it yet. An eery sense of calm settled over my skin, as I recalled on repeat, *I'm walking through the bloody Himalayas on my own! Fuck me! How many humans get to experience this?*

In the last hour, a gorgeous mountain range with a river running below it emitted the most profound energy. Taking me by surprise, the mountains whipped into my mind and delivered a loud message in a strong masculine voice.

You will become a very different person. It will take months to integrate, but you will shift. Your energy shifting allows others to shift. You have such faith, Louise. You are courageous and brave and strong.

Like the father's approval, the message made me cry. I had my well done, my gold star, my affirmation from a higher power that I had done what I needed to do.

I walked on through the veils, through the mountains, through the waters, through Gaia, through the darkness, past the wild dogs, under the stars that lead us all home in the end.

***

The gift of the mountain

I woke to the sound of donkeys and yaks and looked around the room. And playfully shouted, "It's the last bloody night I have to wake up with you lot in my space!"

This group didn't get my silliness typically, but I wasn't going to hide it anymore. I was full of joy this morning! And they played along.

Suzi's face popped out of her sleeping bag. Our group was finally back together again. We were jovial and familiar with each other as we got dressed in our sleeping bags, sharing our stories, wet wipes and toothpaste. It was clear a new bond had been formed between us. We had all overcome something, physically, mentally and emotionally. We had all been on as much of an inner journey as an outer one.

***

On the very final stretch, the adrenaline had worn off and the little food I had eaten was showing. I dragged my body along, feeling civilisation just around the corner, and stopped to take one last look at the view of the valley below, then turned to see the most curious solid green rock, almost like agate. I smiled. I had almost forgotten.

"Is this to be the new kuya for my mesa, Kailash?"

The medicine of this stone holds the gift of courage, the mountain said clearly to my heart.

I had grown from a playful, carefree starseed to a wise medicine woman, an earth chakra shaman who would continue to walk the Earth in divine service to the planetary rebirth and greater life expression. It was with dreams of a new Earth and a renewed motivation that I had pushed through those final moments of my journey around holy Mount Kailash in a state of meditation and peace and deep reverence of the whole.

***

EARTH CHAKRA SHAMAN

Crown Chakra Prayer
Divine Knowing

Mount Kalish, the holiest of mountains on Earth,
I call upon you now.
May I always have the courage and bravery
to shine my love and my light,
awaken the purpose of all
who are willing to fight the good fight
through personal power, purpose and play.
We all claim our divine right
to show up for the Earth
and see the world from great height.
I call upon Kailash to bless all beings that we may be
free.
Every step I take from this day,
I will revere as a sacred journey.

***

CHAPTER 22

Sacred Gifts from the Highest Heights

"Only one who has risked the fight with the dragon and is not overcome by it wins the 'treasure hard to attain'."
~ Carl Jung

We travelled for two days though the Himalayan ranges to get to Everest, past mighty peaks, sacred lakes and farmland, on wide roads and dirt tracks. It was another few hours to basecamp and I was glued to the window watching the lands pass me by and feeling Everest pulling me closer and closer. We pulled over for our first glimpse and my heart beat in a way it had not since starting this earth chakra journey. It was as if I was rushing into the arms of unconditional love. And even though Everest was behind a layer of cloud and I could not see him fully yet, the energy he emitted was like a beacon stretching for a million miles into the universe and into my core.

I had travelled the world and my soul and I had never felt this way before. There were no words. Only a knowing that somehow I belonged to this mountain.

"About 300 people attempt to summit Everest every year," Gelsen shared. "Six to ten of those die trying, so there are about 300 dead bodies up there, which many lamas feel is disrespectful to the mountain god. Everest is 8,848 metres high, the highest mountain in the world, and it is rare to see the peak because of the cloud cover."

"All sacred mountains reveal themselves to me," I said jokingly but not really joking.

I was still gazing out at the windows when I said this. And maybe it was certainty, maybe manifestation, or maybe a command, but when we pulled into basecamp an hour later, the sky was blue and the peak of Everest was in full sight.

"You made it happen, Louise," Gelsen said.

"I never had any doubt!" I replied.

Everest had been waiting for me all my life. I felt a huge sense of freedom. I had completed my entire quest. I was no longer carrying a burden of having to be in service. I was not here to activate any chakra or to give my medicine away. Everest had called me home for me. This was not duty; this was reward.

***

The sacred cave

Our traditional guesthouse was, to my surprise, a huge canvas tent alongside 40 or so others, sitting on what looked like a car park. Some of the tents even had flags waving outside saying 'free WIFI'. Our host greeted us with her daughter who looked about three years old but turned out to be nine. Gelsen explained that children who live at this height above sea level do not grow very quickly, so they all look little and young!

The guesthouse was a beautiful space with four wooden-framed sofas and two ornate wooden tables. In the centre was the most powerful stove I had ever seen pumping out heat and boiling up water. At the back was a bed that covered the width of the tent, where we would all sleep. I was amazed to see another two rooms out the back.

We drank warm tea and gazed around in awe of the comfort and beauty of the traditional Tibetan fabrics. Still, I was itching to get outside into the sunshine and meet Everest properly.

"Drink up, drink up! Let's go on an adventure!" I encouraged the group, my immortal child back to her old self. I hoped she would stick around when I got home.

Gelsen had spoken about a sacred cave at Everest and I had not let it go that I wanted to visit it. Plus, I had a tiny piece of alabaster left that I wanted to give as an offering. We wandered together out of the little guesthouse, through the camp, towards Rongbuk, the highest monastery in the world. It was grand and gorgeous, overlooking the purest-looking river I had ever seen, grey, blue, clear, untouched by humans and so alive! I wanted to stay, to play, to touch the waters, but my heart was being pulled to the monastery.

We climbed up the outside walls so effortlessly now. After all this time, I had finally acclimatized to the altitude! At the top, I stood gazing at Everest's peak. Joy, joy and more joy poured out of me. I raised my arms in the air and praised and danced, thanking Everest for bringing me here.

EARTH CHAKRA SHAMAN

***

The cave was not some dark entrance in the side of a mountain as I had imagined, but down inside a hole in the floor inside of the monastery. No one else was in here and Gelsen told us it wasn't for tourists. Few knew about it, he said.

"Down here is the 4,000-year-old cave of the Lotus Buddha," Gelsen said as I dropped down, reaching with my foot for a ledge to guide me. Inside, I crouched down and was stunned to see a narrow 12-foot long cave containing glass-fronted shrines and so many candles flickering in the dark. It was warm and womb-like. This place was undeniably powerful. I sat in the alcove, the mountain rock curved around my body, hugging me.

Erin, Tom and Jim sat nearby, squashed in together, and I felt such love for them as I saw pure reverence in their expressions and they began to meditate. I smiled. They had come such a long way. We all had.

I crossed my legs, pulled my mesas out of my bag into my lap, rested my hands on my legs and welcomed the peace. Oh this peace!

Immediately, I went deep into vision. My body was lighting up, my third eye was bright, and I began to see a peaceful world. In the world, there were fewer people, fewer cities and less farming, but the relationship between animals, people and the lands was unmistakable. It made me cry to witness the beauty.

In my mind's eye, I walked into the city. The roads were empty and the city was clean. It felt normal to walk here and there was peace everywhere. This was the new Earth I'd prayed for, a world I'd dreamed into being, and I was holding this vision inside of Everest.

When I came around there was no one in the cave. The group had gone, but by the trapdoor in the corner was a monk. Gelsen had told me there was a sole monk here, who lived alone. He had also told me that this was the only monastery that wasn't under surveillance by the government. As I packed my bag, the monk looked up and beckoned me to crouch in front of him. Neither one of us spoke. Time slowed and silent blessings flowed from me. I couldn't stop them. I felt his blessings flowing to me too. The reverence was magical, as if he was Everest himself.

***

I went back to the tent but had itchy feet. I didn't want to stay inside! After dinner, I left the warm cosy space and I walked the 20 minutes back to the cave on my own. The sun was setting on the mountain peak, still not a cloud in the sky!

I had become unafraid of everything, even the wild dogs, even knowing I was putting myself in a vulnerable position. I was choosing this, choosing to go deeper and be more alone with the mountain before we left the next day. I knew the cave was so safe that I could open my entire self to it, to Everest. I had to go there one more time.

I slipped through the trapdoor and I settled in to pray.

"Om mani padme hum," I chanted, then said the Prayer of St Francis.

Everest spoke one sentence that stayed with me.

I am your mountain now.

EARTH CHAKRA SHAMAN

My body lit up and I journeyed deep into the mountain. I felt like I'd been meditating for hours and hours, but it was no more than 15 minutes, before I brought myself back again. Now fully awake, fully conscious, I could feel something in my left palm. It was a pyramid. I could feel the outline of its energy in my palm. I could feel the sides. What was this gift from the mountain? I had to understand what this was, my mind began to rush in. Everest asked me to let go of it all.

Feel it, he said.

I explored it in my hand and looked through one of the facets. There, I saw a horse galloping, then myself walking into a huge cave. I journeyed into the cave, observing the unfolding vision.

There was Gelsen with a wife, keeping warm in a beautiful cave not far from here, with water flowing through it. It was as if I could see his past and that somehow it was connected to mine, but not in this lifetime.

I looked through another facet and saw the same cave with many white horses being led into it. There were many people, too, all wearing white, but the horses were as important as the humans. The creatures were not owned like they are now. This was the future, I realised.

Then I became aware of the waters, separating from my body, then becoming the winds.

I couldn't see through the next facet without turning my hand upside down. In doing so, I connected to the elements. I could see a pond and the pyramid allowed me to spin the water. Out of the pond, I pulled a dog in a cage! I didn't want to look. I wasn't sure what it meant. Was the dog dead?

I opened my eyes, still holding the pyramid, but unable to see it in this three-dimensional world.

"What is this?" I asked Everest. "And why is it only in my left hand?"

You need to learn about the powers first. Then it will grow into your right hand also, came the reply.

Quantum time had once again taken me to other dimensions. I felt like I had been in there for days but it had been less than an hour. I walked back to basecamp, under the most glorious canopy of stars. The sky was so clear and snow-capped Everest glowed in the moonlight. More awake, more connected, more open, I could not have been any happier.

***

Palm pyramids and the light

I could feel Everest's energy pulsating through the canvas of the guest house and had to pinch myself that I wasn't dreaming that, yes, I was indeed sleeping on Mount Everest. I lay with my hands on my belly and heart, energy flowing into my body and journeyed back to the cave where I sat in stillness to learn more about the pyramid.

Each facet seemed to show me past, present and future. One facet took me to a small circle of stones in a room of secrets and showed me that I was a guardian of so many secrets. Indeed, I was. It was peaceful here, a place where the stone structures felt fragile, but they didn't need to be touched. I didn't need to know these secrets. I saw they meant more to the owners than to anyone else. And they were safe here.

I journeyed through the stone tower of secrets and saw it was not as fragile as I had thought. It was solid. I saw that the pyramid could be on my palm or on top of my hand, and by the time I slept, it was in my right hand too.

Through your right hand, the pyramids will join into very powerful merkaba, Everest said.

I drifted in and out of my vision as I fell into a half-sleep. I saw my pyramids joining together, ancient sacred geometry, portals and time travel. The pyramids in my hands came into their own. Light shone as I opened my palms. This was something beyond any energy I had ever felt. This was something else. Unable to move, I stayed in awe but also a little in fear of this power.

Blessings and prayers poured from my heart, for peace and safety of the lands and people, and for a new level of consciousness to touch the Earth.

I called in my spirit guide Xakier. He showed me that he too had pyramids in his palms. Without understanding, I explained to him my fear of using my powers.

"This is too much. What if I hurt someone?"

You have been gifted this power to use it. You will not be able to overwrite the powers of God. That is not something you need to be afraid of. It is not that you will overuse your powers that will be the issue, Louise; it will be that you underuse them.

***

Epilogue

It was November when I dreamt of trying to put some of my alabaster kuya into the centre of the cross at Shaftesbury Abbey. In the dream, I was hiding behind the herbs. I saw a man who worked there, a gardener or keeper of the land, and wanted to ask him to help me but was afraid of being told I couldn't do what I needed to do. I feared that he may catch me and report me to the church!

All the kings were waiting for me to place the alabaster, though. King Alfred the Great, King Arthur, Jesus and Archangel Gabriel talked to me, telling me to put the alabaster medicine stone into the centre of the cross and everything would be transformed. The invisible world would become visible.

Was I being called again? *I have to process this*, I thought when I woke. Then when I checked my Instagram messages later that morning, there was a message from a follower.

"Dear Louise, I have recently moved home and found a copy of *Spheres of Destiny*. I'm happy to send it to you. The book would certainly be going to the perfect new home."

I could see it was a book by Robert Coon, the man who brought the earth chakra grid system to the world. I thanked the guy for his message and didn't give it much more thought. But I kept being nudged to go back and read the message again. When I looked closer at the photo of the book cover, I saw it was called *Spheres of Destiny: The Shaftesbury Prophecy*.

***

It was a full moon on the winter solstice, and we had sung with the Pagan choir as we watched the sun rise through the ancient stones of Stonehenge. Three hours later, we stood at the locked gates of Shaftesbury Abbey. The sign said it was closed between October and April.

I knew this alabaster kuya in my pocket belonged to the sixth chakra of the Earth and had to be given today.

I could see into the Abbey gardens by leaning over the wall, but I wasn't quite courageous enough to be doing a James-Bond-style break-in, so we went for a cup of tea to figure it out. As the girls sipped hot chocolates, something told me to find the phone number and call the Abbey.

"Hello?" said the voice of an older man.

I stumbled, feeling like I was intruding. Was this a home phone line?

"Hello, is this the Abbey?"

"Yes, it is."

"I'm so sorry to bother you, but I have come a long way today to find the Abbey closed. I had a dream that I needed to come and make an offering to the cross."

Realising I sounded like a total fruitcake even to the most religious of people, I added, "I probably sound crazy. Is it okay for me to speak to you about this?"

The man responded shakily.

"Well, it's strange that I'm even here to pick up your call. The Abbey is closed until April. I had only come into the office to get some paperwork. I think you had better come. You will have to come now though."

I flew out of the cafe and ran around the corner to the Abbey, leaving Harry and the girls to their drinks. Tears of excitement, disbelief and wonder flooded me as I pushed open the big black gates. I felt a surge of privilege too, yet it felt somehow *normal* to be doing this. Maybe I had had access to this abbey in previous lifetimes?

The man I'd spoken to on the phone was one of the volunteers and most certainly the helper in my dream from whom I was trying to hide. This time, though, I wasn't going to shy away from him. He was going to help me, just like my dream was trying to show me.

"What is it you want to do?" he asked out of curiosity.

"I have some sacred alabaster. It comes from Egypt. In my dream, Jesus, Archangel Gabriel, King Alfred and King Arthur told me to deliver it right into the heart of the cross at Shaftesbury."

I knew he didn't get it, but he was still struck by the synergy of my divinely timed phone call.

"Why don't you go ahead into the grounds and do what you need to do. I'll leave you to do your work alone and wait here to lock up after you."

"Thank you, thank you, thank you," I said, throwing my arms around him.

I walked past the statue of King Alfred and smiled. As I passed, I felt him, the great protector, with his wildly radical and powerful heart, watching me. Without fear, I ascended the stone steps and reached my arm as high as I could, placing the alabaster in the centre of the cross. I was no longer hiding my magic in these Christian places and it felt like liberation! I placed the alabaster, bowed, then prayed and gave thanks.

On the way out, I hugged the man again, probably a little more than he was used to and left a Christmas kiss on his cheek. I wandered back to Harry and the girls, who were in shock and joy. Harry kissed me softly on my third eye. He could not have been prouder. Never, out of all the people in the world, did I think Harry would be the one human who got me, who got this call. It defied his logic and reason. Yet he was the one to honour the greatest mystery of all. The mystery of the Divine.

***

A few weeks after Christmas, we discovered some fascinating insights about Harry's family. It came to light that Harry's grandfather was the 33rd grandson in a direct line to King Alfred the Great, the king of Wessex, who gifted Shaftesbury Abbey to his daughter. The king from my dreams, the king from my visions who had become my spirit guide. You can't make this stuff up.

To me, Harry carried the light and energy of the divine masculine. Of King Alfred, of King Arthur, of Archangel Gabriel himself. Harry had shown up for me all the way. Somehow, we had found a way to dance with the Divine together. He had even started supporting my retreats, bringing the medicine of the divine masculine, then in writing my first book... (and this one...) When the world spins madly on, he is my anchor back home, back to Gaia, back to the heart chakra of the Earth, back to divine union.

Guinevere of the heart chakra

And then there's me.

I took my place in my personal power.

In February 2019, I stood at the base of Glastonbury Tor, alone in the dark. I was cold and scared, yet I knew there was only one way I had to go. And that was up!

How had I even got here in the darkness of the Tor all alone? I had been with my soul sister Bethany and some other medicine sisters for a weekend of sacred ceremony before Bethany's baby was to be born. We had ended the weekend in an almost biblical Divine Feminine mothers blessing in the sacred waters of the White Springs. Candlelight bounced off the cave like walls onto our beautiful naked bodies. We sang and laughed unaware of the freezing February temperature. This was our own intuitive ancient way to honour the mother and our children of the future.

It was on leaving the town that evening that it hit me hard. I had to deliver the medicine stone from Mount Kailash to the heart chakra of the Earth! And I had to do it now. I asked my friend Carla who was driving us home if she minded doing a stop-off on the way.

"Of course, we can do that. It'll be an adventure," she agreed.

We drove through town and up the dark lanes to the back of the giant Tor.

When we parked up, my friend took a deep breath and said, "Actually, Lou, do you mind if I don't come with you?"

That was not what I was expecting to hear! I felt a sudden fear sensation rise through my body, but desperately tried to mask it so as not to make her feel bad!

"No, of course not. I'll be about half an hour. Is that okay?"

"Absolutely. I don't mind. I just got a feeling when we were driving that I wasn't meant to come with you," she explained.

She looked worried.

"Will you be okay? I'm so sorry."

I put on my bravest face.

"Yes, yes, yes. I'll be fine. Don't worry at all, babe," I replied, trying to convince myself more than anything.

I got out of the car. And looked up. *God it's dark*, I thought instantly. Walking into the blackness was unnerving. The cloud cover was thick tonight and the wind roared. I zipped my coat up to my neck and fear flooded my mind. *What am I doing?*

As I crossed the field leading to the Tor, I reflected on how this had all begun: that life-changing healing and vision almost five years ago, when I had been transported into another world on top of the Tor. In the journey, dragons had sat at my feet, and I was split in two, my blood draining from my body and filling with pure golden light. When I had been 'purified', I was taken into a church, where archangels and kings crowned me and told me that I was Guinevere. I had been *chosen*, they said, and when I received a ruby, I would be ready for my purpose.

I twiddled my ruby ring now, remembering the gift of it five years ago and the strange messages that I was Guinevere. I had come so far. I had had no idea back then what lay before me.

Taking big gulps of air, I faced into the battering wind. Being so dark, I could no longer see in front or behind me. I kept on walking. My heart beat fast now as I walked, and fear-filled thoughts of rape entered my mind. I put my hand into my pocket and felt for my kuya. I remembered the moment I had taken it out of my mesa. Without too much thought, I had to detach from keeping this medicine. *It was never mine to keep*, I reminded myself, *it was always only mine to give*. Still, I had to override my desire to keep it, to hold on for fear that someone would take it and not understand the reverence of it, to follow the logical thoughts of leaving a priceless sacred stone where any one could take it. This was part of the journey. This was what it had all been for: to return courage back to the heart chakra.

I hadn't really thought too much about the Guinevere thing since. I'd only learned one year before that Guinevere was King Arthur's wife. Nor had I fully understood that the two of them were my line to Avalon! Yet, as I walked towards the Tor now, I rose into a deep divine feminine warrioress energy.

The car felt a long way behind me now. *I am safe, I am courageous, I can do this*, I repeated to myself. Thoughts centring on my vulnerability were replaced with presence for my divine mission and purpose.

I entered through the kissing gate and stood at the foot of the steps leading to the top of the Tor. Fear overcame me and I felt an energy that frightened me from spirits I did not know. I couldn't see the spirits, but I could feel them, and they could harm me if they wanted. They wanted to know who I was and why I was here. I touched the kuya in my pocket again and something came from the place of no mind, no thought. A deep voice that didn't sound like mine came from me:

"I am Guinevere. I am here to bring the medicine stone from sacred Mount Kailash, the seventh chakra of the Earth. I am here to deliver the gift of courage back to the heart chakra. Let me through the gate and protect me as I climb the Tor."

The command was strong, and the wind stopped in that instant. I laughed because it had worked to quell the energy, and also because I sounded completely ridiculous! And I had no idea where it had even come from. Thank God there was no one there to witness whatever it was that just happened through me!

I began to climb, singing songs of the earth, medicine songs of the symbols I had been gifted along this great journey. I climbed higher and higher up the winding steps, realising that the wind no longer touched me, although it was all around. It was as if I was in the eye of a storm. While the wind sounded gale force, I was not being blown off the side of the Tor. I was in a clear path of no wind. If I reached out, I could feel the force of it, but not where I was climbing.

"Thank you, thank you, thank you," I said with every step, appreciating the protection of the spirits, and telling the unseen world about my journey as I climbed.

"May this gift of courage expand the heart chakra, birthing utopia and sacred immortality. With this kuya, may all of us humans feel connected to nature, learn to take no more than is needed and find the joy in sharing. May we protect and honour the waters that flow through our bodies and through the earth. May we all see the shadows and heal with love and forgiveness. Let there be abundance for all, for all animals and for all humans who were once enslaved. May they be free. May balance be restored to the people who once suffered in the name of religion. Let shackles and judgments be burned in sacred fires. Let everyone be liberated to dance on the earth, remembering their roots, singing the songs of truth and listening to the guidance of Gaia."

I placed the kuya of courage in the heart chakra of the Earth and I sat with my back against the old stone tower that stands there. As I felt the energy of the lands expanding like a sonic boom, I closed my prayer.

"May all beings feel love. May all beings feel this love, give love and receive love."

And in the cold dark night, I sat there and felt the pinprick of light that I was, flow all around the Earth. I was one. We are all one.

I skipped down the steep hill, laughing and mocking myself.

"I am Guinevere? Bloody hell! Glad no one was around to hear that!" I said out loud, cringing at myself. "I'll be wearing a cape and crown before I know it."

But this was not to be the last of Guinevere. She was just getting started!

***

As for the earth chakras…

In the final throes of completing the first edit of this book, Rainbow Serpent woke me painfully from my sleep. She demanded my presence with two firm commands.

You must return to Uluru and bring the blue stone.
And…
Stay focused and complete this book.

Within hours of handing over my book for editing, miracles began to rain down that were impossible to deny. I had no choice. I had to go. Leaving my family once again, I headed off to witness the worst fires in Australia's memory and to return to Uluru.

On 12 January 2020, I found myself in a huge sacred ceremony at Uluru, about to learn what the future held for planet Earth; that the fires were just the beginning; that this time was prophesied. We would get more than we ever bargained for.

The great turning had begun. Now we *all* have an important role to play in how this unfolds.

***

Thanks

Bon Bon and Bella Boo, my beautiful daughters – for the thousands of kisses you plant on my cheeks when I'm deep in the writing cave and for putting up with your wild mummy getting whisked away by the earth, by people, places and sometimes big caves. I honour that this journey has not always been easy for you and I want you to know how grateful I am for your patience, understanding and most of all your love for me. I love you and am so proud of who you are.

Harry – because, ya know, you're the best and I fucking love you!

Sarah – I am lost for words to describe the gratitude I have for your friendship and the commitment you have had in me and my books. Thank you for all your time and energy in reading, and rereading, and editing. And for holding sacred truthful space for me as I processed the mammothness of this journey. I deeply value your wisdom and your ability to speak and see truth. Thank you for always seeing me. I love you.

Kris – my kickass editor who dances with my dyslexia and honours my very deep and long writing process. I love our relationship and our blossoming friendship. Thank you.

Let's see how the Uluru medicine unfolds on our next journey.

Lizzie, for all your hours and of painting for me, I give thanks to you for your beautiful work and your love and commitment.

I give thanks and deep reverence to the Angel of Abundance, who showed up to play this vital role in the activation of the Earth and my soul.

To the grid workers out there: you are my heroes, and I deeply honour your intuitive, powerful, and often silent work. Thank you for your commitment to the new Earth grid. I love you.

And thank you to the Indigenous shamans and teachers who have shared their medicine teachings with me and others, so we can take our place of service to the Earth. I give the deepest of thanks to you. Munay.

May all beings be free. May there be harmony.

***

About Louise

Louise Carron Harris is a modern-day medicine woman; a shamanic healer, mentor, teacher, storyteller, radio presenter, and public speaker. She lives in the southeast of England with her husband and children.

She lives a life of love, laugher, and contentment, while inspiring others to cultivate courage to follow their own call through transformation experiences, courses, and retreats.

Join the mailing list for free meditations and updates and to join her online community here:
www.louisecarronharris.com
You can contact Louise on: hello@louisecarronharris.com and follow her on social media:
www.facebook.com/louisecarronharris
Instagram @louisecarronharris
Twitter @loucarronharris

***

Printed in Great Britain
by Amazon